Accounting

Related titles in the series

Advertising
Auditing
Book-keeping
Business and Commercial Law
Business Studies
Business French
Business German
Business Italian
Commerce
Cost and Management Accounting
Economics
Financial Management
Information Technology
Keyboarding and Document Presentation
Law
Management Theory and Practice
Marketing
Office Practice
Personnel Management
Psychiatry
Social Services
Statistics for Business
Teeline Shorthand

Accounting

Margaret Weaver

MADE SIMPLE
BOOKS

To Catherine and Victoria

Made Simple
An imprint of Butterworth-Heinemann
Linacre House, Jordan Hill, Oxford OX2 8DP
A division of Reed Educational and Professional Publishing Ltd

℞ A member of the Reed Elsevier plc group

OXFORD   BOSTON   JOHANNESBURG
MELBOURNE   NEW DELHI   SINGAPORE

First published 1997

British Library Cataloguing in Publication Data
Weaver, Margaret
  Accounting
  1.   Accounting
  I.   Title
  657

ISBN 0 7506 3260 7

Typeset by Avocet Typeset, Brill, Aylesbury, Bucks
Printed by Martin's the Printers Ltd., Berwick on Tweed

Contents

List of exercises taken from professional accounting papers   ix
Acknowledgements   xi

1 Introduction to financial accounting   1
Aims of the chapter   1
What is accounting?   1
The users of accounting information   1
Financial accounting and management accounting   2
Book-keeping   2
The accounting profession   2
The regulatory framework   3
The 'true and fair view'   3
Stewardship   4
Summary   4
Exercises   4

2 How book-keeping works   5
Aims of the chapter   5
Why book-keeping is necessary   5
Providing financial information to users   6
The accounting equation   7
The 'separate entity' concept   8
Maintaining the ledger   8
Double-entry book-keeping   10
Account titles   11
Further transactions   13
Summary   15
Exercises   16

3 Summarizing the accounts   21
Aims of the chapter   21
The trial balance   21
The trading and profit and loss account   23
The balance sheet   25
Personal, real and nominal accounts   27
Capital and revenue items   27
Summary   28
Exercises   28

4 Subsequent accounting periods and adjustments   30
Aims of the chapter   30
Balancing off the ledger accounts   30
The next accounting period   31
Calculating the cost of goods sold at the end of the second
trading period   32

	Adjustments for accruals and prepayments	33
	Summary	38
	Exercises	38
5	**Provisions against assets**	**41**
	Aims of the chapter	41
	Depreciation of fixed assets	41
	Provisions for doubtful debts	46
	Accounting treatment of goodwill	47
	Accounting treatment of research and development costs	48
	Leases	48
	Summary	48
	Exercises	48
6	**Preparing final accounts from a trial balance**	**51**
	Aims of the chapter	51
	The extended trial balance	55
	Summary	57
	Exercises	57
7	**Accounting concepts and conventions**	**61**
	Aims of the chapter	61
	Accounting policies	61
	Accounting concepts	61
	Accounting bases	63
	Accounting conventions	63
	Summary	64
	Exercises	65
8	**Discounts, VAT and business documents**	**68**
	Aims of the chapter	68
	Discounts	68
	Value Added Tax (VAT)	70
	Business documents	72
	Summary	76
	Exercises	76
9	**The books used in book-keeping – an introduction**	**79**
	Aims of the chapter	79
	Divisions of the ledger	79
	Other methods of book-keeping	80
	The use of folio columns	80
	Summary	81
	Exercises	81
10	**The cash books and bank reconciliations**	**83**
	Aims of the chapter	83
	Cheques and paying-in slips	83
	The two-column cash book	83
	The three-column cash book	85
	The analysed cash book	86
	Other types of bank and cash ledger accounts	87
	The petty cash book	87
	Bank reconciliations	89
	Summary	92
	Exercises	92

11 The journals and the correction of errors   95
    Aims of the chapter   95
    The sales, purchases and returns journals   95
    Analysed journals   97
    The general journal, journal proper or journal   98
    Errors which do not affect the agreement of the trial balance   99
    Errors which do affect the agreement of the trial balance   100
    The effect of errors on the profit and loss account and balance sheet 102
    Other uses of the suspense account   102
    Summary   102
    Exercises   102

12 Control accounts   105
    Aims of the chapter   105
    Contra entries   107
    Summary   108
    Exercises   108

13 Accounting for stocks and wages   110
    Aims of the chapter   110
    Accounting for stocks   110
    Accounting for wages and salaries   112
    Summary   115
    Exercises   115

14 Preparing accounts from incomplete records   117
    Aims of the chapter   117
    Constructing ledger accounts   117
    Preparing an opening statement of affairs   117
    Other calculations   118
    Summary   121
    Exercises   121

15 Accounting for not-for-profit organizations   124
    Aims of the chapter   124
    Types of transactions in non-profit-making organizations   124
    Surpluses and deficits and the income and expenditure account   124
    The accumulated fund   124
    Trading activities   125
    Records maintained by not-for-profit organizations   125
    Special transactions in not-for-profit organizations   125
    Receipts and payments accounts   126
    Summary   129
    Exercises   130

16 Manufacturing accounts   133
    Aims of the chapter   133
    Classifications of costs   133
    Summary   137
    Exercises   137

17 Partnership accounts   139
    Aims of the chapter   139
    The partnership agreement   139
    Liability of partners   140
    Appropriating the profits (or losses)   140

Capital and current accounts		141
Changes in the profit-sharing ratios of partners		143
Summary		148
Exercises		148
18 Limited company accounts		**151**
Aims of the chapter		151
Setting up a limited company		151
Share capital		152
Appropriating the profits		153
Shareholders' funds		154
Published accounts		155
Auditing the limited company		157
Summary		157
Exercises		158
19 Post-balance sheet events, contingencies, reserves		**162**
Aims of the chapter		162
Post-balance sheet events		162
Contingencies		163
Reserves		163
Summary		164
Exercises		164
20 Cash flow statements		**165**
Aims of the chapter		165
Format of the cash flow statement		165
Summary		169
Exercises		170
21 Interpretation of accounts		**174**
Aims of the chapter		174
Performance (profitability) ratios		175
Solvency (liquidity) ratios		177
Use of assets (efficiency) ratios		178
Capital structure (gearing) ratios		180
Investors' (security) ratios		181
Summary		183
Exercises		183
22 The use of computers in accounting		**187**
Aims of the chapter		187
Computerized v manual systems		187
Hardware and software		187
Types of software of use to accountants		188
Batch v real-time systems		189
Segregation of duties		189
Other security precautions		189
Accounting codes		190
Advantages and disadvantages of computer systems		192
Characteristics of good information		192
Summary		193
Exercises		193
Appendix		194
Solutions to exercises		197
Index		239

Exercises taken from professional accounting papers

The following exercises are reproduced by kind permission of:

5.5x   AAT, June 1992
6.4x   CIMA, November 1995

7.1   CIMA, November 1992
7.2   CIMA, May 1995
7.3x   CIMA, November 1990
7.4   ACCA, June 1994
7.5x   CIMA, November 1987

9.1   AAT, June 1991

11.5x AAT, June 1992

13.3   CIMA, May 1996

15.4   AAT, June 1991

18.3   ACCA, June 1994
18.4x CIMA, May 1995

19.1   AAT, December 1990

20.4   CIMA, May 1995

21.4x CIMA, November 1995
21.5   AAT, June 1992

22.1   CIMA, November 1995
22.3   CIMA, November 1990

Acknowledgements

Thanks to my husband, Chris, who helped with the proofreading and checking of arithmetic, and ensured that I was supplied with food and drink during the many hours spent at my computer. Thanks also to my friend, Mike Ackerley, who provided constant encouragement as I wrote this book. He read through every word to ensure clarity of explanation to non-accountants, and pointed out my errors and omissions, etc., etc. He too helped me proofread the final version, and made the task altogether much more bearable.

Margaret Weaver

1   Introduction to financial accounting

Aims of the chapter

The aims of this chapter are to:

- consider the purpose of accounting
- describe the users and uses of financial information
- distinguish between financial and management accounting
- explain the connection between book-keeping and accounting
- identify the composition of the accounting profession
- outline the regulatory framework of accounting
- explain the role of management as 'stewards' of an organization.

What is accounting?

Accounting is the process by which organizations provide financial information for those who require it.

The users of accounting information

These generally fall into two categories – *external* users and *internal* users.

External users

External users, and the types of information they might require, are as follows:

Lenders, e.g. banks, finance companies, might need to know how much money the organization already has, how much it already owes to others and whether it owns anything of value which could be used as security for any unpaid debts.

Suppliers of goods and services to the organization need to be sure that their bills will be met, so they will be interested in the ability of the organization to access funds quickly; customers need to be assured that the business is a sound and reliable source of supply, and is not likely to close and therefore fail to provide the required goods and services.

Tax authorities, e.g. Inland Revenue and Customs and Excise, need to know how much profit the organization has made, how much tax and national insurance it has deducted from its employees' wages, and how much VAT it has collected or suffered.

Owners, particularly if they are not involved in the day-to-day running of the organization, might need an overview of the state of the organization from time to time – of its profits, amounts owing to or by the organization, and how much cash the organization has.

A prospective buyer or new partner of the business might need to know the value of the items which the business owns, and how much profit it has made in the past.

Financial analysts and advisers will require information for potential investors, or to provide statistical data for publication or submission to the government.

Internal users

Internal users include managers and owners who work in the business, and the types of information they might require includes all of the items mentioned for external users, but in addition they require more detailed information on the day-to-day transactions and the different aspects of the organization, such as costs incurred by individual departments or products.

Internal users also include employees of the organization, who need to be assured of the security of their jobs.

Financial accounting and management accounting

Financial accounting is primarily concerned with providing information for external users. Such information is usually historic, presented in a summarized format, provided at set periods such as annually or quarterly, and is often required to be produced by law. The common method of providing such information is through the trading and profit and loss account, the balance sheet and the cash flow statement. All of these will be discussed in detail later in the book.

Management accounting is primarily concerned with providing information for internal users. The information might be historic, but is often used as a basis for future forecasts. It usually needs to be detailed and provided at frequent intervals or as required.

Financial accounts are expressed in monetary terms, whereas management accounts might be expressed in monetary or non-monetary terms, such as number of units produced or number of hours worked.

This book concentrates primarily on financial accounting.

Book-keeping

Financial information can only be accurately provided if there is a proper system of recording the transactions of the organization. This is known as *book-keeping*. Originally, the records were handwritten in books, but in recent years mechanical, electronic and computerized systems have been developed. They all work on the same principles, so although this textbook appears to explain the operation of a handwritten system, you should easily be able to apply your knowledge to other book-keeping systems.

Only transactions which can be measured in monetary terms are recorded. For example, the payment of wages can be valued in monetary terms according to the amount spent, but the fact that the staff are happy and efficient in their work cannot be measured in this way, and is therefore not a financial transaction.

The accounting profession

Anyone can call themselves an accountant, but a qualified accountant is one who belongs to one of the following professional bodies:

- the Institute of Chartered Accountants
- the Chartered Association of Certified Accountants
- the Chartered Institute of Management Accountants.

In earlier times, accountants were heavily involved in the preparation of accounts, but nowadays the accountant is involved very little in this area, but much more in the area of interpreting and analysing accounts, advising organizations, planning and controlling, decision-making and managing people.

The regulatory framework

Accountants, and the financial information they provide, are governed by a variety of regulations and statements of good practice. Members of the professional bodies are bound by codes of conduct. The accounts prepared by limited companies are regulated by company law. In addition, the accounting bodies formed the Accounting Standards Committee, now called the Accounting Standards Board (ASB). These bodies have produced various Statements of Standard Accounting Practice (SSAPs) and, more recently, Financial Reporting Standards (FRSs), which are gradually replacing the SSAPs. The purpose of these standards is to ensure that, as far as possible, organizations treat items in their accounts in the same manner as each other, so as to prevent the large variations in the accounts prepared by some organizations in the 1960s. This book does not detail the provisions of the standards, but does make reference to them where applicable. To support the SSAPs and FRSs, there are also Statements of Recommended Practice (SORPs), which provide additional guidance on the interpretation of the standards. There are also International Accounting Standards (IASs), which are becoming more widely recognized.

All of these regulations and guidelines are regarded in the UK as 'Generally Accepted Accounting Practice' (GAAP), which does not have any legislative authority and poses the problem of what constitutes generally accepted practice. Basically, if a practice is contained within the above standards or law, and organizations are adhering to it, then it becomes accepted practice.

In addition, the accounting profession adheres to several concepts and conventions, which will be dealt with more fully later in the book.

So that you might understand the need for all these rules and regulations, consider the following simple example of how an organization could treat a basic item of information.

Suppose it buys in 20 items to sell, at a cost of £1 each. It expects to sell them for £5 each. What is their value to the organization? Is it the cost – £20? Or is it the potential selling price – £100? Or is it the expected profit – £80? If you sell them all, but have to pay £2 each for the next set of items, should the value be reduced by this figure? The point here is that the valuation could be subjective – i.e. subject to different opinions – and four different organizations could use four different valuations. The rules and regulations of the accounting profession attempt to introduce a method which is objective – i.e. everyone can agree to a single valuation.

For your information, the rules state that goods should be valued at their cost to the organization – so the items should be valued at £20.

A further part of the regulatory framework is the need for certain organizations to have an annual audit. This is an independent check by a registered auditor that the accounts of the organization are properly prepared. More detail on auditing is given later in the book.

The 'true and fair view'

The financial accounts should provide a true and fair view of the organization's financial results and state of affairs as presented to the users of the accounts. The accounts need not be completely accurate, but they should be free from material mis-statements which might affect the view given by them. The annual audit required by most limited companies results in the declaration that the accounts show a true and fair view.

Stewardship

The management of an organization is responsible for ensuring that the organization employs its capital and assets for the benefit of its users – both internal and external – and that they are used as efficiently as possible. They must be able to show evidence that this is the case, and so they are responsible for maintaining proper books of account. Their aim is to ensure that the organization achieves its objectives and satisfies the needs of all its users.

To this end, management must ensure that the accounting system contains controls and checks over its entries, so as to prevent errors and possible fraud, and must institute procedures to maintain assets securely.

Summary

By the end of this chapter you should recognize the need for organizations to provide financial information for various purposes. You will understand the connection between accounting and book-keeping and appreciate the differences between management and financial accounting. You will know how the accounting profession is comprised, and how its activities are regulated and monitored.

Exercises

1.1 Briefly describe the accounting information required by six different user groups.

1.2 Identify the various guidelines and regulations which govern the preparation and production of accounting information.

The answers to both these questions can be found by re-reading the chapter.

Aims of the chapter

The aims of this chapter are to:

- illustrate why book-keeping is necessary
- introduce the two main financial statements prepared by organizations
- explain the meaning of the terms 'revenues', 'expenses', 'assets', 'capital' and 'liabilities'
- define the 'accounting equation'
- demonstrate the operation of the double-entry book-keeping system.

Why book-keeping is necessary

Imagine P. Lyons starts a business on 1 January 19x6, buying and selling clothes, and has the following financial transactions:

19x6

1 Jan He puts £1,000 of his own money into the business cash drawer
2 Jan P. Smith lends £500 cash to the business
3 Jan He pays the business telephone bill of £100 out of the cash
4 Jan He repays £100 cash to P. Smith
5 Jan He buys equipment for £400 cash
6 Jan He buys clothes intended for sale, for £150 cash
7 Jan He buys equipment worth £200 from L. Peters, but does not pay for it at once
8 Jan He sells some of the clothes (which had cost £100) for £270 to L. Samson, who does not pay at once
9 Jan He receives £10 cash from hiring out some of his equipment
10 Jan He pays L. Peters £50 cash

Suppose you need a quick answer to the following questions:

- How much cash is left in the cash drawer?
- How much does the business owe to other people?
- How much equipment has the business got?
- How much profit (or loss) has the business made by selling clothes?

Try working out the answers without writing anything down. Did you get £710 in cash, £550 owing to other people, £600 for equipment and £170 profit? If you didn't get all these, do not worry – it proves the point that in order to answer such questions quickly and accurately, there needs to be a method of writing down the things which happen in an organization, as they occur. That is what book-keeping does – it provides a method of recording the financial transactions of an organization.

If you got the answers right, well done – but imagine how difficult it would be after 500 transactions had taken place!

Providing financial information to users

Most organizations produce statements of financial information once a year — more often if it is useful. The two most commonly produced statements are:

- the trading and profit and loss account
- the balance sheet.

The trading and profit and loss account

This statement provides information about the profit made during a particular period of time.

Here is a simple trading and profit and loss account for P. Lyons, for the period ending 10 January:

P. Lyons – Trading and profit and loss account for the 10 days ending 10 January 19x6

	£
Sales	270
Cost of goods sold	100
Gross profit	170
Add rent receivable	10
	180
Less telephone	100
Net profit	80

Profit is the difference between the revenue earned by the business and the expenses consumed in earning that revenue.

Revenue is the money earned from the sale or hire of goods and services. Examples include:

- *Sales revenue* – money earned from selling the goods and services which the organization normally deals in
- *Other revenues*, such as:
  - rent receivable from hiring out the assets of the business
  - interest receivable from bank balances
  - commission receivable from selling other people's goods.

P. Lyons had sales revenue of £270 and other revenue (rent receivable) of £10.

Expenses are items which are 'used up' in the running of the business. They do not have any lasting benefit to the organization. There are a great many kinds of expenses depending on the type of organization, but some examples include:

- gas, electricity, telephone, wages, salaries, rent and rates
- rent payable, interest payable and commission payable
- stocks of items which are quickly used up, such as stationery, heating oil and petrol
- stocks of materials and goods which the organization sells in the ordinary course of business.

Only those stocks which are used up are regarded as expenses; any remaining stocks are treated as assets, which will be explained in the next section.

P. Lyons has two types of expenses – goods which were sold and which cost £100, and telephone expenses of £100.

You will note that profit is calculated in two stages. *Gross profit* is the difference between sales revenue and the cost of the goods which were sold. *Net profit* is the final profit after adding any other revenues and deducting any other expenses.

The balance sheet   This statement provides information about the things which the business owns at a particular point in time, and where the money to provide those things has come from.

The balance sheet of P. Lyons at 10 January 19x6 is as follows:

P. Lyons – Balance sheet as at 10 January 19x6

	£		£	£
Assets		*Capital*		
Equipment	600	Capital at the start	1,000	
Stocks	50	Profit for the period	80	
Debtors	270		1,080	
Cash	710	*Liabilities*		1,080
		Loan	400	
		Creditors	150	
				550
	1,630			1,630

Assets are things which an organization owns or possesses, which have not yet been used up. Examples include the following:

- premises, office equipment, motor vehicles and plant and machinery
- stocks of goods intended for sale, raw materials, manufactured goods
- bank balances
- cash balances
- debtors – people who owe money to the organization. Debtors arise when an organization sells goods and services 'on credit', which means that the customers do not pay up at once. Such customers are called 'debtors' and they are regarded as assets because the money which they owe belongs to the organization.

P. Lyons has assets valued at £1,630. Note that the value of stocks shown on the balance sheet is the cost of the stocks remaining unsold at 10 January.

Capital is the money provided to the business by the owner(s). It may have been put in from their private funds when the business started; it might have been added to during the life of the business, either by additional capital being provided, or by profits being made which have been left in the business. If the owner(s) have withdrawn capital, this is known as *drawings* and reduces the amount of capital. P. Lyons started with capital of £1,000 and has made a profit of £80 which has been left in the business.

Liabilities are amounts which the business owes to other people and organizations. Examples include:

- loans from banks or other lenders, mortgages, monies borrowed from friends
- bank overdrafts
- creditors – people to whom the organization owes money because it has purchased goods or services on credit.

P. Lyons has a loan on which £400 is still owing, and creditors of £150.

The accounting equation   You might notice that the balance sheet is presented with two sides, each showing the same total of £1,630. This is because the balance sheet illustrates the *accounting equation*:

$$\boxed{\text{ASSETS} = \text{CAPITAL} + \text{LIABILITIES}}$$

This shows that the organization has assets of £1,630, £1,080 of which have been provided by the owner and £550 by others. You will use the accounting equation in different ways throughout your studies of accounting.

The 'separate entity' concept

An organization is separate from its owner or owners – it has an identity of its own. It can enter into transactions on its own behalf – it gains the benefits and bears the consequences of those transactions. For example, if it borrows money from a lender, it gains the benefit of that money and owes the lender for the amount borrowed.

An organization can also enter into transactions with its owner(s), in the same way as it enters into transactions with 'outsiders'. For example, if a business is provided with money by the owner (instead of from a lender), it gains the benefit of that money and it owes the owner for the amount borrowed. This is because the organization is regarded as being a 'separate entity' from its owner.

The purpose of this is to ensure that the transactions of an organization are distinguished from the personal transactions of the owner. Only business transactions should be recorded in the business books, and personal transactions should be ignored unless they affect the business. For example, the purchase of a washing machine for use in the owner's home, and paid for out of his personal funds, has no effect on the business and should not be recorded in the business books.

Now try Exercises 2.1 and 2.2 at the end of the chapter.

Maintaining the ledger

What is the ledger?

This is where all transactions are recorded. Originally, handwritten ledgers were used, but nowadays mechanical, electronic and computerized systems are widely used. Many organizations require more than one ledger, divided into sections, which we will look at later.

The account

The ledger is divided into pages. Each page will contain a record of the transactions which have taken place on each revenue, expense, asset, liability or capital item. The page is headed up with the title of the item, and is known as an 'account'. For example, the page which records transactions concerning electricity will be called the 'Electricity account'. When we need to know the amount spent on electricity, we simply turn to the electricity account and calculate the total from the information on the page.

Recording transactions in the accounts

A business can choose how many separate accounts it needs. For example, it might combine electricity and gas into a single 'Heat and light account'. Unless you are told otherwise, it is as well to maintain a separate account for each item.

The layout of the account and the information it contains are also a matter of choice. As a minimum, the account should show the date of each transaction, a description of the transaction or a reference number indicating where the description can be found, and the value involved.

Debits and credits

The account also needs to show whether each transaction causes an *increase* or a *decrease* in the value of that item. This can be done in several ways, but the most popular method in examinations is to use the 'two-sided' method, whereby the page is divided into two sides. The left-hand side is called the *Debit* side (abbreviated to DR), and the right-hand side is the *Credit* side (abbreviated to CR).

One side is used for increases, the other for decreases.

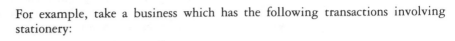

For example, take a business which has the following transactions involving stationery:

19x6
31 March	Paid bill in cash, £100
3 July	Received cash refund for overpayment, £30
30 October	Paid bill by cheque, £90
31 December	Paid bill by cheque, £40

A two-sided ledger account for stationery might appear as follows:

Stationery

19x6	£	19x6	£
31 Mar Cash paid	100	3 Jul Cash refunded	30
30 Oct Cheque paid	90		
31 Dec Cheque paid	40		

In order to calculate the final total for stationery, we need to add up all the increases on the debit side (£230) and deduct all the decreases on the credit side (£30), to arrive at £200 for the year.

Choosing which side of the account to use

Not all accounts use the debit side for increases and the credit side for decreases. The side to use depends on the category of account. You have already seen that there are five categories of account – revenues, expenses, assets, liabilities and capital.

For *revenues, liabilities* and *capital*, the credit side is used for increases and the debit side for decreases.

For *assets* and *expenses*, the debit side is used for increases and the credit side for decreases.

There are lots of different explanations as to why these sides are chosen, but there is no really easy way to remember the rules. The more you practise writing up ledger accounts, the more likely you are to become familiar with the rules, but until then you might find the following table useful to refer to:

Ledger account title

Debit side	*Credit side*
Increases in assets	Decreases in assets
Increases in expenses	Decreases in expenses
Decreases in revenues	Increases in revenues
Decreases in liabilities	Increases in liabilities
Decreases in capital	Increases in capital

It might also help to remember that assets and expenses are both things which an organization spends money to acquire, so they are treated in the same way as each other, while revenues, liabilities and capital all provide money or goods to an organization.

Now try Exercise 2.3 at the end of this chapter.

Double-entry book-keeping

Double-entry book-keeping is the system of keeping records which involves making two entries for every transaction. It is the only proper book-keeping system. Some small organizations use adaptations of the system, sometimes known as *single-entry* systems.

Every financial transaction which takes place has two effects – the effect of value coming into (being received by) the organization and the effect of value going out of (being given by) the organization.

Example

On 1 January, T. Morris lends your business £100 in cash.
This transaction has two effects:

● The business receives £100 cash (value comes into the business)
● T. Morris gives £100 cash (value will go out of the business when Morris is repaid).

Because every transaction has two effects, two accounts are involved in the transaction, and therefore two entries need to be made in the ledger.

The two accounts involved in the above example will be the cash account and T. Morris's account. In order to decide which side of each ledger account to use to record the transaction, we need to determine the category of each account and whether the transaction causes an increase or a decrease in each.

Cash is an *asset*. It is *increasing*. The rule is that increases in assets are recorded on the *debit* side of the account.

T. Morris is a *liability*. The amount owed to him is *increasing*. The rule is that increases in liabilities are recorded on the *credit* side of the account.

Thus, the *two entries* needed to record that transaction are:

● Debit the cash account *and*
● Credit T. Morris's account.

The ledger accounts would appear as follows:

	Cash		
	£		
1 Jan T. Morris	100		

	T. Morris		
			£
	1 Jan Cash		100

Each account contains the name of *the other account* used in the transaction, so that its opposite entry can be traced.

Note that the transaction resulted in a debit entry in one account and a credit entry in the other. This *always* applies, whatever the classification of the accounts involved and whether the effects are increases or decreases.

> The double entry rule is that every transaction requires a debit entry and a credit entry.

Account titles

An organization is entitled to use any titles it wishes for its accounts, but there are some standard titles and some accounts with specific uses.

Purchases

When raw materials and goods intended for sale are bought, they should be entered in an account entitled 'Purchases'. This account should never be used for any other kinds of purchase, such as machinery or stationery. The purchases account is usually classed as an expense account at this stage.

Sales

When goods which the business normally deals in are sold, they should be entered in an account entitled 'Sales'. This account should never be used for any other kinds of sale, such as the sale of plant or equipment. The sales account is classed as a revenue account.

Stock

There is an account entitled 'Stock' which you will look at in the next chapter. However, it is important that you do not use the stock account to record purchases and sales.

Rent, interest and commission

These can be either paid or received by an organization. It is important to have a separate account for each and to state clearly whether it deals with rent, interest or commission *payable* or *receivable*.

Carriage

An organization might incur costs for carriage on goods which it buys or sells. It is important to use separate accounts for carriage inwards (on goods bought) and carriage outwards (on goods sold).

A fully worked example of recording transactions in ledger accounts
On 1 January 19x6, R. Patterson starts a business with £500 in cash and £2,000 in the bank. He intends to open an 'Instant Print' shop selling photocopies and printed matter to the public. He has the following further transactions:

19x6
2 Jan   Buys a motor van for £1,200, paying by cheque
3 Jan   Buys some office equipment from S. Jackson for £450 on credit
10 Jan   Pays rates of £100 cash
12 Jan   Buys paper, inks and chemicals for photocopying and printing, for £500 on credit from Paper Supplies Ltd, and pays carriage charges of £25 cash
14 Jan   Pays S. Jackson £350 by cheque
15 Jan   Sells printed leaflets on credit to P. Walker for £125
16 Jan   Buys more office equipment for £200, paying by cheque
18 Jan   Receives a cheque refund of rates overpaid, of £40
20 Jan   Buys more paper and inks for £230 cash
21 Jan   Pays a gas bill of £140 by cheque
22 Jan   Returns faulty office equipment to S. Jackson, costing £20
26 Jan   Receives rent from a tenant of £50 cash

31 Jan Cash sales of photocopies for the month, £163
The ledger accounts would appear as follows:

Capital

19x6	£	19x6	£
		1 Jan Cash	500
		1 Jan Bank	2,000

Cash

19x6	£	19x6	£
1 Jan Capital	500	10 Jan Rates	100
26 Jan Rent receivable	50	12 Jan Carriage inwards	25
31 Jan Sales	163	20 Jan Purchases	230

Bank

19x6	£	19x6	£
1 Jan Capital	2,000	2 Jan Motor van	1,200
18 Jan Rates refund	40	14 Jan S. Jackson	350
		16 Jan Office equipment	200
		21 Jan Gas	140

Motor van

19x6	£	19x6	£
2 Jan Bank	1,200		

Office equipment

19x6	£	19x6	£
3 Jan S. Jackson	450	22 Jan S. Jackson	20
16 Jan Bank	200		

S. Jackson

19x6	£	19x6	£
14 Jan Bank	350	3 Jan Office equipment	450
22 Jan Office equipment	20		

Rates

19x6	£	19x6	£
10 Jan Cash	100	18 Jan Bank	40

Purchases

19x6	£	19x6	£
12 Jan Paper Supplies Ltd	500		
20 Jan Cash	230		

Paper Supplies Ltd

19x6	£	19x6	£
		12 Jan Purchases	500

Carriage inwards

19x6	£	19x6	£
12 Jan Cash	25		

Sales

19x6	£	19x6	£
		15 Jan P. Walker	125
		31 Jan Cash	163

P. Walker

19x6	£	19x6	£
15 Jan Sales	125		

Gas

19x6	£	19x6	£
21 Jan Bank	140		

Rent receivable

19x6	£	19x6	£
		26 Jan Cash	50

Now do Exercises 2.4, 2.5x and 2.6x at the end of this chapter.

Further transactions

Returning stocks

You have already learnt to keep separate accounts for stocks bought (Purchases) and stocks sold (Sales). The reason for this is that they are valued at different levels – purchases are at cost price and sales are at selling price. Furthermore, not all purchases are sold at once, so a single account would give confusing information.

We also need separate accounts for stocks returned.

Returns outwards (also called Purchase returns)

These are stocks which the organization has sent back to the supplier. The ledger entries to be made when such goods are returned are:

● Debit the creditor (the liability owed to him is decreasing)
● Credit Returns outwards (the expense of purchases is decreasing).

Returns inwards (also called Sales returns)

These are stocks which the organization has received back from its customers. The ledger entries to be made when such goods are returned are:

● Credit the debtor (the asset owed by him is decreasing)
● Debit Returns inwards (the revenue from sales is decreasing).

> Note that these returns accounts are used only for the return of stocks. They are never used for the return of items such as stationery, machinery or equipment. If these are returned, then the stationery, machinery or equipment account is credited.

Returning stocks for an immediate refund

If a refund is given, as might happen if the debtor's or creditor's account has already been paid, the two accounts involved are the relevant returns account and bank or cash.

Example

A business has the following transactions:

19x6		Debit	Credit
1 Jan	Business commences with £10,000 capital in the bank	Bank	Capital
2 Jan	Materials paid by cheque, £5,000	Purchases	Bank
3 Jan	Goods sold on credit to L. Burton for £2,000	L. Burton	Sales
4 Jan	Materials purchased on credit from T. Porter for £1,000	Purchases	T. Porter
5 Jan	Materials costing £50 returned to T. Porter	T. Porter	Purchase returns
6 Jan	Goods sold for £4,000, paid for by cheque	Bank	Sales
7 Jan	L. Burton returns goods worth £100	Sales returns	L. Burton
8 Jan	L. Burton pays £1,900 by cheque	Bank	L. Burton
9 Jan	L. Burton returns goods worth £10 for cheque refund	Sales returns	Bank

The ledger accounts would appear as follows:

Capital

19x6	£	19x6	£
		1 Jan Bank	10,000

Bank

19x6	£	19x6	£
1 Jan Capital	10,000	2 Jan Purchases	5,000
6 Jan Sales	4,000	9 Jan Sales returns	10
8 Jan L. Burton	1,900		

Purchases

19x6	£	19x6	£
2 Jan Bank	5,000		
4 Jan T. Porter	1,000		

L. Burton

19x6	£	19x6	£
3 Jan Sales	2,000	7 Jan Sales returns	100
		8 Jan Bank	1,900

Sales

19x6	£	19x6	£
		3 Jan L. Burton	2,000
		6 Jan Bank	4,000

T. Porter

19x6	£	19x6	£
5 Jan Purchase returns	50	4 Jan Purchases	1,000

Purchase returns

19x6	£	19x6	£
		5 Jan T. Porter	50

Sales returns

19x6	£	19x6	£
7 Jan L. Burton	100		
9 Jan Bank	10		

Bad debts

When it becomes known that a debtor is unable or unwilling to pay all or part of his debt it is wrong to continue treating him as a debtor (and hence as an asset) of the business, and therefore the amount which is unlikely to be received is 'written off'. This amount is known as a *bad debt*.

The ledger entries required are:

- Credit the debtor's account
- Debit a Bad debts written off account

with the relevant amount.

The balance on the bad debts written off account is regarded as an expense of the organization.

Before writing off a bad debt, a reasonable effort should be made to recover the money, unless it is known that the debtor is bankrupt or is unable to be traced.

Recovery of a bad debt

If a written-off debt later appears likely to be paid, the amount is 'written back', by reversing the original entries, i.e:

- Debit the debtor's account
- Credit Bad debts written off.

A worked example

G. Hallam bought goods from the business on 5 January 19x6 for £1,200. On 20 January 19x6 you discover that he is bankrupt and is only able to pay one-quarter of the debt, and you therefore write off the remainder. On 25 February 19x6 you are notified that he can in fact pay half the debt. On 18 March 19x6, he pays £200 towards the debt.

Note that there are several different stages to this – the original writing-off of the bad amount, the writing-back of the extra sum likely to be received, and the receipt of part of the money owing. The ledger accounts would appear as follows:

G. Hallam

19x6	£	19x6	£
5 Jan Sales	1,200	20 Jan Bad debts written off	900
20 Feb Bad debts written off	300	18 Mar Bank	200

Bad debts written off

19x6	£	19x6	£
20 Jan G. Hallam	900	20 Feb G. Hallam	300

Drawings

Drawings are amounts of money, goods or other items taken out of a business by the owner for his own personal use. They are decreases in the amount of capital, and some organizations might debit the capital account with them. In examinations, however, you should open a separate drawings account and debit that. The credit entry will be to whatever item the owner has taken. If stocks have been taken, the credit entry is to the purchases account. If he has used business funds to pay a personal bill, say a telephone bill, and that has been debited to the telephone account, then that account is credited. Other examples include stationery and office equipment.

The value used is always the original cost to the business, even if the normal selling price is different.

Capital introduced

Owners commonly put money into the business, but they might put in other personal items, such as a car or equipment. In such cases, the capital account is credited and the debit entry is to whatever item has been introduced, e.g. motor vehicles or equipment.

Summary

By the end of this chapter you should understand the need for book-keeping and be able to record simple financial transactions using the double-entry system of book-keeping. You should be able to explain the meaning of the terms 'revenues',

'expenses', 'assets', 'capital' and 'liabilities', and be aware of the contents of the trading and profit and loss account and balance sheet. You should also be able to define the 'accounting equation', and appreciate its meaning.

Now do Exercises 2.7, 2.8, 2.9x, 2.10, 2.11x at the end of this chapter.

Exercises

2.1 Prepare a profit and loss account and a balance sheet from the following information:

	£
Cash	250
Sales	400
Cost of stock sold	180
Heat and light	50
Creditors	40
Equipment	100
Premises	700
Wages	30
Debtors	60
Loans	120
Capital	830
Stock remaining	20

2.2 Classify the following into the correct category by heading up four columns, one each for 'assets', 'liabilities', 'revenues' and 'expenses':

Rent receivable; electricity; office machinery; debtors; bank balance; premises; gas; rent and rates payable; wages and salaries; sales; cost of stock sold; bank interest receivable; creditors; cash; loans; stock remaining.

2.3 State the type of account (asset, liability, capital, revenue or expense) for each of the following, and the side of the ledger account which should be used to record the effect:

	Type of account	*Side of ledger account to be used*
Increase in cash		
Decrease in creditor		
Increase in electricity		
Increase in bank balance		
Decrease in debtors		
Increase in sales		
Increase in capital		
Decrease in electricity		
Increase in purchases		
Increase in rent payable		
Decrease in rent receivable		
Increase in machinery		
Decrease in bank balance		
Increase in bank loan		

2.4   Complete the columns given for each of the following transactions (the first is done for you):

		Titles of accounts	Types of accounts	Increase/ decrease	Debit/ credit
19x6					
1 Jan	P. Lyons puts £1,000 of his own money into the business cash drawer	Cash Capital	Asset Capital	Increase Increase	Debit Credit
2 Jan	P. Smith lends £500 cash to the business				
3 Jan	He pays the business telephone bill of £100 out of the cash				
4 Jan	He repays £100 cash to P. Smith				
5 Jan	He buys equipment for £400 cash				
6 Jan	He buys clothes intended for sale, for £150 cash				
7 Jan	He buys equipment worth £200 from L. Peters, but does not pay for it at once				
8 Jan	He sells some of the clothes (which had cost £100) for £270 to L. Samson who does not pay at once				
9 Jan	He receives £10 cash from hiring out some of his equipment				
10 Jan	He pays L. Peters £50 cash				

When you have completed the columns, enter the transactions in the ledger accounts.

2.5x   Complete the columns given for each of the following transactions:

		Titles of accounts	Types of accounts	Increase/ decrease	Debit/ credit
19x6					
1 Feb	F. Brown starts a business selling video cameras, with £18,000 cash of his own money				
2 Feb	He buys fixtures and fittings for £1,750 cash				
3 Feb	He pays rent on his shop of £1,200 cash				
4 Feb	He buys video cameras for £7,000 on credit from I. Poole				
5 Feb	He pays wages of £125 in cash				
6 Feb	He sells fixtures and fittings for £350 to A. Osborne on credit				
7 Feb	He sells video cameras on credit for £5,000 to S. Morrell				
8 Feb	He pays for delivery on the video cameras sold, of £30 cash				
9 Feb	He buys more fixtures and fittings on credit from G. Good for £400				
10 Feb	A. Morrell pays him £3,000, which he pays into the bank				

	Titles of accounts	Types of accounts	Increase/ decrease	Debit/ credit

19x6

11 Feb He receives commission, £50 cash

12 Feb He transfers £50 cash to the bank

When you have completed the columns, enter the transactions in the ledger accounts.

2.6x   Enter the following transactions into the ledger accounts:

19x6

1 Jan   R. Lewis opens a sweetshop, with £1,000 in cash and £4,000 in the bank

2 Jan   He buys fixtures and fittings, paying £1,415 by cheque

3 Jan   He buys fixtures and fittings on credit for £810 from Easifit Ltd

4 Jan   He buys sweets on credit for £2,000 from J. Good & Sons

5 Jan   He sells fixtures to the Crown Hotel for £248, on credit

6 Jan   He takes out a loan of £40,000 and purchases the shop

7 Jan   He pays carriage charges on sweets purchased, of £30 cash

8 Jan   He returns faulty fixtures to Easifit Ltd, costing £60

9 Jan   He pays £125 in cash for the hire of a van

10 Jan He sells sweets for £1,500 cash

11 Jan The Crown Hotel pays £48 cash on account

12 Jan He sells sweets for £400 cash

13 Jan He pays J. Good £1,200 by cheque

14 Jan He pays another £2,000 of his own money into the business bank account

15 Jan He transfers £100 from the bank into the cash till

The following exercises are used again in exercises at the end of Chapters 3 and 4. Leave at least three blank lines between each account, and check your answers carefully.

2.7   P. Roberts starts a business, with £2,500 in the bank and £500 cash, on 1 January 19x6. The following transactions occur:

19x6

2 Jan   He buys raw materials on credit for £700 from J. Martin

3 Jan   He sells goods for £300 on credit to G. Goddard

7 Jan   He sells goods for £1,100 to K. Lemon on credit

12 Jan He buys equipment for £3,000, paying by cheque

17 Jan He returns raw materials worth £150 to J. Martin

18 Jan K. Lemon returns goods worth £240

20 Jan He buys raw materials for £350, paying by cheque

23 Jan He sells equipment for £100 cash

28 Jan He pays J. Martin £250 by cheque

29 Jan He receives notice that G. Goddard expects to pay only 50 per cent of his debt

30 Jan He transfers £200 cash into the bank from his cash box

Record the above transactions in the ledger accounts.

2.8   R. Moss starts a business on 1 January 19x6, with £5,000 in the bank and £500 cash. The following transactions occur:

19x6

3 Jan	He buys fixtures and fittings for £2,000, paying by cheque
4 Jan	He buys raw materials from D. Hill for £3,000 on credit
6 Jan	He returns raw materials costing £800 to D. Hill
9 Jan	He sells goods on credit to A. Clark for £1,700
10 Jan	He draws out £30 cash for himself
11 Jan	He buys raw materials from D. Hill for £1,200 on credit and pays £20 cash for carriage charges on these goods
12 Jan	He pays carriage charges of £50 cash on goods sold to A. Clark
14 Jan	He sells goods for £80 on credit to H. Fielding
17 Jan	He pays D. Hill £1,500 by cheque
19 Jan	A. Clark returns goods worth £200
23 Jan	He sells goods to A. Clark for £1,900 on credit; he pays rent and rates of £60 in cash; he pays gas charges of £40 cash
24 Jan	He receives notice that H. Fielding is bankrupt and is unable to pay his debt
26 Jan	He receives bank interest of £10 paid direct to the bank account
28 Jan	He transfers £100 from the bank into the cash till
29 Jan	He borrows £300 cash from L. Harwood, repayable in five years

Record the above transactions in the ledger accounts.

2.9x   On 1 January 19x6 Sam Small starts a business with £45,000 in the bank and £1,000 cash. During his first six months he has the following transactions:

19x6

10 Jan	He pays rent of £150 cash
20 Jan	He buys a shop for £38,000, paying by cheque
30 Jan	He buys fixtures and fittings for £1,000 on credit from D. Middle
27 Feb	He buys goods for resale on credit from B. Large for £3,000
15 Mar	He returns goods costing £300 to B. Large
4 Apr	He sells goods to R. Little on credit for £2,500 and pays carriage charges of £50 cash on these goods
3 May	He pays rent of £200 cash
10 May	R. Little returns goods worth £100
15 May	He withdraws £400 cash for himself
18 May	He receives a refund of rent overpaid of £50, by cheque
20 May	R. Little pays him £2,000 by cheque
1 Jun	He pays B. Large £1,500 by cheque
20 Jun	He buys goods for resale from B. Large for £900, on credit, and pays carriage charges on these goods of £150 in cash
25 Jun	He pays for heating and lighting, £600 by cheque
26 Jun	He sells goods on credit to T. Turner for £45
30 Jun	He receives notice that T. Turner is unlikely to pay two-thirds of his debt. He receives rent from a tenant of £40 by cheque

Record the above transactions in the ledger accounts.

2.10   On 1 May 19x6 T. Wood starts a business as a plumber's merchant, with £5,000 in the bank. The following transactions occurred during his first month of trading:

19x6

3 May	He bought machinery on credit from J. Lomas for £1,400
5 May	He paid for electricity, £50 by cheque
7 May	He bought plumbing materials on credit from R. Fisher for £800, and paid for their delivery, £25 by cheque
9 May	He sold plumbing materials for £70 cash
10 May	He returned plumbing materials costing £40 to R. Fisher
12 May	He paid the office secretary's wages of £25 in cash
14 May	He sold plumbing materials to E. Wishbone, for £450 on credit
18 May	He sold machinery which had cost £300, for the same sum, in cash
21 May	He received commission of £170 in cash
23 May	He returned machinery costing £200 to J. Lomas Ltd
24 May	E. Wishbone returned plumbing materials worth £80
25 May	He sold plumbing materials on credit for £85 to N. Capstick
27 May	He paid for the delivery of these materials, £35 by cheque
29 May	He received bank interest of £15 paid direct into the bank

Record the above transactions in the ledger accounts.

2.11x Donald Wiston commenced in business on 1 July 19x6 as a dealer in sports equipment. He paid £5,600 into a business bank account and £35 into a cash box. During July the following transactions occurred:

19x6

3 July	He bought 500 hockey sticks at £3 each from Sports Suppliers Ltd, and paid carriage charges of £15 by cheque
7 July	He rented premises for the month, paying £450 by cheque
9 July	He bought stationery for £56 on credit from W.H. Smithers
11 July	He sold 300 hockey sticks for £7 each on credit to Newtown Sports Club
12 July	He paid carriage charges on the hockey sticks sold, of £8 cash
15 July	He paid wages of £75 by cheque
18 July	He bought packing equipment for £1,000 on credit from F. Jacobs
21 July	He paid Sports Suppliers Ltd £1,500 by cheque
23 July	He paid electricity charges of £125 by cheque
25 July	He sold 10 hockey sticks for £8 each, cash
26 July	He paid telephone bills of £230 by cheque
27 July	He discovered that one of the telephone bills, for £35, was for his private telephone
29 July	Newtown Sports paid £1,750 by cheque
30 July	He returned 40 hockey sticks to Sports Suppliers Ltd, receiving a cheque refund
31 July	Newtown Sports returned 5 hockey sticks costing £7 each

Record the above transactions in the ledger accounts.

3   Summarizing the accounts

Aims of the chapter

The aims of this chapter are to:

- explain the purpose of the trial balance
- demonstrate the calculation of the balance on a ledger account
- demonstrate the preparation and agreement of the trial balance
- explain the purpose of, and demonstrate the preparation of, the trading and profit and loss account
- introduce the purpose and use of the stock account
- explain the purpose of, and demonstrate the preparation of, the balance sheet
- discuss alternative classifications of ledger accounts
- explain the nature of capital and revenue transactions.

All businesses need to summarize their accounts from time to time and to prepare information for the various users as outlined in Chapter 1. This is usually done by preparing a trading and profit and loss account and a balance sheet at least annually, or more often if appropriate.

To help them in providing this information, they first need to ensure that, as far as possible, the entries made in the ledger accounts are accurate.

The trial balance

The *trial balance* is a list of all the ledger accounts, showing the position of each one at a particular date. The following is an example of a trial balance for J. Taylor, who commenced in business on 1 March 19x5:

J. Taylor – Trial balance as at 31 March 19x5

	DR £	CR £
Capital at 1.3.19x5		3,500
Cash	300	
Bank	1,150	
Motor van	2,400	
Office equipment	700	
Creditors		600
Rates	80	
Purchases	530	
Returns outwards		70
Carriage inwards	25	
Sales		590
Returns inwards	20	
Debtors	325	
Drawings	30	
Loan		1,000
Electricity	250	
Rent receivable		50
	5,810	5,810

Calculating the balance on an account

The *balance on an account* is the difference between the debit and credit entries made on it.

In the above trial balance is an office equipment account with a balance of £700. The ledger account might have looked like this:

Office equipment				
19x5	£	19x5		£
3 Mar Purvis	850	31 Mar S. Purvis		300
16 Mar Bank	150			

The balance on this account is £1,000 debit less £300 credit, i.e. £700 debit, which indicates that the business has £700 worth of office equipment.

An account will have a *debit balance* if the total of debit entries exceeds the total of credit entries; it will have a *credit balance* if the opposite applies; it will have a *nil balance* if the debit and credit totals are the same.

Preparing the trial balance

The trial balance is an important statement, so it must be properly headed up with the name of the organization and the date at which it is prepared. It is presented with two columns headed 'Debit' and 'Credit'. The accounts are listed in any suitable order and the balance placed in the appropriate column. Some accounts might be grouped together and shown as one total – this often applies to debtors and creditors, especially where there are large numbers of them.

Accounts with a nil balance need not be shown.

Avoid the urge to write anything in the ledger accounts at this stage – if you need to write figures down to help you calculate the balance, then do this on a separate sheet of paper.

Accounts with debit balances are mainly assets and expenses, but will also include drawings and returns inwards. Accounts with credit balances are mainly revenues, liabilities and capital, but will also include returns outwards.

Agreeing the trial balance

When all the ledger accounts have been listed, the two columns are totalled. If the double-entry rule has been carefully applied – i.e. every transaction has been given a debit entry and a credit entry – then the two totals should agree. If they do not, then checks should be made in the following order:

1 Re-total the two columns.
2 Check that all assets, expenses, returns inwards and drawings have been shown as debit balances, and that revenues, liabilities, capital and returns outwards are shown as credit balances.

> Useful tip: Divide the difference by 2 and look for a balance for that amount which might have been recorded in the wrong column.

3 Check through the ledger accounts to ensure that no account has been omitted from the trial balance.
4 Check any balances which have been added together on the trial balance, e.g. debtors.
5 Check that individual balances have been recorded correctly on the trial balance.
6 Recalculate the individual balances.
7 Check the transactions for the possibility of one 'half' of an entry having been omitted from the ledger accounts.

8 Finally, check each transaction back to the ledger accounts.

What the trial balance proves

The trial balance only proves that for every debit entry there is an equivalent credit entry. It does not prove that no errors have been made at all. For example, an entry could be in the wrong account, or a complete transaction could have been omitted – neither of these would prevent the trial balance from agreeing.

In theory, the trial balance should agree before the accounts can be relied upon. Even a small difference can hide two or more larger errors. In practice, a senior person will look at the balances to determine that they appear reasonable, and, if so, it is assumed that the figures can be relied upon for the time being, until there is time to investigate more fully.

Now do Exercises 3.1, 3.2, 3.3x, 3.4 and 3.5x at the end of this chapter.

The trading and profit and loss account

The trading and profit and loss account brings together the revenues earned and expenses used up in earning that revenue. It calculates the profit. As profit is earned *throughout* the period, the trading and profit and loss account covers a *period of time*.

In theory, it consists of two accounts, but most organizations combine the two.

The trading account

The *trading account* is used to calculate gross profit.

Gross profit is the difference between revenue from sales and the cost of making those goods saleable. This cost will include the cost of raw materials or goods, any carriage inwards, and any other costs necessary to make the goods fit for sale. It does not include the cost of *selling* the goods, so it never contains selling expenses or carriage outwards.

In order to prepare the trading account, you need either the trial balance or the ledger accounts in front of you. You also need to know how much stock is remaining, in order to calculate the cost of the stock which has been sold. For the example in the trial balance above, let us say that the remaining stock (called 'closing stock') at 31 March was £300.

The trading account for J. Taylor would appear as follows:

J. Taylor – Trading account for the month ending 31 March 19x5

	£	£
Sales	590	
less Returns inwards	20	
Net sales		570
less Cost of goods sold:		
Purchases	530	
add Carriage inwards	25	
	555	
less Returns outwards	70	
	485	
less Closing stock	300	
Cost of goods sold		185
Gross profit		385

The profit and loss account

The *profit and loss account* is used to calculate net profit. Net profit is the profit remaining after all other revenues have been added to, and all other expenses have been deducted from, the gross profit.

Net profit belongs to the owner(s) of the business, and therefore is added to his capital.

If the expenses exceed the gross profit and other revenues, then a net loss is made, which is deducted from the owner's capital.

The profit and loss account of J. Taylor would appear as follows:

J. Taylor – Profit and loss account for the month ending 31 March 19x5

	£	£
Gross profit (from the trading account)		385
Add Other revenues		50
		435
Less Expenses:		
Rates	80	
Electricity	250	
		330
Net profit		105

The trading and profit and loss account are usually combined.

Now do Exercises 3.6, 3.7, 3.8x, 3.9 and 3.10x at the end of this chapter.

Making entries in the ledger accounts

As the trading and profit and loss account are prepared, each of the accounts which is included is 'transferred' from the ledger into the trading and profit and loss account. This is done by making an entry on the *opposite* side of the account to the one which denotes the balance. For example, the purchases account would require an entry on the credit side, because it has a debit balance. In the above example, the purchases account might be as follows:

Purchases

19x5		£	19x5		£
10 Mar Cash		470	31 Mar Trading account		530
20 Mar Bank		60			

The rent receivable account would require a debit entry, because it has a credit balance:

Rent receivable

19x5		£	19x5		£
31 Mar Profit and loss account		50	30 Mar Cash		50

The 'opposite entry' for each transfer is made in the trading and profit and loss account. The layouts used above do not appear as ledger accounts, but nevertheless the double-entry rule still applies. Revenues are credited to the trading and profit and loss account and expenses are debited.

The stock account

So far we have not used a stock account. For transactions involving stock we have used the purchases, sales and returns account. The stock account is only used at the end of the period when the trading account is prepared. It is opened now to record the closing stock at the end of the period.

As stock is an asset, the account is debited.

For J. Taylor above, the stock account would appear as follows:

Stock

19x5	£	19x5	
31 Mar Trading account	300		

Net profit

This is credited to the owner's capital account. If a net loss is made, that would be debited instead.

Drawings

Drawings are not expenses of an organization, so they do not form part of the profit calculation. They reduce the amount of capital provided by the owner, so at the end of the period the balance on the drawings account is transferred to the capital account. In J. Taylor's books, the two accounts would now appear as follows:

Drawings

19x5	£	19x5	£
12 Mar Cash	30	31 Mar Capital	30

Capital

19x5	£	19x5	£
31 Mar Drawings	30	1 Mar Bank	3,500
		31 Mar Net profit	105

Now do Exercises 3.11, 3.12, 3.13X, 3.14 and 3.15X at the end of this chapter.

The balance sheet

The *balance sheet* is a statement of balances on the ledger accounts at a particular point in time. It is prepared after the trading and profit and loss account have been completed.

Many of the ledger accounts will no longer have balances remaining at this stage – those which have been transferred into the trading and profit and loss account will have nil balances. The accounts which do still have balances remaining will all be assets, liabilities and capital.

The balance sheet for J. Taylor would appear as follows:

J. Taylor – Balance sheet as at 31 March 19x5

	£	£		£	£
Fixed assets			*Capital*		
Motor van	2,400		Opening balance	3,500	
Office equipment	700		Net profit	105	
		3,100			3,605
Current assets			*less* Drawings		30
Stocks	300				3,575
Debtors	325		*Long-term liabilities*		
Bank	1,150		Loan		1,000
Cash	300		*Current liabilities*		
		2,075	Creditors		600
		5,175			5,175

The balance sheet above is presented in two-sided format, but do not think that it is a ledger account. It is presented in this way purely for ease of understanding at this point in your studies.

Note that assets and liabilities have been sub-divided into two groups each.

Fixed assets

These are assets of a major nature, bought with the intention of being retained in the business for some time. Although they might eventually be sold, this is not the main purpose of their acquisition. Examples include land, buildings, plant, equipment and motor vehicles. An asset is usually regarded as fixed if it is intended to be retained for more than twelve months.

Current assets

These are assets of a more temporary nature which will be used up and replaced or sold quickly. Examples include stocks of materials and goods for sale, debtors and bank and cash balances.

Long-term liabilities

These are amounts owed by the business which are not due for repayment in the next twelve months. Examples include mortgages, hire-purchase agreements and bank loans.

Current liabilities

These are amounts owed by the business which are due for repayment in the next twelve months. Examples include creditors and bank overdrafts (even though some businesses regard their bank overdraft as semi-permanent).

The order of assets and liabilities is also important. Within each group, the first item is the one which is most permanent, the last item is the least permanent. This is known as *reverse order of liquidity* – the item most 'liquid', or easily turned into cash, is shown last.

Vertical presentation of the balance sheet

Nowadays it is popular to present the balance sheet in a vertical format. The above balance sheet would appear as follows:

J. Taylor – Balance sheet as at 31 March 19x5

	£	£	£
Fixed assets			
Motor van		2,400	
Office equipment		700	
			3,100
Current assets			
Stocks	300		
Debtors	325		
Bank	1,150		
Cash	300		
		2,075	
less Current liabilities			
Creditors		600	
Net current assets			1,475
			4,575
less Long-term liabilities			
Loan			1,000
			3,575
Financed by:			
Opening capital			3,500
Net profit			105
			3,605
less Drawings			30
			3,575

The main advantage of this layout is that it shows the very important figure of *net current assets* (£1,475). This is the difference between current assets and current liabilities, and it shows the funds of the organization which are available for day-to-day use. Current assets will all be converted into cash in the near future, if they are not already, and after deducting the liabilities which are due for payment soon the remaining balance is the amount of 'liquid funds' which the organization has. This figure is also called *working capital*.

Another advantage is that the layout clearly shows the investment in the business by the owner, in the section entitled 'Financed by'. This figure is sometimes taken to represent the net worth of the business – it is the value which would remain if all assets were sold for the values at which they are shown in the balance sheet, and all outside liabilities were repaid.

The accounting equation

You saw in Chapter 2 that the accounting equation is:

$$\text{Assets} = \text{Capital} + \text{Liabilities}$$

as shown in the two-sided version of the balance sheet. The equation still works with the vertical presentation, except it is restated as

$$\text{Assets} - \text{Liabilities} = \text{Capital}$$

Now do Exercises 3.16, 3.17, 3.18x, 3.19 and 3.20x at the end of this chapter.

Personal, real and nominal accounts

This is another way of classifying accounts. The categories are as follows:

● *Personal accounts* are those which record transactions with people and organizations, e.g. debtors and creditors.
● *Real accounts* are those which record transactions about items which can be touched, e.g. premises, machinery and stocks. This category also usually includes bank and cash accounts.
● *Nominal accounts* are those which record transactions about items involving profits and losses, e.g. revenues and expenses.

Capital and revenue items

This is yet another way of classifying accounts and types of transactions.

● *Capital items* are those which have a long-term effect on the organization. They have no immediate effect on the calculation of profit and are usually shown on the balance sheet. Examples include land and buildings, machinery, long-term investments and loans.
● *Revenue items* are those which have a short-term effect on the organization. They have an immediate effect on the calculation of profit and are usually shown in the trading and profit and loss account. Examples include stocks of materials and goods for sale, revenues and expenses.

Capital and revenue expenditure

The purchase of a capital item is obviously capital expenditure. The amount is debited to the assets account and shown on the balance sheet. Some transactions might be connected with capital items, but might still be revenue transactions. For example, the *repair of* a piece of equipment is *revenue expenditure* because it is an expense which is taken to the profit and loss account, but it is connected with a capital item of equipment. Generally, if the expenditure *improves* the item beyond its original condition, or provides some benefit which did not previously exist, the item is classed as *capital expenditure* and is added to the cost of the item in its ledger account; if it is merely bringing the item back to its original condition, then it is *revenue expenditure* and is charged to the profit and loss account in the period in which it is incurred.

Some common examples which occur in examinations include the following:

- *Capital expenditure*
  - new central heating system, where there was none before
  - double glazing which replaces single glazing
  - painting of a company logo on a building or motor vehicle
  - delivery and installation costs for a new machine
- *Revenue expenditure*
  - new engine in a motor vehicle
  - new roof for a building
  - insurance of premises
  - all kinds of repairs and maintenance

Capital and revenue receipts

These occur when items are sold or insurance monies are received for loss or damage to items. The classification depends on the nature of the item. Monies from the sale or other disposal of revenue items are classed as revenue receipts and would be taken to the profit and loss account. Monies from the sale or insurance proceeds of capital items are classed as capital receipts and would be dealt with by reducing the value of the items on the balance sheet.

Summary

By the end of this chapter you should be able to summarize the ledger accounts using the trial balance, and prepare the trading and profit and loss account and balance sheet. You should be aware of different classifications of ledger accounts, and of the difference between capital and revenue transactions.

Exercises

3.1, 3.2, 3.3x, 3.4, 3.5x   Prepare a trial balance for each of Exercises 2.7, 2.8, 2.9x, 2.10, 2.11x in the previous chapter.

3.6, 3.7, 3.8x, 3.9, 3.10x   Prepare a trading and profit and loss account for each of Exercises 2.7, 2.8, 2.9x, 2.10, 2.11x in the previous chapter. Closing stock figures are as follows: Exercise 2.7 – £200; Exercise 2.8 – £660; Exercise 2.9x – £1,790; Exercise 2.10 – £460; Exercise 2.11x – 155 hockey sticks at £3 each.

3.11, 3.12, 3.13x, 3.14, 3.15x   Transfer the relevant balances for each of Exercises 2.7, 2.8, 2.9x, 2.10, 2.11x in the previous chapter to/from the trading and profit and loss account, and transfer any balance on the drawings account to the capital account.

3.16, 3.17, 3.18x, 3.19, 3.20x   Prepare a balance sheet for each of Exercises 2.7, 2.8, 2.9x, 2.10, 2.11x in the previous chapter.

3.21 Classify each of the following transactions as capital or revenue:

Purchase of plant; delivery costs of plant purchased; repairs to plant; income from the sale of plant; income from the sale of stocks; income from the sale of stationery; expenditure on stationery; insurance claim for stolen motor vehicle; insurance claim for stock destroyed by fire; commission receivable.

4

Subsequent accounting periods and adjustments

Aims of the chapter

The aims of this chapter are to:

- demonstrate the method of balancing off ledger accounts at the end of a period
- explain the method of maintaining ledger accounts in second and subsequent accounting periods
- explain and demonstrate the treatment of opening stock in the calculation of cost of goods sold
- explain and demonstrate the treatment and recording of accruals and prepayments

Balancing off the ledger accounts

Once the trading and profit and loss account and balance sheet have been completed at the end of a period of trading, the ledger accounts will need to be 'balanced off' ready to commence the next period. Balancing off is a kind of 'tidying up' of the ledger accounts, so that the balance is immediately obvious; if this tidying up were not done, ledger accounts would simply grow in length as more debit and credit entries were made, and to determine the balance would be time-consuming.

The procedure for balancing off an account has four stages:

- *Stage 1* – Calculate the balance on the account by adding up the two sides and taking one from the other (which you have already done in preparing the trial balance). Again, resist the urge to write anything in the ledger accounts at this stage.
- *Stage 2* – Enter the balance on the side with the smaller total. The date used should be the last day of the period; the description should be 'Balance carried down' or 'Balance carried forward' if you are at the bottom of a page.
- *Stage 3* – The two sides should now be equal, so total them up to prove that they are. Put the totals on the same level as each other and rule double lines under each total to show that you have no need of them now.
- *Stage 4* – Enter the balance below the total line on the appropriate side of the account, i.e. on the debit side for a debit balance and on the credit side for a credit balance. The date used should be the first day of the next period; the description should be 'Balance carried down' (or 'forward').

Example of an account with a credit balance

Fred Smith Ltd

19x5	£	19x5	£	
5 Apr Returns	600	4 Apr Purchases	4,000	
6 Apr Bank	1,200	7 Apr Purchases	3,000	Enter the totals on the same level
30 Apr Balance c/d	5,200			
	7,000		7,000	
Enter the balance on the side with the smaller total		1 May Balance b/d	5,200	Enter the balance on its correct side

(Note the abbreviations 'c/d' and 'b/d' for 'carried down' and 'brought down'.)

Students are often confused by the various figures involved in the balancing-off process. Stage 1 involves adding up the entries on the two sides, which gives two figures. The difference between the two sides is the balance, which is entered on the smaller side in Stage 2. Stage 3 involves adding up the two sides again to give yet another set of totals. Stage 4 involves the balance from Stage 2 being carried down. Take care that it is the balance which you carry down, and not the totals.

Example of an account with no balance

Some ledger accounts will have no balance remaining, either because the balance has been transferred to the trading and profit and loss account (this will apply to revenues and expenses), or because the debit and credit sides were already equal (e.g. when a debtor has paid in full). In such cases, all that needs to be done is to add up the two sides to ensure that they are equal, and rule them off with double lines.

J. Allen Ltd

19x5	£	19x5	£
5 Apr Sales	2,300	10 Apr Bank	1,200
		20 Apr Bank	1,100
	2,300		2,300

Example of an account with no balance and only one entry on each side

If an account has no balance and only one entry on each side, then there is no point in totalling the two sides to make sure they agree – simply rule off each side.

A. Jordan

19x5	£	19x5	£
16 Apr Bank	1,450	4 Apr Purchases	1,450

Example of an account with only one entry

If an account has only one entry, then the balance is equal to that entry. It need only be recorded on the opposite side, and the two sides can be ruled off without the need for totals.

Machinery

19x5	£	19x5	£
13 Apr Bank	4,500	30 Apr Balance c/d	4,500
1 May Balance b/d	4,500		

All accounts should be balanced off in one of these ways, so that they are ready to start the next period. Check that those with debit balances are assets, and those with credit balances are either liabilities or capital. Remember, though, that the bank balance could be credit if there is an overdraft.

The only exception to the above is the *stock* account, which was created from the entry in the trading account; there is no need to balance this off at all.

Now do Exercises 4.1, 4.2, 4.3x, 4.4 and 4.5x at the end of this chapter.

The next accounting period

Entries in the following period are made on the next available line after the totals. Remember *not* to use the stock account for any transactions in the next period – the purchases account should be used for stock bought, and the sales account should be used for stock sold.

Opening ledger accounts for the next period

Examination questions sometimes give you the balances at the beginning of the second period and ask you to open ledger accounts before proceeding to enter the next period's transactions.

If this happens, as soon as you have opened the ledger accounts, check that the total of debit balances equals the total of credit balances. Examination questions often omit to tell you the capital figure. Thus, if the debits total more than the credits, the difference could be the amount of capital. If you are already given the capital figure and the debits still total more than the credits, this could be because the bank balance should be an overdraft (and therefore should be a credit balance rather than a debit balance).

The next trial balance

At the end of the second period a trial balance will again be produced. The method of preparation is exactly the same as we saw in the previous chapter. Each balance is determined by adding up the entries on the two sides and taking one from the other. Take care to add in the balance which has been brought down from the previous period (if there is one), but you must *not* add in any figures which appear above the balancing totals.

Example

		Fred Smith Ltd			
19x5		£	*19x5*		£
5 Apr	Returns	600	4 Apr	Purchases	4,000
6 Apr	Bank	1,200	7 Apr	Purchases	3,000
30 Apr	Balance c/d	5,200			
		7,000			7,000
8 May	Bank	4,000	1 May	Balance b/d	5,200
12 May	Bank	1,000	23 May	Purchases	3,100

The balance at 31 May 19x5 is £8,300 credit less £5,000 credit, i.e. £3,300 debit.

Every account in the ledger must be listed in the trial balance, including the balance on the stock account, which did not exist at the end of the first period of trading. This balance is the closing stock at the end of the first period, which now becomes the opening stock at the start of the current period.

Calculating the cost of goods sold at the end of the second trading period

As with the first period, the trial balance contains Sales, Purchases, Returns and maybe Carriage inwards, and there will need to be a calculation of closing stock at the end of the second period. In addition, we have an opening stock figure too. The cost of goods sold, therefore, is calculated as follows:

Opening stock + Net purchases – Closing stock

Example

A. Whelan has the following information regarding the cost of goods sold during 19x6:

	£
Stock at 31 December 19x5	2,400
During 19x6 – Purchases	27,500
– Returns outwards	1,500
– Carriage inwards	500
Stock at 31 December 19x6	3,200

Cost of goods sold would be:

	£	£
Opening stock		2,400
Purchases	27,500	
Carriage inwards	500	
	28,000	
less Returns outwards	1,500	
		26,500
		28,900
less Closing stock		3,200
Cost of goods sold		25,700

The trading and profit and loss account and balance sheet are prepared as for the first period, and the ledger accounts are again balanced off.

Entries in the stock account

The stock account requires two entries to be made in it – one to transfer the opening stock out and into the trading account, the other to transfer the new closing stock in from the trading account. The stock account would appear as follows:

Stock

19x5	£	19x6	£
31 Dec Trading account	2,400	31 Dec Trading account	2,400
19x6			
31 Dec Trading account	3,200		

Adjustments for accruals and prepayments

The 'matching' rule and profit

A very important 'rule' in accounting is that revenues earned must be 'matched' with the expenses which have been incurred in earning them. All revenues earned in the period, and all expenses used up in earning that revenue, should be included in the profit and loss account, irrespective of the time of payment.

If revenues and expenses arose at the same time as payment was received or made, there would be no problem in determining the amount earned or used up – it would simply be the balance on the ledger account. But this is not often the case. Many expenses are paid annually or quarterly. Some are paid in advance of being used up, others are paid in arrears (i.e. after being used up). Some, like heating oil or stationery, have stocks at the beginning and end of the period. Income can also be received in advance or in arrears.

There are therefore five situations which can exist at the end of the accounting period:

- Expenses which have been used up but not paid for, e.g. heating and lighting costs. These are known as *accrued expenses*.
- Expenses which have been paid but not yet used up, e.g. insurances. These are known as *prepayments*.
- Stocks which have been acquired but not used up.
- Revenues earned but not yet received, e.g. bank interest paid annually after the year end. This is known as *accrued income*.
- Revenues received but not yet earned, e.g. advance royalties or commissions. This is known as *advance income*.

Declaring assets and liabilities

As well as ensuring that revenues and expenses are correctly calculated in the profit and loss account, it is also important to declare all assets and liabilities on the balance sheet at the end of the period. This means that any expenses accrued or revenues in advance should be included with current liabilities, and any expenses prepaid, income accrued or stocks remaining should be included with current assets.

Ledger accounts involving accruals and prepayments

The ledger accounts for revenues and expenses will commence with any accrued or prepaid amounts from the previous accounting period:

- Prepaid expenses, income accrued or stocks will be shown as debit balances brought forward
- Accrued expenses and advance income will be shown as credit balances brought forward.

As revenues are received and expenses paid, they are entered into the ledger accounts as normal:

- Debit bank, credit revenue account; or
- Credit bank, debit expense account.

At the end of the accounting period, adjustments will be made for accruals and prepayments, prior to preparing the trading, profit and loss account and balance sheet.

Example 1 (accrued expense)

The gas bill is received quarterly in mid January, April, July and October for the previous three months' usage. At 1 January 19x5 a bill of £400 was outstanding. It was received, and paid on time, along with the other three bills received during the year. At 31 December 19x5 it is estimated that gas to the value of £350 has been consumed, for which the bill will arrive in January 19x6.

The gas account, prior to adjusting for gas accrued at the end of the year, would appear as follows:

Gas

19x5	£	19x5	£
15 Jan Bank	400	1 Jan Accrued b/d	400
15 Apr Bank	370		
16 Jul Bank	430		
17 Oct Bank	440		

The trial balance at 31 December 19x5 would show £1,240 debit for gas.

However, this is not the figure needed for the profit and loss account, because an additional amount of £350 has been consumed during the year which is not recorded in the account. The procedure to adjust for this is:

- Debit the account to increase the expense and to give a new balance
- Transfer the new balance to the profit and loss account
- Bring down the accrued amount on the credit side
- Show the resulting credit balance as a current liability on the balance sheet.

Gas

19x5	£	19x5	£
15 Jan Bank	400	1 Jan Accrued b/d	400
15 Apr Bank	370		
16 Jul Bank	430		
17 Oct Bank	440		
31 Dec Accrued c/d	350	31 Dec Profit and loss a/c	1,590
	1,990		1,990
		19x6	
		1 Jan Accrued b/d	350

Point to note:

In the above gas account, you can see that the amount accrued at 1 January 19x5 was well estimated – the bill which arrived was for exactly that amount. This is unusual for some expenses – the estimate is often only a guess based on the previous year's bill, with an allowance for inflation or changed consumption. If the estimate is incorrect, but by only a small amount, we say that it is not 'material' and we do not worry about it. If the actual bill in January 19x5 had been £420, it would simply mean that the profit and loss account for 19x4 had been undercharged by £20 and the profit and loss account for 19x5 would be charged with £1,610 instead of £1,590.

Example 2 (prepaid expense)

Business rates are payable in April each year, covering the period 1 April to 31 March in the following year. The bill for 19x4/5 was £6,000 and the bill for 19x5/6 was £8,400. Both were paid as soon as they arrived. The accounting year end is 31 December. The rates ledger account, prior to adjusting for rates prepaid at the end of the year, would appear as follows:

Rates

19x5	£	19x5	£
1 Jan Prepaid b/d	1,500		
1 Apr Bank	8,400		

The trial balance at 31 December 19x5 would show £9,900 debit for rates.

However, this is not the amount required for the profit and loss account as the 19x5/6 payment covers the period to 31 March 19x6 – thus three months' rates have been paid in advance. This amount (1/4 of £8,400) needs to be taken out of the account. The procedure to adjust for this is as follows:

- Credit the account to decrease the expense and to give a new balance
- Transfer the new balance to the profit and loss account
- Bring down the prepaid amount on the debit side

• Show the resulting debit balance as a current asset on the balance sheet.

Rates

19x5	£	19x5	£
1 Jan Prepaid b/d	1,500	31 Dec Prepaid c/d	2,100
1 Apr Bank	8,400	Profit and Loss a/c	7,800
	9,900		9,900
19x6			
1 Jan Prepaid b/d	2,100		

Example 3 (accrued income)

The business has a deposit account with the bank on which interest is credited annually on 28 February. At 1 January 19x5 it was estimated that interest of £2,300 had been earned on the account during 19x4 but not received until 28 February 19x5. When the interest was credited, it amounted to £2,700. At 31 December 19x5 it is estimated that interest of £1,400 has been accrued. The interest receivable ledger account, prior to adjusting for the interest accrued, would appear as follows:

Interest receivable

19x5	£	19x5	£
1 Jan Balance b/d	2,300	28 Feb Bank	2,700

The trial balance at 31 December 19x5 would show £400 credit for interest receivable.

However, this is not the amount required for the profit and loss account as a further £1,400 has been earned during the period which has not yet been received. This amount needs to be added to the account. The procedure to adjust for this is as follows:

• Show the resulting debit balance as a current asset on the balance sheet
• Credit the account to increase the revenue and to give a new balance
• Transfer the new balance to the profit and loss account
• Bring down the accrued amount on the debit side.

Interest receivable

19x5	£	19x5	£
1 Jan Balance b/d	2,300	28 Feb Bank	2,700
31 Dec Profit and loss a/c	1,800	31 Dec Balance c/d	1,400
	4,100		4,100
19x6			
1 Jan Balance b/d	1,400		

Point to note:
The actual interest received on 28 February 19x5 includes not only the accrued interest from 19x4, but also the interest earned during January and February 19x5.

Example 4 (accrued expense and stock)

Your company keeps a substantial stock of stationery. At 1 January 19x5 the stock was valued at £8,500. During 19x5 several purchases of stationery were made, including one during December 19x5 for which the invoice of £5,400 was not received until 19x6. At 31 December 19x5 the stock of stationery was estimated as costing £7,200. The stationery ledger account, prior to making adjustments at the end of the year, is as follows:

Stationery

19x5	£	19x5	£
1 Jan Stock b/d	8,500		
13 Feb Office Gear Ltd	12,500		
18 Jun Bank	2,400		
21 Sep Paper Products Ltd	13,000		
5 Nov Office Gear Ltd	9,300		

The trial balance at 31 December 19x5 would show £45,700 debit for stationery.

However, this is not the amount required for the profit and loss account as there is an additional purchase which has not been entered in the account *and* there is a stock remaining. The procedure to adjust for these is as follows:

- Debit the account with the additional invoice for £5,400
- Credit the account with the closing stock of £7,200
- Calculate a new balance and transfer it to the profit and loss account
- Bring down the accrued invoice on the credit side *and* the remaining stock on the debit side
- Show the resulting debit balance as a current asset and the credit balance as a current liability on the balance sheet.

Stationery

19x5	£	19x5	£
1 Jan Stock b/d	8,500		
13 Feb Office Gear Ltd	12,500		
18 Jun Bank	2,400		
21 Sep Paper Products Ltd	13,000		
5 Nov Office Gear Ltd	9,300	31 Dec Stock c/d	7,200
31 Dec Accrued c/d	5,400	Profit and loss a/c	43,900
	51,100		51,100
19x6		*19x6*	
1 Jan Stock b/d	7,200	1 Jan Accrued b/d	5,400

The profit and loss account and balance sheet with accruals and prepayments

The profit and loss account (extract) containing the revenues and expenses used in the above examples, would appear as follows:

Profit and loss account for the year ending 31 December 19x5

	£	£
Other revenue:		
Interest receivable		1,400
less Expenses:		
Gas	1,590	
Rates	7,800	
Stationery	43,900	

The balance sheet will show the prepayments as current assets and the accruals as current liabilities. There may be several of these to add together. In the example above, the prepayments total will consist of:

	£
Rates prepaid	2,100
Interest receivable owing	1,400
Stock of stationery	7,200
	10,700

Some organizations would prefer to show the interest receivable owing as an addition to debtors, and the stock of stationery as an addition to stocks.

In the above example, the accruals total will consist of:

	£
Gas accrued	350
Stationery invoice outstanding	5,400
	5,750

Thus, the balance sheet (extract) containing the above figures would appear as follows:

Balance sheet as at 31 December 19x5

Current assets	£
Stock	
Debtors	
Prepayments	10,700
Bank and cash	
less Current liabilities	
Creditors	
Accruals	5,750
Bank overdraft	

Summary

By the end of this chapter you should be able to balance off ledger accounts at the end of a period, and maintain ledger accounts for second and subsequent periods. You should be able to adjust the cost of goods sold for opening stocks, and make appropriate adjustments for accruals and prepayments.

Exercises

4.1, 4.2, 4.3x, 4.4, 4.5x   Balance off the remaining ledger accounts from Exercises 2.7, 2.8, 2.9x, 2.10, 2.11x.

4.6 At 1 January 19x5 the following balances were brought forward in your books, representing amounts accrued or prepaid at that date:

Rent payable account	£150 Debit
Electricity account	£80 Credit
Stationery account	£50 Debit
Interest receivable account	£30 Debit

You are told that:

(a) Rent is payable quarterly in advance on the last day of February, May, August and November, at £150 per quarter.

(b) Electricity is paid as follows:

5 February 19x5	£100 (for the period to 31 January 19x5)
10 May 19x5	£130 (for the period to 30 April 19x5)
8 August 19x5	£150 (for the period to 31 July 19x5)
7 November 19x5	£110 (for the period to 31 October 19x5)

The electricity meter shows that £90 has been used up since the last bill was received.

(c) Stationery purchased during 19x5, on 31 July, and paid for in cash, was £300, and you estimate that £80 worth is still unused at 31 December 19x5.

(d) Interest was received during the year as follows:

2 January 19x5	£25 (for the six months to 31 December 19x4)
3 July 19x5	£60 (for the six months to 30 June 19x4)

You estimate that interest of £30 is owing at 31 December 19x5.

You are required to show the ledger accounts for these four accounts, the amounts to be shown in the profit and loss account for 19x5 and the amounts to be shown in the balance sheet at 31 December 19x5.

State also the meaning of each of the balances brought forward on the ledger accounts at 31 December 19x5.

4.7x At the beginning of 19x5 A. Trader, has, among others, the following balances brought forward in his books:

Rates	£ 30 Debit
Gas	£200 Credit
Rent payable	£300 Credit

You are told that:

(a) Rates are payable in two equal instalments on 30 June and 31 December 19x5, to cover the period from 1 April 19x5 to 31 March 19x6. The amount payable for the year to 31 March 19x6 is £180.

(b) Rent is payable on 1 January, April, July and October for the preceding three months (i.e. the payment made on 1 April covers the period January, February and March). The amount payable has been £1,200 for several years, but increased to £1,600 per annum with effect from the payment made on 1 October 19x5.

(c) Gas is paid during 19x5 as follows:

2 February	£300
3 May	£500
4 August	£400
2 November	£400

The last bill covered the period up to 31 October 19x5. It is estimated that gas consumed during November and December 19x5 was 1,000 therms at 20p per therm.

Prepare all ledger accounts for 19x5. Show clearly the amounts to be transferred to the profit and loss account for 19x5, and the amounts to be shown in the balance sheet at 31 December 19x5.

State the meaning of the balances carried forward at the end of 19x5.

4.8 Your firm paid £3,600 on 8 February 19x5 for rental of premises, covering the period from 1 January 19x5 to 30 June 19x6. However, at the next renewal date (1 July 19x6) an increase in rent payable of 20 per cent per annum was imposed, of which your firm was unaware, and therefore, on 3 July 19x6, they made the payment for the year to 30 June 19x7 at the old rate.

In November 19x6 the mistake was realized, and a cheque for the additional sum was forwarded on 8 November 19x6.

Your firm's year end is 31 December. Prepare the rent payable account for 19x5 and 19x6.

4.9 Your firm purchases heating oil on credit, but it does not keep an account in its purchase ledger for the supplier, as his bill is always paid within seven days. Explain the meaning of all of the items which appear in the following ledger account in your books:

Heating oil

19x5	£	19x5	£
1 Jan Balance	100	1 Jan Balance accrued	80
5 Jan Bank	80		
6 Jul Bank	300		
10 Nov Bank	450	31 Dec Profit and loss a/c	880
31 Dec Balance accrued	120	Balance c/d	90
	1,050		1,050

5   Provisions against assets

Aims of the chapter

The aims of this chapter are to:

- explain the theory of making provisions against assets
- describe the methods of providing for depreciation
- demonstrate the ledger entries required to record depreciation
- demonstrate the treatment of depreciation in the profit and loss account and balance sheet
- demonstrate the ledger entries required to record disposals of fixed assets
- demonstrate the calculation and recording of provisions for doubtful debts
- explain the existence and theory of goodwill and its treatment in the accounts
- describe the various types of research and development expenditure and their respective treatments in the accounts
- explain the amortization of leases.

A *provision* is an amount charged against profits for a known liability, or a reduction in the value of an asset, where the exact amount is uncertain. We have already seen how it is important that the profit and loss account is charged with expenses which have been used up during the accounting period, even if no money has changed hands. It is equally important to ensure that any decreases in the value of assets are also charged to the profit and loss account in the period in which they occur.

There are many different kinds of provisions; this chapter considers some of the most common.

Depreciation of fixed assets

Fixed assets generally decrease in value as time goes on. This decrease in value is called *depreciation*. SSAP 12 states that 'depreciation is the measure of the wearing out, consumption or other reduction in the useful economic life of a fixed asset whether arising from use, effluxion of time or obsolescence through technological or market changes'. It further states that 'depreciation should be allocated so as to charge a fair proportion of cost or valuation to each accounting period expected to benefit from the use of the asset'.

What this means is that organizations charge the profit and loss account with an amount intended to represent the value of the asset which has been used up during the period. This amount is then deducted from the value which is shown on the balance sheet. The result is that over the life of the asset, its cost (less any expected disposal proceeds or residual value) is charged against profits and the value shown on the balance sheet reduces, until eventually it becomes 'written off'.

The amount of depreciation charged each year can only be an estimate, as the organization is unlikely to know for certain how much it has decreased in value, unless the asset is revalued professionally. This does happen with some valuable assets, but for the majority an estimate is satisfactory. This estimate is known as a *provision for depreciation*.

It is not usual to depreciate land, as it does not wear out (unless used for a purpose which does cause wear, such as mining). Buildings, however, are depreciated, even if from time to time their value increases.

Methods of calculating depreciation

The straight-line method

This assumes that the asset decreases in value by the same amount each period, irrespective of its true value or the amount of use it has had. Thus the profit and loss account is charged with the same amount of depreciation in each period.

The formula is as follows:

$$\text{Annual depreciation} = \frac{\text{cost less estimated residual value}}{\text{number of years expected useful life}}$$

Example

An asset cost £22,000 and is expected to last for four years, after which time it will be sold for £2,000. The annual depreciation is:

$$\frac{£22,000 - £2,000}{4 \text{ years}} = £5,000 \text{ per annum}$$

£5,000 is charged to the profit and loss account for each of the four years. The balance sheet will show the reduced value each year, i.e. £17,000 at the end of year 1 (original cost less one year's depreciation), £12,000 at the end of year 2 (original cost less two years' depreciation) and so on. This reduced value is known as the *net book value*; it must not be regarded as the true value as it is only an estimate according to the books of the organization. It is common to show both the original cost and the cumulative depreciation on the balance sheet as well as the net book value.

The fixed assets section of the balance sheet each year would appear as follows:

	Cost	Accumulated depreciation	Net book value
	£	£	£
Year 1	22,000	5,000	17,000
Year 2	22,000	10,000	12,000
Year 3	22,000	15,000	7,000
Year 4	22,000	20,000	2,000

If the asset remains in use after the end of year 4, the remaining £2,000 will be written off in year 5, to leave a nil net book value.

An alternative way of calculating straight-line depreciation is to apply a percentage to the 'cost less residual value'. In this example, the percentage would be 25 per cent (i.e. 100 per cent over four years). It is important to make it clear, though, that the percentage is applied to the cost, not the net book value.

The reducing balance method

This method applies a percentage to the previous net book value.

Example

An asset cost £20,000 and is to be depreciated by 40 per cent per annum using the reducing balance method. The depreciation each year would be as follows:

	£
Year 1 – cost	20,000
– depreciation	8,000 (40% of £20,000)
– net book value	12,000
Year 2 – depreciation	4,800 (40% of £12,000)
– net book value	7,200
Year 3 – depreciation	2,880 (40% of £7,200)
– net book value	4,320
Year 4 – depreciation	1,728 (40% of £4,320)
– net book value	2,592

You can see that the depreciation to be charged to the profit and loss account is much higher in the early years than in later years. The method probably gives more realistic results than the straight-line method, but it is more time-consuming to calculate.

The balance sheets would appear as follows:

	Cost	Accumulated depreciation	Net book value
	£	£	£
Year 1	20,000	8,000	12,000
Year 2	20,000	12,800	7,200
Year 3	20,000	15,680	4,320
Year 4	20,000	17,408	2,592

The revaluation method

This is used for two types of assets.

- Large, expensive or unusual assets which are professionally valued each year; any reduction in the value from the previous year is charged as depreciation. If the valuation gives an increase, certain assets can be revalued upwards, provided that the value is likely to be sustained. You will look at this type of transaction later in the book.
- Small, inexpensive groups of assets, such as tools. The total value is estimated at the end of each year, and the resulting reduction in value is charged as depreciation.

Depreciation in the year of purchase and disposal

It is common to charge a full year's depreciation in the year of purchase, even if the asset is bought part-way through the year; no depreciation is then charged in the year of disposal.

An alternative is to charge a proportion according to the date of purchase. This is known as depreciation on an *actual time basis*. If you are given a date of purchase, assume that you are to charge a proportion.

Ledger entries for depreciation

The cost of fixed assets is debited to the relevant ledger accounts as normal. The annual depreciation is credited, either to that same account, or (as is more likely) to a separate *provision for depreciation* account, and charged to the profit and loss account. It is usual to maintain a separate provision account for each type of fixed asset. As each annual charge is credited to the provision account, the balance on that account increases to equal the accumulated depreciation which is shown on the balance sheet each year.

Example

A machine is bought for £2,000 on 1 January 19x4. Its expected life is five years. Straight-line depreciation is therefore £400 per year, which will be charged to the profit and loss account in each of the five years. The provision for depreciation account will appear as follows:

Provision for depreciation of machinery

	£		£
		31 Dec 19x4 Profit and loss a/c	400
31 Dec 19x5 Balance c/d	800	31 Dec 19x5 Profit and loss a/c	400
	800		800
		1 Jan 19x6 Balance b/d	800
31 Dec 19x6 Balance c/d	1,200	31 Dec 19x6 Profit and loss a/c	400
	1,200		1,200
		1 Jan 19x7 Balance b/d	1,200
31 Dec 19x7 Balance c/d	1,600	31 Dec 19x7 Profit and loss a/c	400
	1,600		1,600
		1 Jan 19x8 Balance b/d	1,600
31 Dec 19x8 Balance c/d	2,000	31 Dec 19x8 Profit and loss a/c	400
	2,000		2,000
		1 Jan 19x9 Balance b/d	2,000

Disposal of fixed assets

When a fixed asset is disposed of, both its cost and its accumulated depreciation are removed from the respective ledger accounts and transferred into a fixed asset disposals account. The proceeds of sale are also credited here (and debited to bank, cash or debtor), and the resultant balance is taken to the profit and loss account. If that balance is a credit balance, then we say that a *profit on disposal* has arisen, which is added to the gross profit as a source of additional revenue; if the balance is a debit balance, then we say that a *loss on disposal* has arisen, which is charged against profit as an additional expense.

A profit on disposal arises when the asset has been sold for more than its net book value; it is not really a profit, it simply means that too much depreciation has been charged in previous years due to incorrect estimation of the true value of the asset. A loss on disposal arises when the asset has been sold for less than its net book value, and thus too little depreciation has been charged in previous years.

Example

Machine A is bought for £1,000 on 1 January 19x5. Machine B is bought for £1,200 on 1 October 19x6. Machine A is sold for £720 cash on 30 June 19x7. The business year end is 31 December. All machinery is depreciated over ten years, straight-line, with a full year charged in the year of purchase.

Workings:

Depreciation for Machine A = £1,000/10 years = £100 per annum from 19x5
Depreciation for Machine B = £1,200/20 years = £120 per annum from 19x6
Total depreciation charged in 19x5 = £100 (Machine A only)
Total depreciation charged in 19x6 = £220 (both machines)

Total depreciation charged in 19x7 and onwards = £120 (Machine B only)
Depreciation charged on Machine A by the time of disposal = 2 years × £100
= £200

Order of entries:

1 Cost of each machine is debited to the Machinery at cost account on purchase
2 Annual depreciation is credited to the Provision for depreciation account in 19x5 and 19x6
3 On 30 June 19x7 the cost and accumulated depreciation of Machine A is removed from the two ledger accounts and transferred to the Disposals account, along with the sale proceeds
4 At 31 December 19x7 the balance on the Disposals account is taken to the profit and loss account as a loss (expense); annual depreciation on the remaining machine is charged.

The ledger accounts would appear as follows:

Machinery at cost

	£		£
1 Jan 19x5 Cash	1,000	31 Dec 19x5 Balance c/d	1,000
	1,000		1,000
1 Jan 19x6 Balance b/d	1,000		
1 Oct 19x6 Cash	1,200	31 Dec 19x6 Balance c/d	2,200
	2,200		2,200
1 Jan 19x7 Balance b/d	2,200	30 Jun 19x7 Disposals a/c	1,000
		31 Dec 19x7 Balance c/d	1,200
	2,200		2,200
1 Jan 19x8 Balance b/d	1,200		

Provision for depreciation – Machinery

	£		£
31 Dec 19x5 Balance c/d	100	31 Dec 19x5 Profit and loss a/c	100
	100		100
31 Dec 19x6 Balance c/d	320	1 Jan 19x6 Balance b/d	100
		31 Dec 19x6 Profit and loss a/c	220
	320		320
30 Jun 19x7 Disposals a/c	200	1 Jan 19x7 Balance b/d	320
31 Dec 19x7 Balance c/d	240	31 Dec 19x7 Profit and loss a/c	120
	440		440
		1 Jan 19x8 Balance b/d	240
31 Dec 19x8 Balance c/d	360	31 Dec 19x8 Profit and loss a/c	120
	360		360
		1 Jan 19x9 Balance b/d	360

Disposal of fixed assets

	£		£
30 Jun 19x7 Machinery at cost	1,000	30 Jun 19x7	
		Machinery depreciation	200
		Cash	720
		31 Dec 19x7 Profit and loss a/c	80
	1,000		1,000

Fixed asset register

In order to keep track of individual fixed assets, many organizations also maintain a *fixed asset register*. It will contain a record of each asset, with details regarding its cost and depreciation, as well as the date of purchase, the supplier, its location, its maintenance history and any other useful information. The fixed asset register can be totalled so as to compare the cost and accumulated depreciation with the figures contained in the ledger accounts. This aids control and confirms accuracy of the ledger accounts.

Provisions for doubtful debts

An organization should look at other assets to determine whether the value at which they are shown is fair. If it is felt that not all debtors will pay in full, then a provision should be made for the estimated doubtful debts. This provision is *in addition to* any known bad debts which are to be written off, which should be dealt with before the provision is calculated.

The estimate is often taken as a percentage of the total debtors, based on previous experience or on suggestions made by trade organizations. The estimate can be made by producing a list of debtors according to how long they have been outstanding – *an aged debt list*. Those outstanding for long periods of time are less likely to pay up than recent debtors, and so a higher percentage is used for those.

The provision is reviewed each year. Any change since last year is then adjusted by making the appropriate ledger entries in the provision for doubtful debts account and the profit and loss account. The change can be up or down, and so the provision can be increased or decreased over the previous period. An increase is treated as an expense in the profit and loss account, while a decrease is treated as revenue. The resulting balance on the provision account is deducted from the debtors figure on the balance sheet.

Example

A business makes a provision for doubtful debts of 5 per cent of debtors at the end of each year, after writing off known bad debts. However, at 31 December 19x3 it decided to reduce this provision to 2½ per cent in the light of recent trends. Information regarding the years 19x1 to 19x4 is as follows:

	Debtors	Bad debts
	£	£
19x1	48,000	4,000
19x2	72,000	nil
19x3	100,000	nil
19x5	120,000	8,000

The resulting provision each year, to be shown on the balance sheet, is as follows:

19x1 5% of £44,000	= £2,200
19x2 5% of £72,000	= £3,600
19x3 2 1/2% of £100,000	= £2,500
19x4 2 1/2% of £112,000	= £2,800

and therefore the change each year, and ledger entries required, are:

Workings	Profit and loss account	Provision account
19x1 £2,200 – nil (no previous provision) = £2,200	Debit £2,200	Credit £2,200
19x2 £3,600 – £2,200 = £1,400 to be charged	Debit £1,400	Credit £1,400
19x3 £2,500 – £3,600 = £1,100 *reduction* in provision	Credit £1,100	Debit £1,100
19x4 £2,800 – £2,500 = £300 to be charged	Debit £300	Credit £300

The provision for doubtful debts account would appear as follows:

Provision for doubtful debts

	£		£
31 Dec 19x1 Balance c/d	2,200	31 Dec 19x1 Profit and loss a/c	2,200
	2,200		2,200
		1 Jan 19x2 Balance b/d	2,200
31 Dec 19x2 Balance c/d	3,600	31 Dec 19x2 Profit and loss a/c	1,400
	3,600		3,600
31 Dec 19x3 Profit and loss a/c	1,100	1 Jan 19x3 Balance b/d	3,600
Balance c/d	2,500		
	3,600		3,600
		1 Jan 19x4 Balance b/d	2,500
31 Dec 19x4 Balance c/d	2,800	31 Dec 19x4 Profit and loss a/c	300
	2,800		2,800
		1 Jan 19x5 Balance b/d	2,800

The balance sheet shows the provision as a deduction from the debtors figure. As an example, the balance sheet at 31 December 19x4 might appear as follows:

	£	£
Current assets		
Stocks		5,000
Debtors	112,000	
less Provision	2,800	
		109,200

Accounting treatment of goodwill

Goodwill is an *intangible asset*. An intangible asset is one which does not have a physical identity. Other examples include trade marks and patents. Goodwill exists where an organization feels that the value of the business is higher than that represented by its net assets. It is not considered good practice to include goodwill in the accounts, unless it is *purchased goodwill*. This arises when one organization buys the assets of another, but pays more for them than they are worth. The difference is goodwill. SSAP 22 defines goodwill as 'the difference between the value of a business as a whole and the aggregate of the fair values of its separable net assets'.

If an organization wishes to include goodwill in its accounts, then a goodwill account is debited with the value. It is recommended, however, that goodwill is written off as soon as possible. This writing off is known as *amortization*.

Accounting treatment of research and development costs

Many organizations incur expenditure on research and development which may or may not lead to additional profit in the future. There are three categories of research and development costs identified in SSAP 13, and their accounting treatment is as follows:

(a) *Pure research* – the search for new knowledge for its own sake. This is unlikely to be used to produce additional profit and should be charged as an expense immediately it is incurred.
(b) *Applied research* – the search for new knowledge for a particular purpose. It may or may not produce additional profit, so because of the uncertainty it too should be charged as an expense immediately.
(c) *Development* – the use of knowledge to develop new or improved products and methods, and which is more likely to lead to additional profit. If this is the case, the expenditure can be treated as capital expenditure and carried in the balance sheet as an asset. The value is amortized when it starts to produce revenue in the future.

Leases

Leases are also amortized over the life of the lease.

Summary

By the end of this chapter you should understand why organizations need to make provisions against assets, and the methods of calculating and recording those provisions for different types of assets. You should understand how provisions are presented in the accounts, and their effect on the values of items contained in the balance sheet.

Exercises

5.1 Machine A cost £1,200 on 1 July 19x6. It had an estimated useful life of twenty years and an expected residual value of £200. It is to be depreciated on the straight-line basis. Machine B cost £2,000 on 1 July 19x7. It is to be depreciated at 10 per cent per annum on the reducing balance basis. The firm has a year end of 31 December.

(a) Show the ledger entries to record the purchases and annual depreciation for every year until 31 December 19x9. Assume that a full year's depreciation is to be charged in the year of purchase. Assume that all transactions are for cash.
(b) Show how the machinery would appear in the balance sheet at the end of each year.

5.2x Your firm buys the following machines:

> Machine A cost £2,200 on 3 September 19x5
> Machine B cost £3,000 on 31 December 19x5

Machine A is to be depreciated on the straight-line basis. It has an estimated useful life of ten years, and an expected residual value of £200. Machine B is to be depreciated at 20 per cent per annum on the reducing balance basis. A full year's depreciation is to be charged in the year of purchase for both machines. The firm's year end is 31 December.

(a) Show the ledger entries to record the purchases and annual depreciation for every year until 31 December 19x9. Assume that a full year's depreciation is to be charged in the year of purchase. Assume that all transactions are for cash.

(b) Show how the machinery would appear in the balance sheet at the end of each year.

5.3 On 1 October 19x5 your firm bought furniture for £4,000, to be depreciated straight-line at 10 per cent per annum on an actual time basis. The firm's year end is 31 December. The furniture was sold for £2,500 on 31 March 19x9. Show the ledger accounts to record the purchase, depreciation and disposal of the furniture. Assume that all transactions are for cash.

5.4 On 1 July 19x1 your firm bought Machine A for £2,000, to be depreciated at 20 per cent per annum straight-line. No scrap value is expected. The machine is sold for £1,000 on 18 May 19x4. On 1 June 19x2, Machine B is bought for £1,000, to be depreciated at 10 per cent per annum straight-line. No scrap value is expected. The machine is sold for £500 on 5 August 19x5. On 29 April 19x3, Machine C is bought for £1,000, to be depreciated at 10 per cent per annum on the reducing balance basis. All machines are to be depreciated for a full year in the year of purchase. Assume that all transactions are for cash.

Show the ledger accounts to record the purchase, depreciation and disposal of the machines.

5.5x Frank Dennis is the proprietor of a mobile burger business consisting of a converted van and some cooking equipment. The van had been purchased on 1 January 1990 for £6,000. The balance sheet for the business drawn up on 31 December 1990 showed that the van had a book value of £4,800 and the balance sheet as at 31 December 1991 showed a book value of £3,480. The equipment had also been purchased on 1 January 1990 at a cost of £2,000. Depreciation on equipment is calculated on a monthly basis at 10 per cent per annum on cost. On 1 January 1991 the equipment was sold for £1,720 and replaced by new equipment costing £3,000. Business continued to be brisk for Frank and on 30 June 1991 he made the decision to buy a second grill costing £500 and on 30 September 1991 a fryer costing £200. All purchases and sales of equipment were settled immediately by cheque.

(a) State which method of calculating depreciation has been used for the van and the annual percentage rate applied in the calculation.

(b) Draw up the Equipment Account, the Provision for Depreciation of Equipment Account and the Equipment Disposals Account as they would appear in the ledger for the year ended 31 December 1991. Show clearly any transfers to or from the profit and loss account and any closing balances.

(c) State separately the book value of the new grill and the book value of the fryer as at 31 December 1991.

(AAT, June 1992)

5.6 Your business has the following information regarding debtors, and the anticipated provision for doubtful debts:

	Debtors	Bad debts to be written off	Provision to be amended to
	£	£	
31 Dec 19x1	12,000	1,000	5%
31 Dec 19x2	14,000	1,200	5%
31 Dec 19x3	11,000	nil	5%
31 Dec 19x4	13,500	500	6%

Write up the provision for doubtful debts account for each year. Show the balance sheet extract with respect to debtors for each year.

5.7x Your business has the following information regarding debtors, and the anticipated provision for doubtful debts:

	Debtors	Bad debts to be written off	Provision to be amended to
	£	£	
31 Dec 19x5	30,000	2,000	5%
31 Dec 19x6	25,000	nil	4%
31 Dec 19x7	20,000	nil	6%
31 Dec 19x8	25,000	1,000	5%

Write up the provision for doubtful debts account for each year. Show the balance sheet extract with respect to debtors for each year.

6   Preparing final accounts from a trial balance

Aims of the chapter

The aims of this chapter are to:

- demonstrate the preparation of final accounts from a trial balance with adjustments
- demonstrate an appropriate method of preparing workings
- explain the purpose and use of the extended trial balance.

Examination questions often ask for final accounts (i.e. a trading and profit and loss account and balance sheet) to be prepared from a given trial balance, with notes as to adjustments which need to be made to the figures during the preparation of the accounts. This chapter works through a typical examination-style question with a comprehensive range of adjustments.

Jack Jackson has the following trial balance:

Jack Jackson – Trial balance as at 31 December 19x5

	DR £	CR £
Capital at 1 January 19x5		53,500
Sales		180,000
Purchases	155,000	
Returns inwards	2,000	
Returns outwards		1,500
Carriage inwards	500	
Stock at 1 January 19x5	20,000	
Debtors	80,000	
Creditors		50,000
Bank		10,000
Loan		34,000
Rates	5,000	
Stationery	1,000	
Gas	6,000	
Wages	4,000	
Drawings	3,500	
Bad debts written off	1,500	
Bank interest receivable		4,000
Bank interest payable	1,000	
Provision for doubtful debts at 1 January 19x5		3,500
Plant and machinery		
– cost	60,000	
– depreciation at 1 January 19x5		10,000
Office equipment		
– cost	20,000	
– depreciation at 1 January 19x5		13,000
	359,500	359,500

At 31 December 19x5, the following points are to be noted:
(a) Stock of raw materials was £29,500
(b) Stock of stationery was £200
(c) Rates paid in advance were £2,000
(d) Gas accrued was £1,000
(e) Provision for depreciation on office equipment is to be 10 per cent on cost
(f) Provision for depreciation on plant and machinery is to be 5 per cent reducing balance
(g) Provision for doubtful debts is to be increased to 5 per cent of debtors.

Prepare final accounts.

The first stage is to look down the trial balance and label each item with T, P&L or BS (trading account, profit and loss account or balance sheet) according to its destination.

The next stage is to prepare a set of 'workings' to assist you. Go through each of the points above, and calculate its effect on the profit and loss account and balance sheet. You are not asked to prepare any ledger accounts, but if you find that it helps to do so, you can. They are, however, time-consuming to prepare.

Remember that double-entry principles always apply. Each of the above points will have two effects – one on the profit and loss account, the other on the balance sheet.

Let us look at them in turn.

(a) Closing stock £29,500. No workings are needed here, but remember that this is the stock figure needed for the balance sheet – not the one in the trial balance. The figure will appear both in the trading account and on the balance sheet.

(b) Stationery stock £200. This needs to be deducted from the trial balance figure as it is not used up during the current period; the balance needs to be shown on the balance sheet:

	£	
Stationery per trial balance	1,000	
less Stock	200	(BS)
Stationery used up	800	(P&L)

The stationery figure in the trial balance can now be ignored, so put a mark or tick against it to show that it has been amended.

(c) Rates paid in advance £2,000. This needs to be deducted from the trial balance figure as it represents rates used up in the next period; the prepayment needs to be shown on the balance sheet:

	£	
Rates per trial balance	5,000	
less Prepaid	2,000	(BS)
Rates used up	3,000	(P&L)

Tick the rates figure in the trial balance.

(d) Gas accrued £1,000. This needs to be added to the trial balance figure as it represents additional expense; the accrual needs to be shown on the balance sheet:

	£	
Gas per trial balance	6,000	
add Accrued	1,000	(BS)
Gas used up	7,000	(P&L)

Tick the gas figure in the trial balance.

(e) Provision for depreciation on office equipment, 10 per cent on cost. This is the amount to be charged for the current period; it needs to be added to the previous balance on the depreciation account to give the accumulated total for the balance sheet:

	£	
Depreciation charge 10% of £20,000=	2,000	(P&L)
Balance at 1 Jan 19x5	13,000	
Balance at 31 Dec 19x5	15,000	(BS)

Tick the depreciation figure in the trial balance.

(f) Provision for depreciation on plant and machinery, 5 per cent reducing balance. Net book value at 1 Jan 19x5 was £50,000.

	£	
Depreciation charge 5% of £50,000	2,500	(P&L)
Balance at 1 Jan 19x5	10,000	
Balance at 31 Dec 19x5	12,500	(BS)

Tick the depreciation figure in the trial balance.

(g) Provision for doubtful debts to be increased to 5 per cent of debtors.

	£	
Provision to be increased to 5% of £80,000 =	4,000	(BS)
Balance at 1 Jan 19x5	3,500	
Increase in provision	500	(P&L)

Tick the provision for doubtful debts figure in the trial balance.

You are now ready to prepare the final accounts. As you use each figure, tick it, either on the trial balance or on the workings above. All items with a T, P&L or BS by them should be ticked. The closing stock figure in note (a) above needs two ticks.

Jack Jackson – Trading and profit and loss account for the year ending 31 December 19x5

	£	£	£
Sales		180,000	
less Returns		2,000	
Net sales			178,000
less Cost of goods sold:			
Opening stock		20,000	
Purchases	155,000		
Carriage inwards	500		
	155,500		
less Returns	1,500		
Net purchases		154,000	
		174,000	
less Closing stock		29,500	
			144,500
Gross profit			33,500
add Bank interest receivable			4,000
			37,500
less Expenses:			
Rates		3,000	
Stationery		800	
Gas		7,000	
Wages		4,000	
Bad debts written off		1,500	
Bank interest payable		1,000	
Depreciation:			
– plant and machinery		2,500	
– office equipment		2,000	
Provision for doubtful debts		500	
			22,300
Net profit			15,200

Jack Jackson – Balance sheet as at 31 December 19x5

Fixed assets		Cost	Accumulated depreciation	Net book value
		£	£	£
Plant and machinery		60,000	12,500	47,500
Office equipment		20,000	15,000	5,000
		80,000	27,500	52,500
Current assets				
Stock		29,500		
Debtors	80,000			
less Provision	4,000			
		76,000		
Prepayments		2,200		
			107,700	
less Current liabilities				
Creditors		50,000		
Accruals		1,000		
Bank overdraft		10,000		
			61,000	
Net current assets				46,700
				99,200
less Long-term liabilities				
Loan				34,000
				65,200
Financed by:				
Capital at 1 Jan 19x5				53,500
Add Net profit				15,200
				68,700
less Drawings				3,500
				65,200

Note: The prepayments figure in Current assets includes both rates prepaid and stationery stock.

The extended trial balance

Accountants commonly use a tabular layout to prepare final accounts from a trial balance. Using the same example as above, here is the extended trial balance for Jack Jackson:

Jack Jackson – Extended trial balance

	Original trial balance		Adjustments		Trading and profit and loss account		Balance sheet	
	Debit	Credit	Debit	Credit	Debit	Credit	Debit	Credit
	£	£	£	£	£	£	£	£
Capital at 1 Jan 19x5		53,500						53,500
Sales		180,000				180,000		
Purchases	155,000				155,000			
Returns inwards	2,000				2,000			
Returns outwards		1,500				1,500		
Carriage inwards	500				500			
Stock at 1 Jan 19x5	20,000				20,000			
Debtors	80,000						80,000	
Creditors		50,000						50,000
Bank		10,000						10,000
Loan		34,000						34,000
Rates	5,000			2,000	3,000			
Stationery	1,000			200	800			
Gas	6,000		1,000		7,000			
Wages	4,000				4,000			
Drawings	3,500						3,500	
Bad debts written off	1,500				1,500			
Bank interest receivable		4,000				4,000		
Bank interest payable	1,000				1,000			
Provision for doubtful debts		3,500		500				4,000
Plant at cost	60,000						60,000	
Depreciation		10,000		2,500				12,500
Office equipment at cost	20,000						20,000	
Depreciation		13,000		2,000				15,000
Adjustments:								
Stock at 31 Dec 19x5			29,500				29,500	
" " " " "				29,500		29,500		
Rates prepaid			2,000				2,000	
Stationery stock			200				200	
Gas accrued				1,000				1,000
Depreciation – plant				2,500	2,500			
– office equipment				2,000	2,000			
Provision for doubtful debts				500	500			
Totals	359,500	359,500	37,700	37,700	199,800	215,000		
Net profit					15,200			15,200
					215,000	215,000	195,200	195,200

The procedure for completion is as follows:

1 List all the original trial balance figures in the first two columns.
2 List all the adjustments for accruals, prepayments, provision and any other items, in the next two columns. First, enter the adjustment against the trial balance item to which it relates. Choose the debit or credit column as you would choose which side to enter the adjustment on in that ledger account. For example, gas accrued would be debited to the gas account. Next, enter the adjustment in the opposite column lower down the page, with a description.
3 Total the first four columns to ensure that the debit totals equal the credit totals.

4 Extend the net total of the first four columns according to whether they appear in the trading and profit and loss account or in the balance sheet.
5 Add up columns 5 and 6 and take one from the other. This produces the net profit or loss (a profit if the credit column is greater than the debit, and vice versa). Enter the difference in the smaller column and total it again to confirm that the debit and credit columns agree.
6 Enter the profit or loss in column 7 or 8 under the balance sheet (credit column for a profit, debit column for a loss).
7 Total columns 7 and 8 to ensure that they agree.

Summary

By the end of this chapter you should be able to prepare final accounts from a trial balance with adjustments, and set out your workings in a clear manner. You should understand the purpose and use of the extended trial balance.

Exercises

6.1 T. Topley has the following trial balance at 31 December 19x5:

	Debit £	Credit £
Stock at 1 January 19x5	2,970	
Debtors	3,350	
Creditors		1,680
Wages and salaries	1,520	
Rent and rates	1,280	
Bad debts written off	110	
Motor vehicles at cost	1,500	
– depreciation at 1 January 19x5		600
Fixtures and fittings at cost	1,400	
– depreciation at 1 January 19x5		400
Purchases	5,930	
Sales		10,600
Bank	520	
Capital at 1 January 19x5		6,850
Drawings	1,440	
General expenses	190	
Provision for doubtful debts at 1 January 19x5		80
	20,210	20,210

At 31 December 19x5, you are told that:

(a) Rent prepaid is £40, and wages unpaid are £40
(b) Provision for doubtful debts is to be increased to 4 per cent of net debtors
(c) Depreciation is to be provided as follows:
    – on fixtures, at 10 per cent reducing balance
    – on motor vehicles, at 20 per cent on cost
(d) Closing stock is £1,780.

Prepare final accounts.

6.2x   K. Kenyon has the following trial balance at 30 June 19x6:

	Debit £	Credit £
Sales		8,000
Purchases	5,500	
Stock at 1 July 19x5	2,000	
Debtors	8,000	
Creditors		5,000
Returns inwards	250	
Returns outwards		150
Bank interest received		400
Bank interest paid	100	
Wages	400	
Gas	600	
Rates	500	
Stationery	100	
Bad debts written off	500	
Provision for doubtful debts at 1 July 19x5		750
Capital at 1 July 19x5		8,350
Bank		1,000
Office machinery at cost	2,000	
– depreciation at 1 July 19x5		1,300
Plant at cost	6,000	
– depreciation at 1 July 19x5		1,000
	25,950	25,950

At 30 June 19x6 you are told that:
(a) Rates paid in advance amount to £200
(b) Gas accrued amounts to £100
(c) Stationery stock amounts to £20
(d) Stock of raw materials is £2,950
(e) Provision for doubtful debts is to be increased to 10 per cent of debtors
(f) Provision for depreciation of office machinery is to be 10 per cent on cost, and provision for depreciation of plant is to be 5 per cent on the reducing balance.
    Prepare final accounts.

6.3   K. Overthorpe has the following trial balance at 31 October 19x6:

	Debit £	Credit £
Sales and purchases	14,500	19,350
Stock at 1 November 19x5	1,630	
Debtors and creditors	3,670	2,740
Carriage inwards	125	
Carriage outwards	160	
Returns in and out	1,020	825
Wages	3,215	
Rent and rates	2,700	
Heat and light	370	
Commission receivable		1,240
Telephone	270	
Bad debts written off	180	
Provision for doubtful debts at 1 November 19x5		200

	Debit £	Credit £
Bank	1,770	
Capital at 1 November 19x5		13,555
Loan, repayable in 10 years		3,500
Loan interest paid	300	
Premises at cost	10,000	
– depreciation at 1 November 19x5		2,000
Equipment at cost	4,000	
– depreciation at 1 November 19x5		500
	43,910	43,910

At 31 October 19x6, you are told that

(a) Provision for doubtful debts is to be increased to 8 per cent of debtors
(b) Provision for depreciation of premises is to be 5 per cent on cost
(c) Provision for depreciation of equipment is to be 12.5 per cent on cost
(d) Commission of £50 is owing to K. Overthorpe
(e) Loan interest accrued amounts to £50
(f) Rates paid in advance amount to £130
(g) Heat and light accrued amount to £95
(h) Closing stock is £5,370.

Prepare final accounts.

6.4x GBA is a sole trader, supplying building materials to local builders. He prepares his accounts to 30 June each year. At 30 June 1995, his trial balance was as follows:

	Debit £	Credit £
Capital at 1 July 1994		55,550
Purchases and sales	324,500	625,000
Returns	2,300	1,700
Discounts	1,500	2,500
Stock of building materials at 1 July 1994	98,200	
Packing materials purchased	12,900	
Distribution costs	17,000	
Rent, rates and insurance	5,100	
Telephone	3,200	
Car expenses	2,400	
Wages	71,700	
Provision for doubtful debts at 1 July 1994		1,000
Heat and light	1,850	
Sundry expenses	6,700	
Delivery vehicles – cost	112,500	
Delivery vehicles – depreciation at 1 July 1994		35,000
Equipment – cost	15,000	
Equipment – depreciation at 1 July 1994		5,000
Debtors and creditors	95,000	82,000
Loan		10,000
Loan repayments	6,400	
Bank deposit account	15,000	
Bank current account	26,500	
	817,750	817,750

The following additional information at 30 June 1995 is available:

(i) Closing stocks of building materials £75,300
Closing stocks of packing materials £700
There was also an unpaid invoice of £200 for packing materials received and consumed during the year

(ii) Prepayments:
- rent, rates and insurance £450

(iii) Accrued expenses:
- heat and light £400
- telephone £500

(iv) Wages includes £23,800 cash withdrawn by GBA

(v) Debtors have been analysed as follows:
- Current month £60,000
- 30 to 60 days £20,000
- 60 to 90 days £12,000
- over 90 days £ 3,000

and provision is to be made for doubtful debts as follows:

- 30 to 60 days 1%
- 60 to 90 days 2.5%
- over 90 days 5% (after writing off £600)

(vi) Sundry expenses includes £3,500 for GBA's personal tax bill

(vii) The loan was taken out some years ago and is due for repayment on 31 March 1996. The figure shown in the trial balance for 'loan repayments' includes interest of £800 for the year

(viii) The Bank deposit account was opened on 1 January 1995 as a short-term investment; interest is credited at 31 December annually; the average rate of interest since opening the account has been 6% per annum

(ix) At 1 July 1994, GBA decided to bring one of his family cars, valued at £8,000, into the business. No entries have been made in the business books for this introduction

(x) Depreciation is to be provided as follows:
- at 20% on cost for delivery vehicles
- at 25% on the reducing balance for the car
- at 25% on the reducing balance for equipment

(a) Prepare a trading and profit and loss account for the year ended 30 June 1995
(b) Prepare a balance sheet at 30 June 1995
(c) Explain to GBA why FOUR of the transactions which have occurred in his business during the year have affected his bank balance but have not affected the calculation of his profit for the year.

(CIMA, November 1995)

Aims of the chapter

The aims of this chapter are to:

- explain the difference between accounting policies, accounting concepts and accounting bases
- identify and describe the four fundamental accounting concepts and other concepts
- explain the historical cost convention and its alternatives.

In Chapter 1 we mentioned that accountants have a number of rules and guidelines which they use to assist them in making judgements about the treatment of certain items. Some of these rules and guidelines are known as *concepts* and *conventions*. Some are laid down in legislation, others are simply accepted standards. SSAP 2 defines accounting policies, accounting concepts and accounting bases.

Accounting policies

SSAP 2 states that

'Accounting policies are the specific accounting bases selected and consistently followed by a business enterprise as being, in the opinion of management, appropriate to its circumstances and best suited to present fairly its results and financial position'.

Before a company can determine the policies which it considers to be appropriate to its circumstances, it must first consider the 'fundamental accounting concepts' and 'accounting bases' which might be applicable.

Accounting concepts

SSAP 2 identifies four 'fundamental accounting concepts'. These are given additional weight in the Companies Act 1985, which calls them 'fundamental principles'.

The four fundamental accounting concepts are as follows:

The going concern concept

This assumes that the business is going to continue to operate for the foreseeable future, and therefore that assets will continue to be available for use in future accounting periods. If the business is not going to continue, then its assets should be valued at their *exit values*, i.e. the value which they would realize if disposed of under an enforced sale. This value might be lower than the original cost or present net book value of the assets.

The accruals concept

This states that revenues and expenses should be recognized when they are earned or incurred and not necessarily when the money is received or paid; in addition, revenues should be matched with their associated expenses and dealt with in the accounting period to which they relate. For example, revenue from the sale of an item in a particular period should be matched with the cost of that item, even if it was incurred in a different accounting period.

The consistency concept

The accounting treatment of like items should be consistently applied from one period to another. Methods of treatment and valuation should not be changed unless essential. The application of this concept ensures that comparison can be made between the results of different accounting periods.

The prudence concept

This states that a business should not recognize revenues and gains until they are reasonably certain of being realized, and should not overstate assets, but that all known or expected expenses, losses or liabilities should be provided for as soon as they are anticipated. If there is any doubt or conflict between one or more concepts, the prudence concept prevails.

The Companies Act 1985 also states that the requirement to show a true and fair view overrides the fundamental principles.

Other concepts

There are other accounting concepts which businesses apply. Some of these are as follows.

The business entity concept

A business is a separate entity from its owners. We looked at this concept in Chapter 2.

The money measurement concept

Transactions are only recorded if they can be expressed in monetary terms. Some aspects of an organization's operations cannot be expressed in monetary terms, and yet they might be very important in determining the wealth of the organization. For example, an organization with a loyal and content workforce has a valuable asset which is not recorded because it cannot be expressed in monetary terms.

The cost concept

Items are initially recorded at their cost to the organization. This is a fair concept, in that cost can be proved and evidenced by invoice values. However, if items are considered to be worth less than their cost, they should be written down to that lower value – this is known as the *Net Realizable Value*, which is calculated as the expected sale proceeds, less any costs incurred in bringing the items to a saleable condition.

The stability of currency concept

This assumes that no distinction needs to be made between the value of currency from one period to another. If an organization buys two identical assets in different years, it will probably pay different prices for them, and no attempt will be made to value them at the same level.

The dual aspect concept

This is the basis of double-entry book-keeping, in that every transaction has two effects, the end result of which is that assets equal liabilities and capital (the accounting equation).

The realization concept

This states that profit is only earned when there is a legal right to receive the revenue. This is usually when the goods change hands or the service has been completed and accepted. The usual evidence is an invoice. In some cases, profit is not realized until some later date – for example, where goods are sold on sale or return, the revenue is not earned until the date for return has been reached. The payment of money is not necessarily an indication of revenue having been earned.

The materiality concept

This states that items which significantly affect a user's understanding of the accounts should be separately stated. Items which do not can be amalgamated with other items to avoid unnecessary detail in the accounts. The determination of what is meant by 'significant' is based on whether or not the item would affect the true and fair view given by the accounts, and hence would affect any decision made by the user of those accounts. Generally, items with a small value are not material unless they would change a profit into a loss or vice versa.

Accounting bases

SSAP 2 defines accounting bases as 'the methods developed for applying fundamental accounting concepts to financial transactions and items, for the purpose of financial accounts, and in particular

(a) for determining the accounting periods in which revenues and costs should be recognised in the profit and loss account and
(b) for determining the amounts at which material items should be stated in the balance sheet'.

Examples of accounting bases are the methods which companies choose to depreciate their fixed assets or to value stocks (see Chapter 13 for methods of stock valuation).

Accounting conventions

Over the years, accountants have considered different policies for the treatment of accounting items, and as a result 'standard' policies have been developed which most organizations adhere to. These are known as *accounting conventions*. They do not remain static – opinions change from time to time, and new conventions are developed. Some of these are successful, and remain in use; others are short-lived; yet others are still in the course of development.

The historical cost convention

In your studies so far, you have used this convention, perhaps without realizing it. It utilizes the cost concept mentioned above, with the result that, in the first instance, all transactions are recorded at their cost to the business. Any depreciation or reduction in values is based on that cost, which is a past cost, i.e. it is historical.

The greatest advantage of using historical cost is that it is completely objective.

The theory of capital maintenance

In Chapter 1 you saw an example of how different values could be placed on stocks. The example cited the purchase of 20 items at a cost of £1 each, and an expected selling price of £1.50 each. You then considered what value to put on those items. Is it the cost – £20? Or is it the potential selling price – £30? Or is it the expected profit – £10? You also considered what value to use if you had to pay £1.20 each to replace them. Chapter 1 stated that items should normally be valued at their cost to the business.

Let us say that this business commenced with capital in cash of £20 – enough to buy the first batch of stock. Suppose it also pays out £7 in expenses. Having sold them for £30, it now has £23 capital – the original £20 plus £3 profit. Is that good? Well, no, not if you realize that the cost of the next batch is going to be £24 (20 items at £1.20 each) – and you have only £23. The capital has not been maintained at a sufficient level to enable the business to continue trading at its present rate. You could say that the business has not made a profit in 'real terms'.

It is not only stocks which affect the maintenance of capital. Any asset which will require replacing at some time in the future will affect the amount of capital available. Fixed assets will require replacement eventually, and if no charge is made for their depreciation then the profit is being overstated, and hence the capital figure in the balance sheet is higher than it ought to be. Depreciation must be charged in order to bring the capital figure down to a 'fairer' level.

In recent years, accountants have suggested many different ways of dealing with this problem and have devised methods of calculating profit which attempt to show more realistically whether or not a business has maintained its capital, and hence whether it has made a profit in real terms. Two of these methods are mentioned next.

Current Purchasing Power (CPP) accounting

This method adjusts the accounts of the business by applying a factor equivalent to the change in the Retail Price Index (RPI). The main criticism of the CPP method is that the goods in which a particular business deals might not alter in line with the RPI. The method therefore fell out of favour in 1975.

Current Cost Accounting (CCA)

Sir Francis Sandilands headed a committee which looked into the problems of incorporating adjustments for inflation into company accounts (known as *inflation accounting*). The committee produced a report which recommended that companies should restate their accounts using specific indices for individual assets. Companies were then required by law to produce accounts which conformed to *both* the historical cost convention and the CCA recommendations.

This method fell out of favour in 1985. The calculations involved were time-consuming and subjective; comparisons between businesses could no longer be made with confidence, and arguments were raised as to whether all assets should be adjusted for inflation, including cash.

The problem of accounting for changing price levels still remains, and accountants still strive to find a solution.

Summary

By the end of this chapter you should understand the difference between accounting policies, concepts and bases, and be able to explain how they affect the way in which financial transactions are recorded and reported. You should understand how the historical cost concept operates, its limitations, and that the various attempts which have been made over the years have not succeeded in producing an alternative approach which is acceptable to all.

Exercises

7.1 The managing director of a company has recently returned from a conference on the techniques of business valuation. She has now realised that the accounts prepared by the company for publication probably understate the value of the company by:

(i)   the exclusion of goodwill
(ii) the valuation of fixed assets at cost; and
(iii) the treatment of the costs of research.

She has asked you to draft a report stating why the accounting treatment of these items understates the value of the company.

You are required to draft an appropriate report, making reference to accounting concepts where applicable.

(CIMA, November 1992)

7.2 SBJ's fixed asset register gives the cost and depreciation to date for every fixed asset held by the company. Prior to charging depreciation for 1994, the total net book value of all fixed assets on the register at 31 December 1994 was £147,500.

At the same date, the fixed asset accounts in the ledger showed the following balances:

	Cost £	Depreciation to date £
Motor vehicles	48,000	12,000
Plant and machinery	120,000	30,000
Office equipment	27,500	7,500

You are told that:

(i)   An item of plant costing £30,000 has been sold for £23,500 during 1994. The loss on disposal was £800. No entries have been made for this disposal in the ledger, but the asset has been removed from the fixed asset register.

(ii) A motor car was purchased on 1 October 1994, and correctly recorded in the nominal ledger. Its cost was made up as follows:

List price of vehicle	£24,000
Trade discount	20%
VAT added at 17.5%	
Insurance	£360
Vehicle licence (road fund tax)	£130
Painting of company name	£100 (no VAT)

The vehicle has not been entered in the fixed asset register.

(iii) Office equipment was purchased during 1994, entered in the fixed asset register, but not in the ledger. Until the omission can be investigated fully, its cost is deemed to be the difference between the balances on the fixed asset register and the ledger account at 31 December 1994 (prior to charging depreciation for the year).

(iv) Depreciation for 1994 is to be charged as follows:

   – on motor vehicles, at 25% per annum straight-line, with a full year's depreciation in the year of purchase
   – on plant and machinery, at 10% per annum straight-line, with a full year's depreciation in the year of purchase

— on office equipment, at 10% per annum reducing balance, with a full year's depreciation in the year of purchase.

Requirements:
(a) Calculate the correct balances at 31 December 1994 for cost and depreciation to date on the three fixed asset accounts in the ledger (prior to the charging of depreciation for 1994)
(b) Calculate the depreciation for each class of fixed asset for 1994
(c) Explain why an organisation charges depreciation on fixed assets, and the accounting concepts and principles which govern the charging of depreciation.

(CIMA, May 1995)

7.3x AB, a sole trader, commenced trading on 1 January 1990. He has provided you with the following details of his telephone costs:

	£
Quarterly rental payable in advance on	
1 January, 1 April, 1 July and 1 October	15
Telephone calls payable in arrears:	
January to March 1990, paid 1.4.1990	159
April to June 1990, paid 1.7.1990	211
July to September 1990, paid 1.10.1990	183

He is to prepare his first accounts to 31 October 1990 and estimates that the cost of calls for October 1990 will be £74.

AB also pays rent quarterly in advance for his premises and has made payments as follows:

	£
1 January 1990	600
1 April 1990	750
1 July 1990	750
1 October 1990	750

You are required to:

(a) prepare AB's ledger accounts for telephone and rent for the period from 1 January 1990 to 31 October 1990, showing clearly the amounts to be transferred to his profit and loss account for the period together with any balances carried forward on 31 October 1990
(b) explain the accruals concept in relation to profit measurement theory.

(CIMA, November 1990)

7.4 (a) Define each of the following terms as used in financial accounting:

(i)   asset
(ii) revenue
(iii) expense
(iv) matching.

(b) Explain the purposes, and the weaknesses, of a balance sheet
(c) It has become common in recent years, particularly in the UK, for companies not to provide any depreciation on their freehold buildings, which simply remain in the balance sheet at the same cost figure each year.

Describe arguments for and against the validity of this treatment, and explain whether you regard this policy as acceptable.

(ACCA, June 1994)

7.5x Describe the main limitations of preparing balance sheets and profit and loss accounts on an historic cost accounting basis in times of inflation.

(CIMA, November 1987)

Discounts, VAT and business documents

Aims of the chapter

The aims of this chapter are to:

- explain the calculation and treatment of trade and cash discounts
- explain the calculation and treatment of value added tax
- describe the contents and purpose of a range of business documents.

Discounts

The prices at which goods and services are bought and sold can be affected by *discounts*. A discount is a reduction in the 'normal' price payable. There are two types of discount – *trade discount* and *cash discount*.

Trade discount

This is a discount given when a business sells to particular customers. It might be given to customers who purchase large quantities (a *quantity discount*), to new customers (an *introductory discount*), to staff (a *staff discount*) or for a variety of other reasons.

The original price might have a variety of descriptions, including 'List Price', 'Catalogue Price', 'Recommended Retail Price' or 'Gross Value'. Once offered, the price is fixed at that reduced level, which is called the *net value*.

The gross value is *never* entered in the ledger accounts; nor is the trade discount. Only the net value is entered, and it is the net value which is used in any further calculations.

Example
You sell goods with a catalogue price of £100 to L. Poole, giving a trade discount of 40 per cent.

	£
Gross value	100
less Trade discount	40
Net value	60

The ledger entries required to record this sale will be:

	£
Credit sales	60
Debit L. Poole	60

At no time is the full value of £100 shown in the ledger accounts.

Trade discounts on returns

If goods are returned on which trade discount was originally given, remember to deduct the same proportion of trade discount when calculating the value of the return.

Cash discount (settlement discount)

Cash discount is deducted if payment is made within a specified time. Payment does not have to be immediate; nor does it have to be in cash. Time periods are often seven or ten days, and even as long as thirty-one days. The objective is to encourage prompt payment.

Unlike trade discount, the cash discount is deducted *only if payment is made within the specified time limit*. This may be some time after the goods change hands. The sale is recorded in the ledger accounts without any reduction for the cash discount; only when the payment is made is any adjustment made for the discount.

Cash discount allowed

This occurs when a business allows its customers to pay a reduced amount in return for prompt payment. It is an expense of the business and is debited to the profit and loss account.

Cash discount received

This occurs when a business pays a reduced amount to its suppliers in return for prompt payment. It is revenue to the business and is credited to the profit and loss account.

If trade discount is also given, this is deducted prior to calculating the amount of cash discount.

Example

On 20 January 19x5 your business buys goods from P. Goodwin which have a list price of £200, less trade discount of 20 per cent, and subject to cash discount of 5 per cent for payment within ten days. The ledger entries required on 20 January to record the purchase are:

Debit Purchases   £160   (£200 less trade discount of £40)
Credit P. Goodwin   £160

Note that there has been no reduction for the cash discount as yet.

If the business pays on 24 January, within the time limit, then cash discount of £8 (5 per cent of £160) can be deducted from the payment. The payment then becomes £152, and the ledger entries required to record that payment are:

Debit P. Goodwin   £152
Credit Bank   £152

This transaction, however, does not completely clear the account of P. Goodwin. A credit balance of £8 remains on the account, indicating that the business still owes this sum. Of course, this is not true, as cash discount has been given. To clear the account, the following entries are to be made:

Debit P. Goodwin   £8
Credit Discounts received   £8

and P. Goodwin's account is then clear.

To summarize, P. Goodwin's account would appear as follows:

P. Goodwin			
	£		£
24 Jan Bank	152.00	20 Jan Purchases	160.00
Discounts received	8.00		

If payment is not made in time, then the full amount of £160 is payable.

Value Added Tax (VAT)

VAT is a tax which the government requires consumers to pay on many of the goods and services we buy. The tax is added to the value of the item and the final consumer must pay the total amount, including VAT, to the seller.

If the seller is a registered trader for VAT purposes (and most businesses are), then he does not keep the VAT paid to him, but sends it to the government, via Customs and Excise. In effect, the seller is a collector of tax on behalf of the government.

Because the seller cannot keep the VAT, he does not include it in his sales figures, but instead records the VAT as a liability to Customs and Excise until it is paid over. This VAT is called *output* VAT.

If the buyer is also registered for VAT purposes, then although he has to pay over the full amount to the seller, the VAT portion can be reclaimed from Customs and Excise. The buyer therefore does not incur the VAT and so does not include it in his purchases figure, but instead records the VAT as an asset due from Customs and Excise. This VAT is called *input* VAT.

If the goods are subject to trade discount, this is deducted prior to calculating the amount of VAT. The current standard rate of VAT is 17.5 per cent.

Example (Output VAT)

A. Customer buys goods from A. Retailer with a list price of £800, less trade discount of 25 per cent, and subject to VAT at 17.5 per cent. In the books of A. Retailer, this would be recorded by the following entries:

Credit Sales	£600
Credit Output VAT	£105
Debit A. Customer	£705

When the VAT is paid over to Customs and Excise, the ledger entries would be:

Debit Output VAT	£105
Credit Bank	£105

Example (Input VAT)

The same retailer buys those goods from A. Wholesaler for £200 plus VAT of 17.5 per cent. In the books of A. Retailer, this would be recorded by the following entries:

Debit Purchases	£200
Debit Input VAT	£35
Credit A. Wholesaler	£235

and when the VAT is recovered from Customs and Excise, the ledger entries would be:

Credit Input VAT	£35
Debit Bank	£35

In practice, businesses submit a quarterly 'return' of their input and output

VAT and offset one against the other, making a single payment or receiving a single refund. They may also maintain a single VAT account rather than separate input and output VAT accounts. The balance would be shown either as an asset or a liability on the balance sheet.

The effect of VAT on profits

In a registered business, VAT normally has no effect on profits. For A. Retailer above, his sales would be £600 and his purchases £200, giving £400 profit – which is exactly the same as if VAT had not existed.

If a business is not registered for VAT, then it is not allowed to add VAT to its sales, but it may suffer VAT on its purchases. If this were the case for A. Retailer, his sales would be £600, but his purchases would have to include VAT, as the amount could not be reclaimed. Purchases would therefore be £235, and his profit only £365.

The same happens if a business buys goods on which the VAT cannot be reclaimed – examples include motor cars and items taken by the owner for his own use.

VAT on other items

VAT is not applied only to sales and purchases, but also to many fixed assets and expenses, including services such as accountancy fees. These are given the same treatment as in the examples above, i.e. the asset or expense account is debited only with the net amount, and the VAT is debited to the VAT account.

VAT on returns

When goods are returned, remember to add VAT to the net value. VAT on returns inwards is debited to the Output VAT account (because it is reducing the amount of output VAT), and VAT on returns outwards is credited to the Input VAT account.

VAT and cash discount

There are special rules regarding VAT where cash discount is also offered. The VAT is to be calculated *on the assumption that the cash discount will be taken*. This produces a lower amount of VAT than would have otherwise been the case. If the cash discount is not taken, there is no need to adjust the VAT.

Example

A business buys goods for £100, plus VAT at 17.5 per cent, subject to discount of 10 per cent for prompt payment. The VAT calculation is 17.5 per cent of £90, i.e. £15.75.

The cash discount itself (of £10) is not deducted at this stage. The ledger entries for the purchase would be:

Debit Purchases	£90.00
Debit Input VAT	£15.75
Credit the supplier	£105.75

and when settlement is made, assuming it is made on time, the entries would be:

Debit the supplier	£105.75
Credit the supplier	£ 95.75 (actual amount received)
Credit Discounts received	£10.00

If payment is not made in time, then the full £105.75 is payable, with no adjustment for either cash discount or VAT.

Business documents

The purpose of documents

Every transaction must be accompanied by documentary evidence. A document performs the following functions:

- It provides evidence that the transaction took place
- It can contain additional information for which there is no space in the ledger accounts
- It prompts the book-keeper to make the necessary ledger entries
- It can be adapted to contain confirmation that the ledger entries have been made
- It can be used as evidence of authorization for the transaction.

Some documents originate outside the organization, and are therefore a reliable source of evidence for audit purposes. Other documents originate inside the organization, and are therefore less reliable unless there are strict controls over their issue.

Here are some of the common business documents. The invoice is perhaps the document most widely used by the book-keeper, but the other documents are equally important. They are described here in the order in which they would originate in a business.

The purchase requisition

When a department or individual in an organization wants to order goods or services, he should complete a *purchase requisition* with details of his requirements. This is sent to the purchasing officer, if the firm is large enough to have one.

The purchase order

The purchasing officer is responsible for ordering the goods and services required from outside suppliers. He should raise a *purchase order*, on which details of the items ordered are given, and should sign it as evidence of authorization, otherwise goods could be ordered which are not strictly required. There are two copies of the order – one goes to the supplier, the other is retained by the purchasing department. Suppose that the Gardening department of M.J. Arkwright & Co requires ten spades and twenty trowels. The head of the department submits a requisition to the purchasing officer, who decided to order these goods from Smith, Jones and Watson Ltd by placing a purchase order with them.

The delivery note

When goods are delivered to the business, a *delivery note* should be received with them, which should be checked and signed by the person receiving the goods. The delivery note goes back to the supplier, although a copy may be retained by the receiving business.

The goods received note

The business receiving the goods raises a *goods received note* (GRN) to confirm the quantity and quality of goods received. This is sent to the purchasing department to be compared with the original order.

The invoice

An *invoice* is a document prepared by the seller to show details of the goods or services supplied. It is sent to the buyer to document the transaction and to act as a request for payment. It might contain a tear-off slip, or include a second copy for the buyer to use when forwarding payment.

There are many different styles of invoice. Here is an example:

SMITH, JONES AND WATSON LTD
3 Hilltop Rise, Westbridge, Cheshire, SK10 4YP
Tel: 01625 615364 Fax: 01625 672575
VAT Reg No. 123 5621 89

INVOICE

M.J. Arkwright & Co
68 Wellington Road
Appleton
Leicestershire
LE4 3BX

No: 5678

Date: 10 January 19x5

Order No 9203

Quantity	Catalogue number	Description	Catalogue price	Trade discount	Net value
			£		£
10	GDN123	Spades	31.25	20%	250.00
20	GDN406	Trowels	10.00	25%	150.00
Terms: Cash discount 5% (£20) for payment in 10 days			Total net value		400.00
			VAT @ 17.5%		66.50
			Total invoice value		466.50

The invoice might contain additional information, such as details regarding delivery. It might also contain items with different rates of trade discount (as in this example) and different rates of VAT.

There may be several copies of the invoice. The seller will treat his copy of the invoice as a sales invoice and use it to record the sale in his books; the buyer will treat his copy as a purchase invoice and use it to record the purchase in his books. The invoice should be passed to M.J. Arkwright's purchasing officer to be checked with the GRN and original order to ensure that it is for goods he has received and that the prices and calculations are correct.

The credit note

A *credit note* is raised by the seller when giving a reduction on a previous invoice. The reduction might be due to an overcharge, a miscalculation, or because the buyer has returned goods for some reason.

It should contain the same information as the invoice, perhaps with additional details such as the reason for the credit and the original invoice number. Remember that trade discount should be deducted and VAT added if these were on the original invoice.

Some buyers raise their own document when requesting a credit note – this is called a *debit note*. Obviously, only one of the documents can be used to initiate the ledger entries.

The remittance advice

Some invoices are sent in duplicate to the buyer; others might contain a tear-off strip with brief details of the invoice value. This is called the *remittance advice*, and the buyer uses it when he pays up to indicate which items are being paid for.

The statement

Many suppliers send a monthly reminder (*statement*) to their customers of transactions during the month, together with outstanding transactions from previous months. If there have been several invoices, it is probably more convenient to wait for the statement and pay the total, rather than to pay each individual invoice. The statement will include invoices, credit notes, payments received, cash discounts and any other adjustments, together with a note of the current outstanding total. It might also include a remittance advice to accompany payment.

There are many styles of statement. Here is an example:

SMITH, JONES AND WATSON LTD
3 Hilltop Rise, Westbridge, Cheshire, SK10 4YP
Tel: 01625 615364 Fax: 01625 672575
VAT Reg No 123 5621 89
STATEMENT

M.J. Arkwright & Co
68 Wellington Road
Appleton   Date: 31 January 19x5
Leicestershire
LE4 3BX

Date	Reference	Debit	Credit	Balance
		£	£	£
19x5				
1 Jan	Balance b/fwd			1,000.00
3 Jan	Inv 5047	805.60		1,805.60
8 Jan	Cheque received		950.00	
	Discount		50.00	805.60
20 Jan	Inv 5678	466.50		1,272.10
25 Jan	C/N 102		100.00	1,172.10
30 Jan	Inv 5801	900.00		2,072.10

The statement shows that there was an outstanding balance from the previous month of £1,000. Three invoices have been issued during the month, and a credit note. In addition, payment was made of £950, which appears to be for the opening balance less a cash discount of 5 per cent. The outstanding balance at 31 January is £2,072.10.

Layout of the statement

This statement is presented in three-column format, which is most common for statements. The format is also becoming common for ledger accounts, the advantage being that the balance is calculated after each transaction and is readily visible. A disadvantage is that there is no check on the accuracy of the balance as there is when a two-sided ledger account is totalled up. The statement is a copy of the customer's account in the books of the supplier. Thus, M.J. Arkwright & Co, being debtors of Smith, Jones and Watson Ltd, will have a debit balance on the account. Invoices will be debited, and credit notes and payments will be credited.

In the customer's books there will be a ledger account for the supplier, who is a creditor and therefore will have a credit balance.

Reconciling the statement with the ledger account

The statement must be carefully checked by the customer against his own ledger account for that supplier to ensure that it contains the correct invoice values and any credit notes and payments made, including the correct allowance for cash discounts.

Suppose that the ledger account of Smith, Jones and Watson Ltd in the books of M.J. Arkwright & Co appears as follows:

Smith Jones and Watson Ltd

	£		£
5 Jan Bank	950.00	1 Jan Balance b/fwd	1,000.00
Discount	50.00	5 Jan Invoice 5047	805.60
27 Jan C/N 102	100.00	23 Jan Invoice 5678	466.50
29 Jan D/N 945	40.00		
30 Jan Bank	500.00		
31 Jan Balance c/d	632.10		
	2,272.10		2,272.10
		Jan 31 Balance b/d	632.10

The first stage is to compare the two records and eliminate those entries which appear correctly in both.

The second stage is to look at the entries in the ledger account which do not appear on the statement. Here there is the debit note on 29 January which has not yet been converted to a credit note by Smith, Jones and Watson Ltd. When it is, it will reduce the balance on the statement by £40. There is also the payment on 30 January of £500 which has not yet reached Smith, Jones and Watson Ltd. This is called *cash in transit*. Again, when it does reach them, it will reduce the balance on the statement.

The third stage is to look at the entries on the statement which do not appear in the ledger account. There is one invoice, 5801, which was obviously on its way to Arkwright, but has not yet arrived. When it does, it will increase the balance in the ledger account.

These differences are adjusted on the reconciliation statement which can now be prepared:

	£
Balance per supplier's statement	2,072.10
less Debit Note 945	40.00
	2,032.10
less Cash in transit	500.00
Revised statement balance	1,532.10
Balance per ledger	632.10
add Invoice 5801 not received	900.00
Revised ledger balance	1,532.10

This then shows that when all outstanding transactions have gone through the two businesses, the balances will agree.

The receipt

Receipts are given when payment is made in cash, and act as evidence that payment has been made; receipts for cheque payments are less common, and not necessary as the cheque acts as evidence for the payment. The receipt must be signed by the person receiving the money. It might also be signed by the person authorizing payment. An example is as follows:

Receipt

No 462   Date:...........................

Received by:..............................

The sum of:..............................   £

For:...

Signed...   Authorized.......................

The receipt might be handwritten, as above, or produced by a cash till, although these are not normally signed so are less reliable as proof of payment.

Summary

At the end of this chapter you should be able to calculate and record trade and cash discounts and VAT. You should know that trade discount is never recorded in the ledger accounts and is always deducted prior to calculating VAT and/or cash discount. You should recognize and be able to use a range of business documents, and be able to reconcile a supplier's statement with the ledger account of the firm. You should also appreciate the need for accuracy and control over business documents as sources of evidence of transactions.

Exercises

8.1 Moss & Son buy the following from T. Gosling on 2 January 19x5:

30 carpets with a recommended retail price of £200 each, less trade discount of 20 per cent.

Cash discount is offered for payment by the end of the month, of 2 per cent.

(a) Record the purchase in the ledger accounts of Moss & Son.
(b) Record the subsequent payment by cheque on 20 January 19x5.

8.2 J. Clifford has the following details regarding sales and purchases during January 19x5:

	Total gross value £	Trade discount	Cash discount for payment in 7 days	Date paid
Purchases				
1 Jan	100	20%	2.5%	Jan 5
2 Jan	150	33⅓%	nil	Jan 7
3 Jan	500	10%	5%	Jan 14

	Total gross value £	Trade discount	Cash discount for payment in 7 days	Date paid
Sales				
1 Jan	400	25%	10%	Jan 6
2 Jan	1,000	20%	5%	Jan 10
3 Jan	200	15%	nil	Jan 18

VAT is charged at 17.5 per cent in all cases. For each item, calculate the net value, the VAT and the amount paid, and then calculate for the whole of January 19x5:

(a) the total to be debited/credited to purchases and sales
(b) the total to be paid over or reclaimed in respect of VAT
(c) the total of cash discounts allowed and received.

8.3 P. Walton receives the following statement of account from her supplier, J. Barber Ltd:

J. BARBER LTD
2 Old Road, Newtown, Longbridge, LO1 2BN
Tel. 0171 429 3606

STATEMENT OF ACCOUNT

To:
P. Walton
Spot Lane
Middletown
MD4 3OL

Date: 31 January 19x5

Date	Details	Debit £	Credit £	Balance £
19x5				
1 Jan	Balance b/fwd			3.000 Dr
1 Jan	Invoice 012	1,000		4,000 Dr
13 Jan	Invoice 016	3,600		7,600 Dr
15 Jan	Cash received		2,800	4,800 Dr
16 Jan	Credit note 0062		50	4,750 Dr
20 Jan	Invoice 019	500		5,250 Dr
29 Jan	Invoice 026	800		
	Credit note 0070		100	5,950 Dr

P. Walton has the following ledger account for J. Barber Ltd:

J. Barber Ltd

19x5	£	19x5	£
13 Jan Cash	2,800	1 Jan Balance b/fwd	3,000
Discount	200	15 Jan Invoice 012	1,000
18 Jan Credit note 0062	50	17 Jan Invoice 016	3,600
30 Jan Cash	1,400	22 Jan Invoice 019	500
31 Jan Debit note 65	300		
Balance c/d	3,350		
	8,100		8,100

Reconcile the two balances. Assume that the cash discount taken on 13 January is allowable.

9   The books used in book-keeping – an introduction

The aims of this chapter are to:

- describe various methods of dividing the ledger
- examine the purpose of subsidiary books
- describe the use of folio columns in ledgers and subsidiary books.

Small organizations may need only one book or ledger in which to record all their transactions. Larger organizations find that one book is insufficient. With a large number of transactions, a single book would be too small, and more than one person would be needed to keep the records up to date. It is common to find that larger businesses divide up the responsibilities for maintaining the accounts between several people, and even between several departments. This also gives the opportunity to incorporate controls to prevent and detect errors and fraud as each person provides a check on the other person's work. It also enables individuals to become 'experts' in the area in which they work.

Divisions of the ledger

Any means of dividing the ledger which is appropriate to the needs of the organization is acceptable. However, a common division is as follows:

- All debtors' accounts maintained in the *sales ledger* (debtors' ledger)
- All creditors' accounts maintained in the *purchase ledger* (creditors' ledger or bought ledger)
- All cash and bank accounts maintained in a *cash book*, with perhaps a *petty cash book* as well
- All other accounts maintained in a *general ledger* (nominal ledger).

Each ledger can be further sub-divided if necessary. For example, the sales ledger could be split into alphabetical sections or according to areas of the country. The nominal ledger could be split into fixed assets, expenses, and so on as required.

The double-entry rules are not affected by dividing the ledger, but it will often happen that the debit entry is made in one division, with the credit entry made in another division. It follows that all the divisions will need to be brought together in order to prepare the trial balance and final accounts.

Subsidiary books

In addition to the ledger accounts, a business might also maintain other books, records and lists which, although not part of the ledger, are used to help in the recording of transactions. In many instances they save space in the ledger accounts by recording details outside the ledger and producing totals of like transactions so that a single total rather than several individual items can be entered in the ledger. For example, a business might make several cash payments for postage stamps in the course of a week; rather than crediting the cash account and debiting the postage account with each payment, it might help to keep a list of all postage payments and debit a single total to the postage account at the end of the week. It does mean that the postage account is not up to date during the week (and hence the ledger accounts would not balance), but it does help to save space.

It is common to use these subsidiary books to record transactions *prior* to entering them in the ledger accounts, and so they might be referred to as *books of prime entry* or *books of original entry*. They are often written up on a daily basis and so are also known as *day books* or *journals*.

Transactions to be entered in the cash and bank accounts are *never* grouped together or left until later to be entered in the ledger. Incorrect or delayed recording of cash and bank items might lead to insufficient money being available; therefore transactions involving cash and bank are always entered individually and immediately in the cash and bank accounts (or cash books) although the 'other half' of the transaction might be grouped or saved up. Thus cash books are books of prime entry *as well as* being divisions of the ledger.

Subsidiary books are not used *instead of* ledger accounts; the ledger accounts must still conform to double-entry principles, and every transaction must result in equal debit and credit entries in the ledger. The subsidiary books are used *in addition to* ledger accounts.

The types of subsidiary book commonly in use are as follows:

- the sales journal (for the sale of goods on credit)
- the purchases journal (for the purchase of goods and services on credit)
- the returns inwards and returns outwards journals
- the cash book and petty cash book
- the 'general' journal or 'journal proper' – often referred to simply as 'the journal' (for the recording of any transaction which does not fit into any of the other books of prime entry).

Other methods of book-keeping

The double-entry system is the only complete book-keeping system. Some businesses adapt this to suit their needs by taking 'short cuts'. For example, if customers pay up very quickly it might be considered time-consuming to open up ledger accounts for every customer; it might be satisfactory to credit each sale to the sales account and place a tick at the side of it when the money is received, debiting the cash or bank account at that time.

Some businesses maintain only bank and cash accounts, and extract information for the final accounts from them.

Some businesses use the *slip system*, which means they use files of invoices, receipts, cheque counterfoils, etc. as their recording system. Invoices are marked 'paid' when the money is received, so a total of debtors is found by adding up those not so marked.

These alternative systems do not provide the control and security checks which a proper double-entry system provides.

The use of folio columns

When a business uses several different books to record its transactions, tracing the 'opposite half' to a transaction can be difficult. Ledger accounts and journals therefore require a *folio column*, which is used to denote the book and page number in which the opposite half can be found. For example, SL 19 tells us that the entry is in the sales ledger on page 19; PDB 32 tells us that the invoice is on page 32 of the purchase day book.

Recording the folio number also acts as confirmation that the entry has been made in the ledger, if it is recorded at that time.

Summary

By the end of this chapter you should be able to identify the divisions of the ledger and subsidiary books, and understand how they assist in recording financial transactions. You should also appreciate how the use of folio columns assists in the cross-referencing of transactions.

Exercises

9.1(a) You are employed by a company which distributes electrical goods to electrical shops and other retail outlets. You receive a telephone call from John Drayton, the proprietor of Drayton Electrical, who is interested in purchasing 60 of the new halogen toasters which you are stocking. The toasters normally sell for £50, but you are able to offer a 20% discount and, in addition, a cash discount of 5% provided that payment is made within 14 days. John Drayton asks you to give him a verbal quotation of exactly how much he would have to pay for the toasters.

(*Note:* VAT should be ignored in this question.)

(i) Clearly showing your workings, calculate how much in total Drayton Electrical would have to pay for the toasters if payment was made within 14 days of the sale.

(ii) Calculate how much would have to be paid if payment was not made within 14 days.

(iii) Assuming that the sale takes place, state what double entry (debits and credits and amounts) would be carried out by your company relating both to the sale and to the receipt of a cheque from Drayton Electrical within 14 days of the sale).

(b) Whilst talking to you on the telephone, John Drayton queries the balance of a statement sent to him as at 31 May 1991. You look up the account in the ledger which shows the following:

Drayton Electrical			
1991	£	*1991*	£
10 May Sales	1,420	14 May Returns	20
18 May Sales	860	22 May Bank	1,260
20 May Sales	903	22 May Discount	140
3 June Sales	746		

In discussing the account it appears that Drayton Electrical have not recorded in their books the returns shown on 14 May. John Drayton is quite confident, however, that the returns took place, but no documentation has been received from your company.

(i) State in which ledger you would have found the account of Drayton Electrical.

(ii) State what document should have been sent to Drayton Electrical on 14 May.

(iii) State which book of original entry would have been used by your company to record the document referred to in (ii).

(iv) Calculate the balance of the statement sent out to Drayton Electrical on 31 May.

(c) John Drayton decides to go ahead with the purchase of the toasters, which are delivered to him and an invoice is issued.

List 10 items of data which are normally shown on an invoice

(AAT, June 1991)

The cash books and bank reconciliations

Aims of the chapter

The aims of this chapter are to:

- describe the various documents used and transactions encountered in the banking system
- demonstrate the operation of the two-column and three-column cash book
- describe the purpose and use of the analysed cash book
- describe the operation of the petty cash book, and explain the control features of the Imprest system of petty cash
- explain the treatment of VAT in cash books
- demonstrate the preparation of a bank reconciliation statement.

All transactions involving cash and bank accounts are entered in one of the cash books. A business might have different cash books for different bank accounts or cash points; in addition, many businesses maintain a petty cash book for small cash payments.

Cheques and paying-in slips

Money is generally taken out of a bank account by *the drawer* writing out a cheque. The cheque is passed or posted to the creditor (*the payee*), who pays it into his bank account. The banking system directs the cheque to the drawer's bank, who take the money out of the account. The cheque is now considered 'cleared'. This process can take several days. The ledger entries to record a cheque paid out should be made as soon as the cheque is written – it should not be delayed until it is cleared. The drawer should record the details of the cheque on the cheque-book counterfoil ('stub').

Money is paid into a bank account by taking or posting cheques and cash received to the bank, and completing a paying-in slip. The details of items paid in should be recorded on the counterfoil of the paying-in book.

The two-column cash book

This book contains both the cash account and the bank account, with separate columns for each. It operates in exactly the same way as having two separate accounts – it is merely the layout which is different:

Cash book

Date	Details	Folio	Cash	Bank	Date	Details	Folio	Cash	Bank

Unless it is a new business, the book will have balances brought forward from the previous period, to be entered on the appropriate side. Remember that the bank balance might represent an overdraft, so would be recorded on the credit side.

As each transaction takes place it is recorded in the normal manner, using the appropriate column. Some special transactions are mentioned below:

1 *Transfers between bank and cash.* You have encountered these before, but using separate ledger accounts. Thus, a transfer of cash to the bank would require a credit entry to the cash account and a debit entry to the bank account. This rule still applies, although it seems strange to see both the debit and the credit entries appearing on the same page, as a debit in the cash column and a credit in the bank column. These are known as *contra entries* and a 'c' is normally entered in the folio column.

2 *Cash received and banked immediately.* This can be entered directly into the bank column.

3 *Cheques received but not banked immediately.* Even if these are placed in a cash drawer, they cannot be spent as cash. They should be recorded in the bank column, and banked as soon as possible.

4 *Money transferred to or from other cash books.* A common transfer is cash withdrawn for a petty cash box which is maintained elsewhere. Credit the Cash or Bank column – the other half of the entry will be in the petty cash book.

5 *Dishonoured cheques.* These occur when a customer's cheque is returned by the bank for some reason (usually because the debtor has insufficient funds in his bank account). The cheque will have been debited to the bank column in the cash book and credited to the debtor's account. This will now have to be reversed, i.e. credit the bank column in the cash book and debit the debtor's account. Some other means of obtaining the money will then have to be explored, or the debt written off.

6 *Bank charges and interest paid/received.* The bank makes these adjustments to a business bank account, often without notification until after the event. The amounts will appear on the bank statement and need to be entered in the cash book – bank charges and interest paid on the credit side, interest received on the debit side.

7 *Standing orders and direct debits.* These are amounts taken out of your bank account automatically to avoid the need to write out cheques. Although there is a difference between the two, their treatment in the ledgers is the same. They should be credited in the bank column.

8 *Bank giro credits.* These are amounts paid into your account at another bank, and maybe without your knowledge. They should be debited in the bank column.

Example

Your business maintains a two-column cash book. At 1 January 19x5 there is a balance of £500 with the bank and £50 in cash. During January the following transactions occur:

1 Jan Received a cheque from R. Jones for £270
3 Jan Received cash from sales of £300
5 Jan Received cash from sales of £250
9 Jan Paid £350 cash into the bank
11 Jan The bank dishonoured the cheque from R. Jones
18 Jan Paid rates by direct debit, £130
20 Jan Paid wages to a labourer, £150 cash
23 Jan Sold goods for £100 cash, paid direct into the bank
25 Jan Received a cheque from L. Turner for £500, but put it in the cash drawer
28 Jan Withdrew £200 from the bank for petty cash
29 Jan Paid L. Bowden £210 by cheque

The cash book would appear as follows:

Cash book

Date	Details	Folio	Cash £	Bank £	Date	Details	Folio	Cash £	Bank £
1 Jan	Balances b/fwd		50	500	9 Jan	Cash banked	c	350	
1 Jan	R. Jones			270	11 Jan	R. Jones			270
3 Jan	Sales		300		18 Jan	Rates d/d			130
5 Jan	Sales		250		20 Jan	Wages		150	
9 Jan	Cash banked			350	28 Jan	Petty cash			200
23 Jan	Sales			100	29 Jan	L. Bowden			210
25 Jan	L. Turner			500	31 Jan	Balances c/d		100	910
			600	1,720				600	1,720
1 Feb	Balances b/d		100	910					

In practice, an organization would record cheque numbers and perhaps paying-in slip numbers in the cash book, but these are rarely expected in examinations. This example also omits the folio numbers, as these are rarely expected in examinations.

The three-column cash book

This operates in an identical manner to the two-column cash book, but with an additional column for cash discounts allowed and received, on the appropriate side of the book. These discount columns are known as *memorandum columns*, because they act as reminders of entries still to be made. They are not ledger accounts. For example, if cash discount allowed is entered in the discount column of the cash book, it is there as a reminder that the discounts allowed account is to be debited with that amount. The purpose of the column is to collect together all occasions of discount allowed and/or received and to debit and/or credit a single total to the discounts allowed and/or discounts received accounts.

The cash and bank columns operate as with the two-column cash book, i.e. the amounts paid and received will be entered in these columns. If the payment or receipt is after deducting cash discount, then the amount of the discount is entered in the discount column. The total of the payment plus discount is debited or credited to the debtors or creditors account.

For example, if, on 23 May 1997, a customer, F. Smalley, pays an invoice of £100 less cash discount of 5 per cent, by cheque, the actual amount received will be only £95. The cash book would appear as follows:

Cash book

Date	Details	Disc £	Cash £	Bank £	Date	Details	Disc £	Cash £	Bank £
23 May	F. Smalley	5		95					

The full £100 will be credited to F. Smalley's account. The £5 discount will remain in the memorandum column until the end of the month, when the columns will be totalled and the total of cash discounts allowed and/or paid will be debited/credited to the respective ledger accounts.

Example
Your business operates a three-column cash book and has the following details relating to February 19x5:

Balances at 1 February 19x5 – cash £50 debit
                                – bank £1,000 debit

1 Feb   Received a cheque from A. Brown for £300
8 Feb   Paid a cheque of £200 to B. Carter in respect of an invoice for £220
9 Feb   Received a cheque from C. Davies for £100 representing payment of an invoice for £110, subject to cash discount of £10
11 Feb Paid wages of £40 in cash
19 Feb Paid D. Evans an invoice for £300 less cash discount of 3 per cent, by cheque
22 Feb Sold goods for cash for £150
25 Feb Received a cheque from E. Ford in respect of an invoice of £500, less cash discount of 3 per cent
27 Feb Paid £100 from the cash box into the bank account

The cash book would appear as follows:

Cash book

Date	Details	Disc £	Cash £	Bank £	Date	Details	Disc £	Cash £	Bank £
1 Feb	Balances		50	1,000	8 Feb	B. Carter	20		200
	A. Brown			300	11 Feb	Wages		40	
9 Feb	C. Davies	10		100	19 Feb	D. Evans	9		291
22 Feb	Sales		150		27 Feb	Cash to bank		100	
25 Feb	E. Ford	15		485	28 Feb	Balances c/d		60	1,494
27 Feb	Cash to bank			100					
		25	200	1,985			29	200	1,985
1 Mar	Balances b/d		60	1,494					

Those entries with discount require extra care. The total of the payment plus the discount must be entered in the personal account. For example, the entry on 8 February will result in £220 being debited to B. Carter to clear the balance there. On 9 February, the total of the receipt and discount of £110 will be credited to the account of C. Davies.

At the end of the period, the discount columns are totalled and the totals will be entered in the nominal ledger accounts, i.e. debit Discounts allowed £25 and credit Discounts received £29.

The analysed cash book

Organizations which have mainly cash transactions rather than credit transactions might use the cash book to analyse the receipts and payments. The analysis would also include VAT if applicable. An example of the credit side of an analysed cash book is as follows:

Cash book (credit side)

Date	Details	Cash £	Bank £	VAT £	Purchases £	Stationery £	Wages £	Petrol £	Other £
1 Jan	Stationery	11.75		1.75		10.00			
4 Jan	Goods		235.00	35.00	200.00				
7 Jan	Goods		470.00	70.00	400.00				
9 Jan	Stationery	47.00		7.00		40.00			
12 Jan	Wages		150.00				150.00		
15 Jan	Petrol	23.50		3.50				20.00	
17 Jan	Gas		200.00						200.00
20 Jan	Goods		352.50	52.50	300.00				
27 Jan	Petrol		23.50	3.50				20.00	
	Totals	82.25	1431.00	173.25	900.00	50.00	150.00	40.00	200.00

The cash book will be balanced off as usual, and the totals of the analysis columns will be debited to their respective nominal ledger accounts.

VAT in cash books

In the above example, where a payment was made which included VAT, the amount of VAT was entered in the VAT column and only the net amount was analysed to 'Purchases', 'Stationery', etc. This only happens where immediate payment is being made. If the payment is to a *creditor*, i.e. in respect of an earlier purchase, then the VAT will already have been dealt with when the invoice was entered in the purchases journal or other book of prime entry.

The debit entry will need to be made to the creditor's account in the purchase ledger. Therefore an additional column for 'purchase ledger' will be added, into which the *total payment* will be entered, including the VAT. There will be no entry in the VAT column.

Similar treatment should be given where money is received from a debtor, by adding a 'Sales ledger' column to include the total receipt.

Other types of bank and cash ledger accounts

There are many other different layouts of bank and cash accounts to suit particular purposes. Larger organizations might need a column to record each individual receipt, with a total column to record the amount banked at the end of the day.

The petty cash book

Most businesses try to restrict the use of cash because of its inconvenience and the risk of loss or fraud. If possible, they encourage all customers to pay by cheque or directly to the bank; if customers do pay in cash, it should be banked as soon as possible. However, there are often occasions when cash payments are unavoidable, usually because the amount involved is small and a cheque would be unacceptable. In such cases, the firm might set aside a sum of cash to be used for these small cash payments, known as *petty cash payments*. They are recorded separately from the main cash book, in a petty cash book. Because of the small amounts involved, petty cash can usually be controlled by a relatively junior member of staff.

The Imprest system

This operates by giving the petty cashier a fixed float of cash at the beginning of the period. This float is used throughout the period to make the payments. At the end of the period, the float is reimbursed by the main cashier to bring the balance back to its original level. This is known as 'restoring the Imprest'. The system aids security, as the maximum amount of cash in circulation at any time is restricted to the original float.

Petty cash vouchers

Every payment should be evidenced by a till receipt, invoice or similar. In addition, the petty cashier should raise a *petty cash voucher* for each payment, giving brief details of the transaction. The vouchers should be pre-numbered so that none can be omitted. The voucher is signed by the person receiving the money, and in some cases authorized by a more senior member of staff.

At the end of the period, the total of the vouchers issued should equal the amount needed to restore the Imprest.

Analysis columns

As with the analysed cash book, the use of *analysis columns* in the petty cash book enables small transactions to be 'saved up' and debited to the nominal ledger accounts at the end of the period.

Uses of the petty cash book

Petty cash is normally used only for payments. The only receipt should be the reimbursement of the amount spent at the end of the period. Most payments are for expenses such as postage, stationery, travelling and cleaning; thus there will be analysis columns for these.

Sometimes payments are made to creditors who request cash payment for small invoices; similarly, small refunds are sometimes given to debtors who require cash for credit notes. These need to be debited or credited immediately to the creditors' or debtors' accounts and not left until the end of the period; therefore an additional column for immediate ledger entries is added to enter the folio number of the personal account concerned as proof that the entry has been made.

If any of the payments include VAT, an additional column for Input VAT is required.

Maintaining the petty cash book

As there is only one receipt of cash each period, the debit side consists only of a single monetary column, sharing the 'Date' and 'Details' column with the credit side. The book will commence with the opening float, as restored at the end of the previous period. As each payment is made, its total will be entered in a 'Total' column. Any VAT will be entered in the 'VAT' column, and the net amount in the appropriate analysis column, unless the payment is to a creditor or debtor, in which case the full amount is entered in the ledger column.

At the end of the period, the credit side of the book is totalled and the individual columns cross-added to agree with the total column. These analysis columns (except for the ledger column) will then be debited to their respective nominal ledger accounts.

The Imprest might be restored *before* the account is balanced off, or *afterwards*.

Example
The Imprest balance at 1 January was £80. The following petty cash payments were made during January:

	£
3 Jan Postage stamps	10.00
7 Jan Cleaner's wages	13.00
14 Jan Post office (parcel post)	2.00
17 Jan Stationery, including £1.40 VAT	9.40
19 Jan Cleaner's wages	7.00
23 Jan Stationery, including £2.80 VAT	18.80
25 Jan Postage stamps	6.00
28 Jan Paid A. Timpson, creditor	5.00

Petty cash vouchers start at 023 and are used sequentially.

The petty cash book would appear as follows:

Petty cash book

Debit	Date	Details	PCV	Total	VAT	Post	Wages	Stationery	Ledger Fo.	Amt
£				£	£	£	£	£		£
80.00	1 Jan	Balance								
	3 Jan	Postage	023	10.00		10.00				
	7 Jan	Cleaner	024	13.00			13.00			
	14 Jan	Parcel post	025	2.00		2.00				
	17 Jan	Stationery	026	9.40	1.40			8.00		
	19 Jan	Cleaner	027	7.00			7.00			
	23 Jan	Stationery	028	18.80	2.80			16.00		
	25 Jan	Postage	029	6.00		6.00				
	28 Jan	S. Timpson	030	5.00					PL23	5.00
				71.20	4.20	18.00	20.00	24.00		5.00
	31 Jan	Balance c/d		8.80						
80.00				80.00						
8.80		Balance b/d								
71.20		Bank								
80.00	1 Feb	Balance								

On 31 January, the analysis column totals will be debited to Postage, Wages, Stationery and Input VAT. The entry to S. Timpson's account will have already been made on 28 January.

Bank reconciliations

As well as the bank account which is maintained by the organization in its cash book, the bank also maintains an account of transactions. Periodically, it sends a copy of this – the *bank statement* – to the organization. It is important that the organization compares its cash book with the statement and identifies any differences.

Debits and credits

In theory, the statement should be identical to the organization's own records, except that it will be in reverse order, i.e. a debit balance in the organization's cash book will appear as a credit balance on the bank statement. This is simply because the organization regards money in the bank as an asset, whereas the bank regards it as a liability – the bank has *borrowed* the money from the organization, which is entitled to have it repaid.

If the account is in overdraft, the organization regards it as a liability and the bank regards it as an asset.

It follows that debit entries in the cash book will appear as credit entries on the statement.

Differences between cash book and statement

Differences will arise for a variety of reasons, some of which are as follows:

- Errors, usually by the organization but occasionally by the bank
- Omissions from the cash book because the transaction did not originate with the organization, e.g. bank charges, interest paid or received, credit transfers and dishonoured cheques
- Amounts received by the organization at the end of the period but not added to the account by the bank until the beginning of the next period (common where the items were taken to the bank at the end of a day, or lodged in a night safe); these are known as *receipts not yet credited by the bank*

● Amounts paid out by the organization which have not yet been cleared (this is explained at the beginning of this chapter); these are known as *unpresented cheques*.

The first two reasons will require investigation and amendments to be made in either the cash book or in the bank's records.

The last two reasons do not require any action to be taken, except to check that the items do appear on the next bank statement when it arrives.

Reconciling the two records

The two records must be compared, any errors or omissions corrected, and any reasons for remaining differences identified. A statement is then prepared, explaining the differences and reconciling the two balances. The procedure is as follows:

1 Compare the two opening balances; these might be different because of receipts not credited by the bank, or unpresented cheques from the previous period. Locate them on the bank statement and tick off these and the opening balances as now agreeing.
2 Compare the two records and tick off any items which appear correctly on both.
3 Examine items not ticked on the statement. These often include bank charges and interest of which the organization was not aware; they might also include credit transfers, dishonoured cheques and direct debits or standing orders which the organization has forgotten about. In all cases, assuming the items are correct, these need to be debited or credited to the cash book. They can then be ticked off too, and a new balance on the cash book is calculated.
4 Examine items not ticked in the cash book. These are normally receipts not yet credited by the bank, or unpresented cheques. No action is needed for these, but they should appear on the reconciliation statement, which is prepared to show that when these items have been passed through the bank, the two records will agree.

Example

Your business receives the following bank statement at 31 March 19x5:

Bank statement				
Date	Details	DR £	CR £	Balance £
1 Mar	Balance			260
3 Mar	234113	20		240
5 Mar	Credit transfer, J. Brown		50	290
7 Mar	234114	5		285
11 Mar	Paid in		40	325
13 Mar	Royal Insurance SO	15		
	Credit transfer, L. Tripp		25	335
19 Mar	Rates DD	45		290
25 Mar	234116	30		260
27 Mar	234118	35		225
29 Mar	Dishonoured cheque	40		185
30 Mar	Bank charges	10		175

The cash book for March (bank columns only) is as follows:

Cash book						
Date	Details	Bank £	Date	Details		Bank £
1 Mar	Balance b/d	240	5 Mar	M. White	234114	5
4 Mar	J. Brown	50	13 Mar	Insurance	SO	15
10 Mar	M. Smith	40	15 Mar	A. Black	234115	16
31 Mar	P. Green	100	24 Mar	L. Grey	234116	30
			25 Mar	T. Yates	234117	12
			26 Mar	H. Hill	234118	35
			31 Mar	Balance c/d		317
		430				430
31 Mar	Balance b/d	317				

Now compare the two records, as follows:

1 The opening balance per the cash book is £240 debit, whilst the bank statement shows £260 credit (a debit balance would be highlighted as an overdraft). Notice that the first cheque number in the cash book is 234114, whereas the bank statement includes cheque 234113. This must be because cheque 234113 was entered in the previous month's cash book and was an unpresented cheque at the end of last month. Now that it has been presented, the bank statement balance agrees with the cash book, and the two opening balances, plus cheque 234113, can be ticked.

2 Tick items correctly appearing in both records. These are:
   ● cheques 234114, 234116 and 234118
   ● insurance standing order
   ● receipts from J. Brown and M. Smith.

3 Examine items on the statement which are not ticked, and take the following action:
   ● credit transfer, L. Tripp – debit the cash book
   ● direct debit for rates – credit the cash book
   ● dishonoured cheque – credit the cash book (it appears to be the cheque from M. Smith)
   ● bank charges – credit the cash book

Amend the cash book with these transactions and calculate a new balance:

Cash book					
		£			£
31 Mar	Balance b/d	317	31 Mar	Rates D/D	45
	L. Tripp	25		M. Smith	40
				Bank charges	10
				Balance c/d	247
		342			342
1 Apr	Balance b/d	247			

4 Examine items not ticked in the cash book. These require no action, but will be used to reconcile the two balances. The items consist of receipts from P. Green not credited by the bank, and unpresented cheques to A. Black and T. Yates.

The reconciliation statement can now be compiled:

Bank reconciliation at 31 March 19x5

	£	£
Balance per bank statement	175	
add Receipts not credited:		
P. Green	100	
	275	
less Unpresented cheques:		
234115	16	
234117	12	
	28	
Corrected balance per cash book	247	

The 'true' bank balance

The true balance, after all transactions have passed through, is £247 – the corrected balance per the cash book. This is the figure which management should use to determine their financial position, and is the figure which should be included on the balance sheet.

Summary

By the end of this chapter you should be able to prepare a two-column and a three-column cash book. You should be able to operate a petty cash book using the Imprest system and be able to explain the control aspects of this system. You should be able to prepare a bank reconciliation statement.

Exercises

10.1 Your business operates a three-column cash book and has the following balances at 1 March 19x5:

– bank £1,200 debit
– cash £250 debit

During February the following transactions occur:

1 March	Received a cheque from A. Harris for £300
8 March	Paid a cheque of £400 to B. Purvis in respect of a debt of £420
9 March	Received a cheque from C. Denver for £150, representing payment of an invoice of £160
11 March	Paid wages of £140 in cash
19 March	Paid D. Eversley for an invoice of £400 less cash discount of 3 per cent, by cheque
22 March	Sold goods for cash for £180
25 March	Received a cheque from E. Farrow in respect of goods with a total invoice value of £500, deducting cash discount of 5 per cent
27 March	Paid £200 from the cash box into the bank account

Write up the cash book for March and balance off. What entries would be made in the cash discounts allowed and received accounts?

10.2x Your business operates a three-column cash book. During March 19x5, the following transactions occur:

1 March Cash balance, £300 debit; bank balance, £565 debit

3 March   Received a cheque from L. Lloyd for £650 in full settlement of a debt of £700

5 March   Received a rent refund of £50 cash

7 March   Paid for stationery of £60 in cash

8 March   Paid Y. Yates a cheque for £345 in full settlement of a debt of £350

10 March Paid P. Patterson £70 in cash, in respect of a debt of £74

12 March Received a cheque for £65 from T. Trotter

15 March Paid £40 in cash to the petty cashier

18 March T. Trotter's cheque is returned unpaid by the bank

21 March Received a cheque from W. Wilson for £890, in respect of a debt of £900

24 March Paid for motor vehicle by cheque, £2,000

27 March Paid bank charges of £45

28 March Withdrew £100 from the bank to put in the cash till

31 March Paid insurance by direct debit, £120

Write up a three-column cash book and balance off.

10.3 Your business operates a petty cash system with an Imprest balance of £75. The transactions during March 19x5 were as follows:

3 March   Paid cleaner's wages, £5

6 March   Paid L. Lomas (a creditor), £14

8 March   Bought postage stamps, £3

10 March Bought cleaning materials, £11.75, including VAT of £1.75

14 March Bought printer ribbons, £4.70, including VAT of £0.70

18 March Paid for parcel post, £8

23 March Bought pens and pencils, £7.05, including VAT of £1.05

26 March Bought postage stamps, £7

29 March Bought stationery, £2.35, including VAT of £0.35

The petty cash vouchers commence at 401. Write up the petty cash book for March 19x5, with analysis columns for Cleaning, Postage and Office supplies as well as Ledger. Balance off and restore the Imprest at 31 March.

10.4 Your business receives the following bank statement at 28 February 19x6:

Date	Details	Debit	Credit	Balance
19x6		£	£	£
1 Feb	Balance			200
3 Feb	Cash and cheques		350	550
10 Feb	Cheque 345436	25		
	Cheque 345437	130		395
15 Feb	Cheque 345438	60		335
20 Feb	SO Halifax BS	20		315
24 Feb	Credit transfer, L. Tudor		100	415
25 Feb	Bank charges	40		375
26 Feb	Cash and cheques		30	405
27 Feb	Cheque 345439	195		210
28 Feb	Cheque 345442	220		10 DR

Your cash book shows the following:

Cash book						
Date	Details	Bank	Date	Details		Bank
19x6		£	*19x6*			£
1 Feb	Balance b/d	550	8 Feb	B. Barton	345436	25
26 Feb	Cash sales	30		C. Clifford	345437	130
28 Feb	J. Harrison	300	10 Feb	F. Graham	345438	60
			17 Feb	A. Archer	345439	195
			20 Feb	E. Ellis	345440	150
			26 Feb	J. Johnson	345441	75
			27 Feb	F. Forster	345442	220
			28 Feb	Balance c/d		25
		880				880
28 Feb	Balance b/d	25				

Correct the cash book and bring down the corrected balance. Prepare a bank reconciliation statement as at 28 February 19x6.

10.5x On 31 December 19x5 the cash book of A. Smith showed a balance of £582 debit. You are informed that:

(a) A cheque received by Smith for £28 was entered in his cash book on 30 December, but was not banked until 4 January 19x6.
(b) No entry has been made in Smith's cash book for a bank giro credit for £114, which was credited to his account by the bank on 28 December.
(c) Cheques drawn by Smith on 29 December 19x5, totalling £157, were not presented to the bank until 3 January 19x6.
(d) On 31 December 19x5 the bank debited Smith's account with £12 for bank charges, for which no entry has been made in his cash book.
(e) On 27 December 19x5 a standing order for £14 to the IPD was paid by the bank. No entry has been made in Smith's cash book for this.
(f) On 28 December 19x5 the bank dishonoured a cheque from a customer of Smith's, for £10. No entries have been made in Smith's cash book for this.

Correct the cash book balance and prepare a bank reconciliation statement. State the correct bank balance to be shown in the balance sheet.

11   The journals and the correction of errors

The aims of this chapter are to:

- demonstrate the use of the sales, purchases and returns journals
- demonstrate the use of the general journal
- identify and demonstrate the correction of errors which do not affect the agreement of the trial balance
- demonstrate the correction of errors which do affect the agreement of the trial balance, and to calculate their effects on profit and the balance sheet figures.

There are five types of journal:

- the sales journal
- the purchases journal
- the returns inwards and outwards journals
- the general journal.

The sales, purchases and returns journals

These are used for sales and purchases and returns on credit. Only sales which are credited to the sales account are entered here; in theory, only purchases which are debited to the purchases account are entered here too, but many businesses extend this to include purchases of expenses and fixed assets, by adding extra columns to the book.

Items which are sold or purchased for immediate payment are not entered here, but in the cash book.

Layout of the sales and purchases journals

The layout will depend on the requirements of the business, but the following is a common layout for a business registered for VAT and with only a single type of sales or purchases:

Date	Invoice/ Credit note number	Name	Folio	Net value £	VAT £	Invoice total £

Operation of the journals

As each invoice or credit note is raised or received, it will be entered in the journal. As it is important to keep debtors' and creditors' accounts up to date, their accounts will be debited or credited at once, but no entries will be made in the nominal ledger for sales, purchases, returns or VAT. These entries will only be made at the end of the day, week or month, as required, by totalling up the columns of the journal, checking their accuracy, and entering the totals in the nominal ledger accounts, thus completing the double-entry.

Example

Your business has the following transactions regarding sales and returns inwards during January 19x5:

3 Jan   Invoice 145 to A. Brown List price £400, less trade discount 10 per cent
10 Jan Invoice 146 to C. Black List price £250
13 Jan Credit Note 65 to A. Brown List price £80, less trade discount 10 per cent
15 Jan Invoice 147 to A. Brown List price £120, less trade discount 33⅓ per cent
24 Jan Credit Note 66 to C. Black List price £40

All items are subject to VAT at 17.5 per cent. Remember that neither the list price nor the trade discount are entered in the accounts – only the net value is used.

The sales journal would be written up as follows:

| Sales journal | | | | | Page 9 | |
Date	Invoice/ number	Name	Folio	Net value	VAT	Invoice total
19x5				£	£	£
3 Jan	145	A. Brown	SL2	360.00	63.00	423.00
10 Jan	146	C. Black	SL1	250.00	43.75	293.75
15 Jan	147	A. Brown	SL2	90.00	15.75	105.75
		Total for January		700.00	122.50	822.50
				NL27	NL85	

The individual debtors' accounts would be debited immediately with each invoice total, while the sales and VAT accounts would be credited at the end of the month with the total of the relevant column, the folio numbers of those accounts in the nominal ledger (NL27 and NL85), being written underneath (*note* – all folio numbers are imaginary). The totals should be cross-checked beforehand (£700.00 + £122.50 = £822.50).

The returns inwards journal would be written up as follows:

| Returns inwards journal | | | | | Page 4 | |
Date	Credit note number	Name	Folio	Net value	VAT	Invoice total
19x5				£	£	£
13 Jan	65	A. Brown	SL2	72.00	12.60	84.60
24 Jan	66	C. Black	SL1	40.00	7.00	47.00
		Total for January		112.00	19.60	131.60
				NL28	NL85	

The ledger accounts would appear as follows:

In the sales ledger:

C. Black *(Folio SL1)*

Date 19x5	Reference	Folio	£	Date 19x5	Reference	Folio	£
10 Jan	Inv 146	SJ9	293.75	24 Jan	C/N 66	SRJ4	47.00

A. Brown *(Folio SL2)*

Date 19x5	Reference	Folio	£	Date 19x5	Reference	Folio	£
3 Jan	Inv 145	SJ9	423.00	13 Jan	C/N 65	SRJ4	84.60
15 Jan	Inv 147	SJ9	105.75				

In the nominal ledger:

Sales *(Folio NL27)*

				Date 19x5	Reference	Folio	£
				31 Jan	Sales–Jan	SJ9	700.00

Returns inwards *(Folio NL28)*

Date 19x5	Reference	Folio	£	Date 19x5	Reference	Folio	£
31 Jan	Returns – Jan	SRJ4	112.00				

VAT *(Folio NL85)*

Date 19x5	Reference	Folio	£	Date 19x5	Reference	Folio	£
31 Jan	Returns – Jan	SRJ4	19.60	31 Jan	Sales–Jan	SJ9	122.50

The double-entry is now complete, and the ledgers should balance.

Analysed journals

As mentioned previously, additional columns can be added to the journals to cater for other types of purchase or to analyse stock purchases.

Suppose a furniture shop buys in two types of goods for sale – carpets and furniture – and wants separate totals for each; in addition, it records stationery purchased on credit in the purchases journal too. The purchases journal might appear as follows:

Purchases journal								
Date	Invoice number	Supplier	Folio	Net value			VAT	Total value
				Furniture	Carpets	Stationery		
19x5				£	£	£	£	£
1 Jan	123	Smith	PL8	100.00	200.00		52.50	352.50
3 Jan	124	Jones	PL4	400.00			70.00	270.00
8 Jan	125	Burton	PL2	120.00	80.00		35.00	235.00
10 Jan	126	Hope	PL3			50.00	8.75	58.75
18 Jan	127	Smith	PL8	100.00			17.50	117.50
25 Jan	128	Hope	PL3			50.00	8.75	58.75
		Totals for January		720.00	280.00	100.00	192.50	1,092.50

As before, the creditors' accounts in the purchase ledger will be credited with the total value immediately; the remaining entries at the end of the month will be to debit the column totals to Furniture purchases, Carpet purchases, Stationery and Input VAT, all in the nominal ledger.

The general journal, journal proper or journal

This is used as the book of prime entry for all transactions which cannot be recorded in one of the other journals or in the cash books. Examples of transactions which are commonly found in the journal are as follows:

- the purchase and sale of fixed assets on credit
- writing off bad debts
- correcting errors in the ledger
- making adjustments in the ledger accounts for accruals and prepayments
- making end-of-year adjustments for depreciation
- transferring amounts between accounts, e.g. when preparing the trading and profit and loss account.

Layout of the journal

As usual, this will depend on the needs of the business. A common layout is as follows:

The journal				
Date	Details	Folio	Debit £	Credit £

Each transaction is entered, together with a description, explanation or 'narrative' of the transaction.

Although the columns are headed 'Debit' and 'Credit', remember that this is *not* the ledger – the columns merely indicate which side of the ledger account to use when making the entries there.

Example

Your business has the following transactions to enter into the journal:

5 Jan Purchased office equipment from T. Trotter for £1,000, and from P. Roper for £1,600, plus VAT at 17.5 per cent
7 Jan Wrote off A. Allen, £250, and B. Bell, £100, as bad debts
12 Jan Discovered that goods had been sold to T. Simpson for £100, but had been debited to T. Simms' account in error
31 Jan Charged depreciation on office equipment of £500 for the month

The journal for January is shown on the following page.

The journal				
Date	Details	Folio	Debit	Credit
			£	£
3 Jan	Office Equipment Input VAT T. Trotter P. Roper (being purchase of fixed assets on credit – see Invoice Nos. 901 and 902)	NL56 NL43 PL14 PL10	2,600 455	 1,175 1,880
7 Jan	Bad debts written off A. Allen B. Bell (being bad debts written off in January)	NL98 SL45 SL52	350	 250 100
12 Jan	T. Simpson T. Simms (being Invoice No. 475 debited to wrong account)	SL78 SL75	100	 100
31 Jan	Profit and loss account Depreciation office machinery (being depreciation charge for January)	NL999 NL104	500	 500

The entries would then be made in the respective ledger accounts.

Errors which do not affect the agreement of the trial balance

A trial balance which agrees indicates that for every debit entry there has been an equivalent credit entry or entries. It does not prove that all the entries are for the correct amount or are made to the correct accounts. There are six types of error which can occur but which do not affect the agreement of the trial balance.

1 *Error of omission.* This occurs where a transaction has been completely omitted from the ledger accounts. For example, a sales invoice 345 to A. Bolton for £1,000 was omitted from the accounts.

2 *Error of commission.* This occurs where one half of a transaction has been entered in the wrong account, but where the error does not affect the view given by the final accounts, i.e. the correct account and the incorrect account are of the same type (e.g. both debtors, both expenses). For example, your business pays A. Robins £2,000 by cheque, but debits A. Robinson's account by mistake.

3 *Error of principle.* This is similar to an error of commission, but the error does affect the view given by the final accounts, i.e. the correct account and the incorrect account are of different types (e.g. one is an asset, the other an expense). For example, your business buys plant for £1,200 cash, but debits the purchases account by mistake. This error will affect the profit and the balance sheet, and this is why it differs from an error of commission.

4 *Compensating errors.* These occur where there are two errors which offset one another. For example, in totalling the sales journal an item has been misread as £110 instead of £10; in addition, a figure in the purchase returns journal has been misread as £500 instead of £600. These two errors result in the sales account being 'overcast' by £100, and the purchase returns account being 'overcast' by £100 – the two errors offsetting one another.

5 *Error of original entry.* This occurs where the wrong figure has been used for the entire transaction, so both debit and credit entries are incorrect. For example, stationery purchased on credit from G. Holden for £140 has been recorded as £14 in both the stationery and G. Holden's account.

6 *Reversal of entries*. This occurs where the entries for a transaction are reversed – the account which should be credited is debited and vice versa. For example, furniture is purchased for £500 on credit from G. Underwood. The entries made were Debit G. Underwood and Credit furniture.

Correcting the errors

The errors are corrected via the journal in the first instance, and then in the ledger accounts. The six errors above, and the journal entries needed to correct them, are as follows:

1 A sales invoice 345 to A. Bolton for £1,000 was omitted from the accounts. To correct this, A. Bolton needs a debit entry and Sales needs a credit entry.
2 Your business pays A. Robins £2,000 by cheque, but debits A. Robinson's account. To correct this, A. Robins needs a debit entry and A. Robinson needs a credit entry.
3 Plant is purchased for £1,200 cash, but the purchases account is debited. To correct this, the plant account needs a debit entry and the purchases account needs a credit entry.
4 The sales account is overcast by £100 and the purchase returns account is overcast by £100. To correct this, the sales account needs a debit entry and the purchase returns account needs a credit entry.
5 Stationery purchased on credit from G. Holden for £140 has been recorded as £14 in both the stationery and G. Holden's account. To correct this, the stationery account needs a further debit entry and G. Holden's account needs a further credit entry of £126.
6 Furniture is purchased for £500 on credit from G. Underwood. The entries made were Debit G. Underwood and Credit furniture. To correct this, two stages are required. First, G. Underwood needs a credit entry and Furniture needs a debit entry of £500 to take out the entries which have been made. This brings the accounts back to the position they were in prior to the purchase. Then to record the purchase properly, G. Underwood needs a further credit entry and Furniture needs a further debit entry of £500.

Errors which do affect the agreement of the trial balance

There are many errors which do affect the agreement of the trial balance. They often occur where one side of a transaction is correctly dealt with but the other is not. The result is that one column of the trial balance will be smaller than the other. Ideally, the error should be found as quickly as possible, but in some cases it is not possible to do so, and rather than hold up production of the profit and loss account and balance sheet, these need to go ahead. So that the accounts balance, a fictitious balance is created; this is entered in a *suspense account*, either debit or credit depending on which column is smaller.

The final accounts will include a debit balance on the suspense account as a current asset, or a credit balance as a current liability.

As soon as possible, the difference must be investigated; often the errors come to light by chance. As they are discovered, corrections are recorded in the journal and then in the ledger accounts, including the suspense account if necessary.

The suspense account is also used where the correct ledger account for one half of an entry is not known: for example, where a business receives a cheque from someone who does not appear in the sales ledger as a debtor. The bank account will be debited, but the credit entry will be to the suspense account. When the identity of the debtor is discovered, the suspense account will be debited and the correct account credited.

Example

Your firm's trial balance at 31 December 19x5 is out of agreement. The debit side totals £35,000 and the credit side totals £34,800. A brief check does not reveal the errors, so an amount of £200 is credited to the suspense account. In addition, a cheque received on 31 December, from Boothby and Son for £30, is credited to the suspense account, as no trace can be made of this amount being owing. Subsequently, the following errors are discovered:

19x6
3 Jan   J. Collins, a debtor, has been debited with £100 for sales of £180
8 Jan   Sales were undercast by £300
11 Jan The cheque from Boothby and Son is discovered to be for commission receivable
20 Jan A gas bill for £420 has been recorded as £400 in the gas account
24 Jan Purchases of office equipment of £3,000 were debited to the purchases account

Correct the items via the journal, and show the entries in the suspense account.
The journal would appear as follows:

	The journal		
Date	Details	Debit	Credit
19x6		£	£
3 Jan	J. Collins	80	
	Suspense account		80
8 Jan	Suspense account	300	
	Sales		300
11 Jan	Suspense account	30	
	Commission receivable		30
20 Jan	Gas	20	
	Suspense account		20
24 Jan	Office equipment	3,000	
	Purchases		3,000

Note that the last item does not affect the suspense account – it is one of those transactions which does not prevent the agreement of the trial balance.
The suspense account would appear as follows:

		Suspense account				
		£				£
19x5			*19x5*			
			31 Dec	Trial balance		200
				Boothby & Son		30
8 Jan	Sales	300	3 Jan	J. Collins		80
11 Jan	Commission rec.	30	20 Jan	Gas		20
		330				330

The suspense account is now clear.

The effect of errors on the profit and loss account and balance sheet

Examination questions often ask candidates to recalculate one or more of the figures in the final accounts after the errors have been corrected. Using the journal can help, in that corrections which necessitate a debit entry to the ledger account either decrease profits or increase net assets; entries which necessitate a credit entry to the ledger account either increase profits or decrease net assets.

In the above example, suppose the net profit for the year to 31 December 19x5 was £17,500. The revised net profit would be calculated as follows:

	£
Original net profit	17,500
Add:	
Sales	300
Commission receivable	30
Reduction in purchases	3,000
	20,830
Less:	
Gas	20
Revised net profit	20,810

If the net assets were £125,000 prior to the discovery of the errors, this will be revised as follows:

	£
Original net assets	125,000
Add:	
J. Collins	80
Office equipment	3,000
Suspense account cleared	230
Revised net assets	128,310

Other uses of the suspense account

The suspense account is also used to record an entry where the correct ledger entry is uncertain or unknown. The entry is recorded in the suspense account until its true destination is discovered, and then it is transferred out.

Summary

By the end of this chapter you should be able to operate the various journals and to understand how they provide a means of control over the financial transactions. You should be able to identify the various errors which can occur during the maintenance of the books of account, be able to correct them, and calculate their effect on the reported profit and balance sheet figures.

Exercises

11.1 Enter the following transactions in the purchases and purchase returns journals. Post the items to the ledger accounts as appropriate.

5 Jan Purchased goods for £350 from D. Evans on Invoice No. 83
15 Jan Purchased goods for £120 from E. Ford, less trade discount of 10 per cent, on Invoice No. 84
20 Jan Returned goods costing £140 to D. Evans, receiving Credit Note No. 901
25 Jan Purchased goods costing £230 from D. Evans on Invoice No. 85
28 Jan Returned goods costing £40 to E. Ford, receiving Credit Note No. 904
All items are subject to VAT at 17.5 per cent.

11.2 Your firm has the following trial balance at 31 December 19x5:

	Debit £	Credit £
Rates	50	
Wages	200	
Sales		6,000
Capital 1 January 19x5		8,250
Stock 1 January 19x5	1,000	
Bank and cash	2,000	
Purchases	4,000	
Creditors		2,000
Motor vehicles	1,000	
Premises	5,000	
Debtors	3,000	
	16,250	16,250

Although the trial balance appears to be correct, you discover the following errors:

(a) A. Hurst (a creditor) has been debited with a cheque for £1,000 which has been paid to A. Hunt.
(b) Motor vehicles and sales were both undercast by £500.
(c) Sales of goods on credit of £600 to A. Brunt were completely omitted from the books.
(d) Rates paid in cash of £150 have been recorded as £50 on both sides of the respective ledger accounts.
(e) Purchases of goods for resale on credit from L. Jones, costing £400, have been debited to L. Jones' account and credited to the purchases account.
(f) Goods sold on credit for £100 to A. Green have been credited to the sales account and debited to the wages account.

In each case, state the type of error, and prepare journal entries to correct them. Produce a corrected trial balance.

11.3 Record the following items in the journal:

19x5
  8 Jan Office equipment costing £340 and stationery costing £70 purchased on credit from H. Young
10 Jan Office equipment which had cost £1,000, and which had been depreciated by £800, sold for £250 on credit to B. Brownlow
15 Jan J. Ashworth is both a debtor (owing £250) and a creditor (owed £350) of your business. The two balances are to be offset against each other
21 Jan A. Briggs, a debtor, is declared bankrupt and is unable to pay £300 of his debt
27 Jan Provision for doubtful debts is to be made of £180

11.4 Your firm's trial balance at 31 December 19x6 is out of agreement. The debit side totals £42,500 and the credit side totals £44,000. A brief check does not locate the errors, so the difference is entered into a suspense account. On the same date, a cheque is received from P. Jepson for £20, and no trace can be made of this amount being owing. The following are discovered:

2 Jan Purchases for December were overcast by £900

4 Jan The cheque from P. Jepson is for rent received

7 Jan Purchase of goods for £2,000 plus VAT at 17.5 per cent had been recorded by debiting purchases with £2,000 and crediting the creditor (C. Taylor) with £2,350

9 Jan An invoice for stationery of £250 had been credited to both bank and stationery accounts

10 Jan The return of a motor vehicle costing £1,000 has been credited to the sales account

Correct the items via the journal, and amend the suspense account. Prior to correcting the errors, net profit had been calculated at £7,450 and net assets at £40,400. Calculate revised figures for both of these.

11.5x You are employed by Micromart plc in the accounts department. The department is divided up into various sections and the one in which you work is responsible for the journal, the purchases day book and the returns outwards day book. The following list represents all the transactions which took place on Monday 8 June. Some of these require action by your section, others will be passed on to different sections.

1 An invoice is issued to P. Davies for goods costing £246.

2 A new motor van is purchased on credit from Banford Autos for £6,240.

3 Cash purchases of £211 are made from D. Foster.

4 A credit note is received from C. Evans for £26.

5 An invoice is received from J. Hunter. £500 of goods had been ordered from Hunter, who has now allowed a trade discount of 10% and an additional cash discount of 5% if payment is made within 7 days.

6 It is discovered that a sale of goods to T. Smith on 1 June for £40 has been entered in the account of J. Smith.

7 Goods costing £63 are returned to H. Farrell, a credit supplier, and the relevant documentation is issued.

8 A modification costing £294 is made to one of the machines and is paid for immediately by cash.

9 An invoice is received from K. Winston for goods costing £426.

10 A credit note for £51 is issued to P. Nolan.

11 E. Branston, a credit customer who owes £117, is declared bankrupt. It is considered highly unlikely that any payment will be received.

12 Some fixtures originally bought on credit for £70 from L. Perry have proved to be unsuitable and are returned to L. Perry, who gives a full allowance.

13 N. Mullins purchases £23 of goods on credit from Micromart plc.

14 It is discovered that a payment of £50 made by cheque to T. Morris on 1 June had been entered in the books as a receipt from the same person.

15 New machinery costing £2,000 is purchased from B. Bracewell Ltd. Payment is made by cheque.

Enter the transactions belonging to your section into a Journal, a Purchases Day Book and a Returns Outwards Day Book as appropriate. Folio numbers and journal narratives are not required.

(AAT, June 1992)

Aims of the chapter

The aims of this chapter are to:

- explain the purpose of control accounts
- demonstrate the maintenance and operation of control accounts.

When the ledger is divided into sections, *control accounts* can be introduced to check on the accuracy of each section of the ledger. A control account contains the same information as the individual ledger accounts which it 'controls', but in total – hence it is sometimes known as a *total account.* For example, if a business keeps a separate sales ledger, then it might also have a sales ledger control account to check on the accuracy of the sales ledger. The sales ledger control account will take its totals of sales and returns from the sales and returns journals; it will take its totals of monies received and cash discounts allowed from the cash books; totals of bad debts are taken from bad debts lists, and so on.

The control account may or may not form part of the double-entry system. If the individual debtors' accounts are kept in the system, then the control account is not, otherwise entries would be duplicated. But many large organizations take the individual debtors' accounts out of the system and maintain them as a separate system; the control account then forms part of the double-entry system and is kept in the nominal ledger. The same applies to creditors and the purchase ledger control account.

A control account can be maintained for any part of the ledger, but the two common control accounts are the *sales ledger control account* and the *purchase ledger control account.* They operate on the principle that whatever is entered in an individual's account is also entered in the control account. It follows that the balance on the control account must equal the total of individual balances on the ledger which it controls.

The control account can also speed up the preparation of the trial balance, as it requires only a single balance to be calculated rather than every debtor's balance.

Example

Your firm has 3 debtors with the following balances at 1 January 19x5:

A   £50 debit
B   £300 debit
C   £800 debit

The following transactions occur during January 19x5:

Sales on credit	B	£400 (3 Jan)
	C	£1,200 (8 Jan)
Returns inwards	B	£80 (10 Jan)
	C	£10 (12 Jan)
Bad debt written off	A	(15 Jan)

Cash received   B   £195 in payment of a debt of £200 (20 Jan)
                C   £1,000 (23 Jan)

The control account would appear as follows:

Sales ledger control account

		£				£
1 Jan	Balances b/d	1,150	31 Jan	Returns		90
3 Jan	Sales	1,600		Cash		1,195
				Discount allowed		5
				Bad debts w/o		50
				Balances c/d		1,410
		2,750				2,750
	Balances b/d	1,410				

and the individual debtors' accounts would appear as follows:

Debtor A

		£			£
1 Jan	Balance b/d	50	15 Jan	Bad debts w/o	50

Debtor B

		£			£
1 Jan	Balance b/d	300	10 Jan	Returns	80
3 Jan	Sales	400	20 Jan	Cash received	195
				Discount allowed	5
			31 Jan	Balance c/d	420
		700			700
1 Feb	Balance b/d	420			

Debtor C

		£			£
1 Jan	Balance b/d	800	12 Jan	Returns	10
8 Jan	Sales	1,200	20 Jan	Cash	1,000
			31 Jan	Balance c/d	990
		2,000			2,000
1 Feb	Balance b/d	990			

The total of the individual balances should be checked with the balance on the control account as follows:

List of sales ledger balances at 31 January 19x5

Debtor B	£420
Debtor C	£990
Total as per control account	£1,410

If the total does not agree with the control account, then this may indicate that the trial balance is also out of agreement, and that the error is somewhere within the sales ledger or its control account. Check backwards in reverse order of compiling the figures – i.e. check the calculation of the control account balance, then the totalling of the list of sales ledger balances, then the extraction of total sales, receipts, discounts, etc. from the books of prime entry, and so on until eventually you will have to check the entries with the original transactions.

Contra entries

Some organizations have debtors who are also creditors, and therefore maintain accounts for them in both the sales and purchase ledgers. To avoid unnecessary transactions, e.g. the debtor paying the organization, and the organization paying the creditor, the two balances are offset against each other. This is done by transferring the account with the smaller balance into the account with the larger balance. The transfer is known as a *contra entry*.

For example, P. Wilson is both a debtor and a creditor. The balance on the sales ledger account is £500 debit, while the balance on the purchase ledger account is £450 credit.

The purchase ledger account has the smaller balance, so it is transferred into the sales ledger account, the entries being:

Debit purchase ledger account   £450
Credit sales ledger account   £450

The resulting balance on the sales ledger account will be £50 debit, and this can then be settled by a single payment.

Credit balances in the sales ledger and debit balances in the purchase ledger

Credit customers normally have debit balances and credit suppliers have credit balances. Sometimes a customer is owed money and a supplier owes money. In such cases, the customer will have a credit balance (and, strictly speaking, is a creditor) and the supplier will have a debit balance (and is a debtor). Rather than transfer them between ledgers, the account remains in its original ledger with a balance on the opposite side to the normal balance. These balances must always be totalled and shown separately in the control account, as one of the rules of accounting is to highlight material items – and a customer with a credit balance is unusual enough to be regarded as material.

Customers with credit balances are often given refunds; suppliers with debit balances might give refunds.

A second example

Examination questions often give candidates a list of figures to be incorporated into a control account. Here is an example of a completed sales ledger control account with a comprehensive range of transactions, but with the final debit balance omitted:

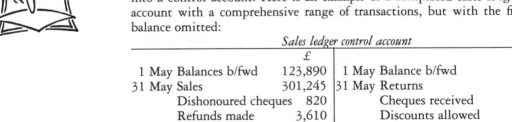

Sales ledger control account

	£		£
1 May Balances b/fwd	123,890	1 May Balance b/fwd	8,450
31 May Sales	301,245	31 May Returns	12,830
Dishonoured cheques	820	Cheques received	242,160
Refunds made	3,610	Discounts allowed	1,950
Credit balances c/fwd	7,280	Bad debts written off	490
		Contras to purchase ledger	2,070
		Debit balances c/fwd	?

The debit balances carried forward need to be established by calculating the balance (£168,895) and then they need to be compared with the total of the individual debtors' accounts in the sales ledger. Note that there were credit balances at the start of May of £8,450, and that during May refunds of £3,610 were given, and yet the closing credit balances at the end of May amount to £7,280. If this confuses you, remember that new credit balances might have arisen during May, and existing credit balances may have been converted to debit balances by the customer purchasing more goods.

Summary

By the end of this chapter you should understand the purpose and operation of control accounts, and be able to use them to check on the accuracy of the ledger accounts and to identify areas of possible error.

Exercises

12.1 From the following information, prepare a purchase ledger control account for the month of January 19x5:

	£
Opening creditors	2,000
Credit purchases for January	12,000
Cheques paid to suppliers	8,500
Cash discount received	500
Purchase returns for January	1,200

12.2x From the following information, prepare a sales ledger control account for the month of January:

	£
Opening debtors	7,000
Sales for January on credit	25,000
Cash sales for January	2,200
Cheques received from debtors	18,500
Cash discount allowed	400
Bad debts written off	1,000
Sales returns for January	800
Dishonoured cheques	450
Contra to purchase ledger	150

12.3 The following balances are extracted from your sales ledger at 1 March 19x5:

Debit balances	£124,600
Credit balances	£ 1,600

The sales ledger control account shows a net balance of £125,000.
    You discover the following errors:

(a) Credit balances totalling £400 have been listed as debit balances on the list of debtors taken from the sales ledger
(b) Cash discounts allowed of £300 have been omitted from the control account
(c) A credit note for £2,000 plus VAT at 17.5 per cent has been recorded in the sales day book as £1,000 plus VAT. It has been correctly entered in the sales ledger
(d) A dishonoured cheque for £1,200 has been omitted from the sales ledger
(e) Bad debts written off, amounting to £500, have been omitted from the control account
(f) A provision for doubtful debts of £375 has been credited to the control account, but no entries have been made in the sales ledger.

    Correct the sales ledger control account and the sales ledger balances.

12.4x An error has been made in the trial balance of Jones at 31 May 19x5. To try to locate the error you are asked to prepare a sales ledger control account and a purchase ledger control account from the following information:

	£
31 May 19x5 – purchase ledger balances	12,000
– sales ledger balances	15,000

Totals extracted from the books of original entry at the end of May were as follows:

	£
Purchase journal	40,000
Sales journal	70,000
Returns inwards journal	5,000
Returns outwards journal	4,000
Cheques paid to suppliers	38,000
Cash and cheques received from customers	60,000
Discounts allowed	2,000
Discounts received	1,000
Bad debts written off	2,500

You discover that the amount received from customers includes cash sales of £300.

At 31 May 19x5, you obtain a list of balances from the sales and purchase ledgers, which show the following:

		£
Purchase ledger balances	– credit	9,500
	– debit	500
Sales ledger balances	– debit	15,500
	– credit	250

Locate the ledger which contains the error, and state its amount.

Aims of the chapter

The aims of this chapter are to:

- demonstrate the three main methods of valuing stocks
- consider the provisions of SSAP 9 regarding the net realizable value of stocks
- demonstrate the calculation of gross and net wages
- demonstrate the ledger entries required to record wages.

Accounting for stocks

Records of stocks are not normally included in the double-entry system. We have already seen how we use sales, purchases and returns accounts for stock movements, and a stock account for end-of-year stock. Most organizations keep a separate record of stocks, outside the ledger, by maintaining an individual record of the transactions of each type of stock held.

These records might be kept on 'bin cards', which normally record only quantities, or on stock records, which record values as well.

The quantity held is checked by means of a physical stock check at the end of the year, or alternatively by a continuous stock check on selected items throughout the year.

Methods of valuing and recording stocks

There are many different methods of arriving at the value of stocks consumed or closing stocks. The most accurate, but time-consuming, method is for each item to be labelled with its cost and, when it is sold, the cost notified to the accounts department. However, this is not practical in most organizations, especially where stocks are bought in bulk, and where no distinction is made between old stocks and new stocks. Therefore stocks must be valued using certain assumptions.

The following example of stock movements of Material X is used to illustrate the three common methods of stock valuation covered in this chapter:

1 July	Opening stock	10 items @ £10 each
13 July	Purchases	5 items @ £16 each
20 July	Issues	8 items
25 July	Issues	3 items
30 July	Purchases	12 items @ £18 each

First In First Out (FIFO)

This method assumes that the stocks which were received first are issued (used) first. Thus stocks remaining at the end of the period are assumed to be those which were received most recently.

The stock record card using the FIFO method would appear as follows:

Date	Receipts			Issues			Balance		
	Qty	Value each	Total value	Qty	Value each	Total value	Qty	Value each	Total value
		£	£		£	£		£	£
1 July							10	10	100
13 July	5	16	80				5	16	180
20 July				8	10	80	2	10	
							5	16	100
25 July				2	10				
				1	16		4	16	64
30 July	12	18	216				4	16	
							12	18	280

The balance is recalculated after each transaction. The issue on 20 July was of the earliest items at £10 each; this left a balance of 2 items at £10 plus 5 items at £16. The issue on 25 July consisted of items at *both* values because there were not enough of the £10 items to satisfy the issue.

Last in First Out (LIFO)

This method assumes that the stocks which were received most recently are issued first. Thus stocks remaining at the end of the period are assumed to be those which were received earliest.

The stock record card using the LIFO method would appear as follows:

Date	Receipts			Issues			Balance		
	Qty	Value each	Total value	Qty	Value each	Total value	Qty	Value each	Total value
		£	£		£	£		£	£
1 July							10	10	100
13 July	5	16	80				5	16	180
20 July				5	16				
				3	10		7	10	70
25 July				3	10		4	10	40
30 July	12	18	216				4	10	
							12	18	256

This time, the issue on 20 July consisted of items at both values; the £16 items are issued first, but as there are only 5 of them it is assumed that 3 of the £10 items are issued too.

Comparing the closing stock value with the FIFO method indicates that, in times of rising prices, the FIFO method gives a higher closing stock value than the LIFO method, and hence a lower cost of goods sold figure and a higher profit figure. For this reason, the Inland Revenue will not accept the LIFO method as a valid method, and therefore it is less popular.

Remember that these valuations are based on the *assumption* that stocks are issued in this way; they may not be in practice.

Average Cost (AVCO)

This method calculates a new 'average cost' each time a purchase is made. This average cost is then used for all issues until another purchase is made. In times of rising prices, this results in stock values which are rising but which are in between the FIFO and LIFO methods. It appears to be a sensible compromise, but it does mean that a new average needs to be calculated with each purchase.

The stock record card using the AVCO method would appear as follows:`

Date	Receipts			Issues			Balance		
	Qty	Value each	Total value	Qty	Value each	Total value	Qty	Value each	Total value
		£	£		£	£		£	£
1 July							10	10	100
13 July	5	16	80				15	12	180
20 July				8	12		7	12	84
25 July				3	12		4	12	48
30 July	12	18	216				16	16.50	264

The new average is calculated by dividing the new total value by the new quantity.

Net Realizable Value

SSAP 9 states that 'stocks should be valued at the lower of cost and net realizable value'. Net realizable value is the expected selling price less any costs of bringing the items into a saleable condition. If this is less than cost, then it should be substituted for the FIFO, LIFO or AVCO valuation in the accounts. The accounting concept involved here is that of prudence.

Accounting for wages and salaries

Calculation of gross wages

The starting point for wages calculations is to determine the *gross wages* before any *deductions*. If an employee is paid a fixed amount, then this is simply the annual salary divided by twelve months, or a fixed weekly wage. If the employee is paid a variable amount, this might depend on the hours worked or the amount of work done. Different rates of pay might be used for different levels of activity; for example, work done in addition to normal hours might be paid at a higher rate (known as *overtime rate*); there may be several different overtime rates according to the number of hours worked, time of day or day of the week.

Time-based wages

Time-based wages are calculated on the number of hours worked, with overtime for additional hours.

Example

Howard is paid £5 per hour for a basic 40-hour week, with overtime at basic rate plus 50 per cent (called 'time and a half'). During Week 8, he worked 46 hours. His gross wage would be:

40 hours at £5 per hour	£200.00
6 hours at £7.50 per hour	£ 45.00
Total gross wages	£245.00

Output-based wages

Output-based wages are based on the level of output or number of items produced, again with a higher rate for larger numbers to improve productivity. This method is sometimes called the *piece-work method*.

Example:

Shirley is paid £1 per item for up to 150 items, and £2 per item thereafter. During Week 8, she produces 200 items. Her gross wage would be:

150 items @ £1 each	£150.00
50 items @ £2 each	£100.00
Total gross wages	£245.00

There is often a minimum wage with this method, to avoid the situation where productivity is low due to no fault of the employee, for example because of machinery breakdown or the slowness of other operators on whom the employee relies.

Calculation of deduction from gross wages

Neither of the above employees will be able to take home all of their gross wages; various deductions will be made – some statutory, some voluntary – to arrive at the net wages.

Income tax

This is a statutory deduction. Most employees will have a tax-free allowance, which means that part of their gross wages will be free of tax and only the amount above that will be taxed. The calculation of tax is complex, and is not part of your studies here. The rate of income tax varies frequently, and so this book uses fictitious rates and allowances.

Suppose that Shirley (in the example above) has a tax-free allowance of £75 per week, and the remainder is taxed at 25 per cent. The tax will be 25 per cent of £170, i.e. £42.50.

This amount is deducted from Shirley's wages and is eventually paid over to the Inland Revenue; for the time being it should be recorded as a liability. The system used for deducting tax 'at source' in this way is called the *Pay As You Earn* scheme (PAYE).

Employee's National Insurance

This is also a statutory deduction with complex calculation. Suppose that Shirley pays 10 per cent National Insurance on her gross wages. She will pay 10 per cent of £245, i.e. £24.50. This too is deducted from her wages and paid over to the Inland Revenue together with the tax.

Employer's National Insurance

Employers also have to pay National Insurance to the Inland Revenue. Assuming the same rate of 10 per cent, a further £24.50 is to be paid over to the Inland Revenue. However, this is not deducted from Shirley's wages, but is an expense of the employer.

Other deductions

These are mainly voluntary and include items such as pension contributions, payments to savings schemes and sports and social club contributions. Some pension contributions reduce the amount of tax paid, but for the purpose of your studies · at this stage, assume they do not. These deductions are taken out of the employee's wages and paid over to the organization concerned, e.g the pension scheme.

Suppose that Shirley pays 6 per cent of her gross wages to the pension scheme.

This will be 6 per cent of £245, i.e. £14.70.
   Suppose that she also pays £2 a week to the social club.

Calculation of net pay

Shirley's net pay is calculated as follows:

	£	£
Gross wages		245.00
Deductions:		
Income tax	42.50	
National Insurance	24.50	
Pension scheme	14.70	
Social fund	2.00	
		83.70
Net pay		161.30

Ledger entries

The total gross wage is an expense of the organization; so is the employer's National Insurance, which is not mentioned in the calculation of Shirley's net pay. These two amounts will be debited to the wages expense account. The liabilities for tax, National Insurance, pension contributions and social fund are all credited to those accounts until paid. The net pay is either credited to an account entitled 'Wages creditor' (if not being paid at once), or to the bank if immediate payment is made. The ledger entries regarding Shirley would be as follows:

Gross wages expense

	£		£
PAYE creditor	245.00		
Employer's National Insurance	24.50		

PAYE creditor

	£		£
		Wages creditor – tax	42.50
		Wages creditor – employee's NI	24.50
		Employer's NI	24.50

Pension scheme creditor

	£		£
		Wages creditor	14.70

Social fund creditor

	£		£
		Wages creditor	2.00

Wages creditor

	£		£
		Net wages	161.30

The creditors' accounts will all be cleared when payment is made.

Summary

By the end of this chapter, you should be able to complete stock record cards using the FIFO, LIFO and AVCO methods of stock valuation, and appreciate the implications of SSAP 9 with respect to stocks valued at net realizable value. You should be able to calculate gross and net wages, and make the appropriate entries in the ledger.

Exercises

13.1 From the following details, prepare stock record cards for each of the stock valuation methods FIFO, LIFO and AVCO:

1 January	Opening stock	– 10 units at £30 each
3 January	Purchases	– 8 units at £35 each
8 January	Sales	– 6 units
15 January	Sales	– 7 units
23 January	Purchases	– 10 units at £40 each
30 January	Sales	– 12 units

13.2x Your firm has the following transactions regarding stock item LPD:

January	Opening stock	– 20 units at £20 each
	Sales	– 12 units
February	Purchases	– 15 units at £24 each
	Sales	– 10 units
March	Purchases	– 15 units at £26 each
	Sales	– 17 units
April	Sales	– 8 units
May	Purchases	– 15 units at £28 each
June	Sales	– 10 units

(a) Prepare stock record sheets using the three stock valuation methods of FIFO, LIFO and AVCO.
(b Calculate the gross profit for each method, using a selling price per unit of £40.
(c) Comment on the effect of each method on closing stock values and profits in times of rising prices

13.3 You are assistant accountant with GTZ Ltd, which is a small commercial organization. You have recently encountered several problems which have highlighted weaknesses in the accounting system. As a result, you propose to suggest some improvements in the controls exercises by the accounting staff, and to discuss these improvements with the company's auditor.

(a) For each of the following problems, suggest controls which could be introduced which would help to improve the reliability of the accounting system:
   (i) a supplier refusing to supply further goods until payment has been made for an invoice issued six months ago, of which GTZ has no record
   (ii) a debtor's ledger account being credited with a credit note which was never issued
   (iii) a cheque from a regular cash sale customer being returned by the bank and being filed in the cashier's drawer without any ledger entries being made
   (iv) a refund being given from petty cash to a customer already refunded by cheque.
(b) You are given the following details regarding stock movements during April 19x6:

1 April	100 units on hand, valued at £10 each
8 April	Stock sold for £360 with a mark-up of 50%
18 April	38 units purchased for £480 less trade discount of 5%
20 April	50 units sold
23 April	35 units sold
28 April	20 units purchased for £260

Prepare a stock record card using both the FIFO and AVCO methods, in order to determine the quantity and value of closing stock at 30 April 19x6.

(c) If the physical stock check carried out at 30 April revealed a closing stock quantity of 50 units, suggest TWO possible reasons for the discrepancy.

(CIMA, May 1996)

13.4 Four people are employed by your firm – A, B, C and D. A and B are employed on a time basis, earning £3 per hour for the first 40 hours and time-and-a-half for subsequent hours. C and D are employed on a piece-work basis, receiving £1 per unit for the first 100 units, £1.50 per unit for the next 20, and £3 per unit thereafter.

During Week 29, the work done by each employee was as follows:

A – 55 hours; B – 30 hours; C – 130 units; D – 110 units

Each employee pays income tax at 25 per cent on earnings above £65 per week. Superannuation contributions are 6 per cent of gross earnings, and National Insurance is 10 per cent each for both employee and employer. Each employee pays £1 per week in trade union subscriptions. Employees A and C each pay 5 per cent of their gross wages into a savings scheme.

Compute the net wages for each employee, and make the necessary ledger entries to record the wages calculations at the end of Week 29. (Do not record the payment of net wages or the payments made to the deductions creditors.)

14

Preparing accounts from incomplete records

Aims of the chapter

The aims of this chapter are to:

- demonstrate the calculation of figures from incomplete records
- demonstrate the method of preparation of final accounts where full double-entry ledger accounts have not been maintained
- explain the purpose and preparation of a statement of affairs.

Small organizations might find that they do not need to keep all their accounting records in double-entry form, but can manage well enough with subsidiary books and documents and a cash book with analysis columns. Because they will still want to prepare final accounts, some of the figures needed will require ledger accounts to be 'constructed' from the books, records and other information available.

Constructing ledger accounts

There is no single method or approach to preparing accounts from incomplete records, as much depends on what information is available and how it is presented. However, there are certain accounts which commonly need to be constructed, especially where only a cash book has been maintained, so that missing figures can be ascertained. The procedure is to construct the account from the data given in the question, and the figure required to balance the account will be the missing one. Some examples of accounts which might need to be constructed are as follows:

- *Sales ledger control account.* This will enable figures such as credit sales, opening or closing debtors, cash received, discounts allowed, or any of the other figures contained in the account to be ascertained.
- *Purchase ledger control account.* This will enable similar figures concerning credit purchases to be ascertained.
- *Cash book or cash and bank summary.* This will enable the balance to be ascertained, or confirmed if it is already available; alternatively, it can be used to highlight a missing figure for monies banked or withdrawn.
- *Sundry expense accounts*, as required. These will enable adjustments to be made for accruals and prepayments, or for missing figures to be ascertained.

The above examples by no means cover all possibilities. Every situation will be different, in that it will have different figures to be ascertained and different accounts will be involved.

Preparing an opening statement of affairs

Examination questions frequently omit the figure for opening capital. To calculate this, or any other missing opening figure, it is necessary to draw up an opening balance sheet. Because it is being drawn up from given data rather than ledger balances, it is called a *statement of affairs*. The layout is as for any balance sheet, except that in examination questions it is not normally necessary to break it down into the different sub-headings.

The missing figure is found by using the accounting equation:

> Assets – Liabilities = Capital

Other calculations

Other calculations which might be required include calculations of depreciation, loan interest and capital repayments, and provisions for bad debts.

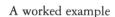

A worked example

Henry Hodgson is a mobile motor engineer who does not keep proper records. During 19x5 his bank statement provided the following figures:

	£
Receipts from customers	49,300
5-year loan from ABC Finance	10,000
Payments:	
– purchase of van	12,000
– purchase of tools	2,000
– motor expenses	1,200
– creditors for spare parts	18,400
– wages	10,800
– stationery	750
– loan repayments – capital	1,500
– interest	500

Tools at 1 January 19x5 were valued at £5,000 and at 31 December 19x5 were valued at £6,000. It is assumed that any imbalance on the bank account is cash withdrawn. This cash was used to pay wages (£4,200), cash purchases of spare parts (£2,400) and the remainder is assumed to be drawings. Credit sales for 19x5 amounted to £54,200. Depreciation on the motor van is to be 20 per cent on cost.

He also provides you with the following list of other assets and liabilities both at 1 January 19x5 and at 31 December 19x5:

	1 Jan 19x5	31 Dec 19x5
	£	£
Bank balance	4,100	1,300
Debtors	?	7,200
Stocks of spare parts	3,100	4,200
Creditors	1,800	1,600
Wages accrued	250	300
Motor expenses prepaid	120	130
Loan interest accrued	nil	180

Stage 1

Prepare bank and cash summaries for the year:

Bank summary for 19x5	£	Cash summary for 19x5		£
Opening balances	4,100	Cash withdrawn		14,950
Receipts, per list above	59,300	*less* Payments:		
	63,400	Wages	4,200	
less Payments, per list above	47,150	Spare parts	2,400	
	16,250			6,600
less Closing balance	1,300	Drawings		8,350
Cash withdrawn	14,950			

Stage 2

Construct a sales ledger control account for the year:

Sales ledger control account

	£		£
Opening debtors	?	Receipts	49,300
Sales	54,200	Closing debtors	7,200
	56,500		56,500

The opening debtors figure is that required to balance the account, i.e. £56,500 − £54,200 = £2,300.

Stage 3

Construct a purchase ledger control account for the year:

Purchase ledger control account

	£		£
Payments made	18,400	Opening creditors	1,800
Closing creditors	1,600	Purchases	?
	20,000		20,000

The purchases figure is that required to balance the account, i.e. £20,000 − £1,800 = £18,200. In addition, there are cash purchases of £2,400, making total purchases £20,600.

Stage 4

Prepare an opening statement of affairs to calculate opening capital:

Henry Hodgson – Statement of affairs at 1 January 19x5

	£	£	£
Assets – tools	5,000		
– stocks	3,100		
– debtors	2,300		
– prepayments	120		
– bank	4,100		
			14,620
less Liabilities – creditors		1,800	
– accruals		250	
			2,050
			12,570

Stage 5

Make adjustments for accruals and prepayments. You can either use ledger accounts, or make calculations as follows:

			£
Wages	Bank payments		10,800
	Cash payments		4,200
			15,000
	less Accrued at 1 Jan 19x5		250
			14,750
	add Accrued at 31 Dec 19x5		300
			15,050
Motor expenses	Bank payments		1,200
	add Prepaid at 1 Jan 19x5		120
			1,320
	less Prepaid at 31 Dec 19x5		130
			1,190
Loan interest	Bank payments		500
	add Accrued at 31 Dec 19x5		180
			680

Stage 6

Provide any other calculations as required:

Depreciation — motor van — 20% of £12,000 = £2,400

	— tools	— previous valuation	£5,000
		— additions during year	£2,000
			£7,000
		— valuation at end of year	£6,000
		— depreciation for the year	£1,000
Loan outstanding		— amount borrowed	£10,000
		— repaid during year	£ 1,500
		— closing balance	£ 8,500

The final accounts can now be prepared:

Henry Hodgson — Trading and profit and loss account for the year to 31 December 19x5

	£	£
Sales		54,200
less Cost of goods sold:		
Opening stock	3,100	
Purchases	20,600	
	23,700	
less Closing stock	4,200	
		19,500
Gross profit		34,700
less Expenses:		
Wages	15,050	
Motor expenses	1,190	
Stationery	750	
Loan interest	680	
Depreciation	3,400	
		21,070
Net profit		13,630

Henry Hodgson – Balance sheet as at 31 December 19x5

Fixed assets	Cost or valuation £	Accumulated depreciation £	Net book value £
Motor van	12,000	2,400	9,600
Tools	7,000	1,000	6,000
	19,000	3,400	15,600
Current assets			
Stocks	4,200		
Debtors	7,200		
Prepayments	130		
Bank	1,300		
		12,830	
less Current liabilities			
Creditors	1,600		
Accruals	480		
		2,080	
			10,750
			26,350
less Long-term liabilities			
Loan			8,500
			17,850
Financed by:			
Opening capital			12,570
Net profit			13,630
			26,200
less Drawings			8,350
			17,850

Summary

By the end of this chapter you should be able to calculate a variety of missing figures using other given figures. You should be able to construct a trading and profit and loss account and balance sheet from given information for an organization which has not kept full double-entry records.

Exercises

14.1 From the following information, calculate the total purchases for April:

	£
Opening creditors	14,000
Closing creditors	18,000
Payments to creditors	51,200
Cash purchases	2,500

14.2 From the following information, calculate the amount of money received from debtors during August:

	£
Opening debtors	3,800
Closing debtors	4,800
Sales, including £3,200 cash sales	62,400

14.3 Calculate the rent payable during 19x5 from the following information:

	£
Rent prepaid at 1 January 19x5	1,200
Rent paid during 19x5	16,500
Rent refunded during 19x5	800
Rent prepaid at 31 December 19x5	1,400

14.4 From the following information, calculate the amount withdrawn by the owner of a business during 19x5:

	£
Cash balance at 1 January	6,500
Receipts during the year:	
– from debtors	44,430
– from cash sales	1,000
– from loan account	10,000
Payments during the year:	
– to suppliers	32,000
– for fixed assets purchased	14,000
– for stationery	1,500
Cash balance at 31 December	12,000

14.5 Your firm owned plant costing £50,000 on 1 January 19x5, on which depreciation of £10,000 had been charged to date. During 19x5, plant costing £12,500 was purchased. At the end of the year, the plant had a net book value of £43,000. How much depreciation had been charged for the year?

14.6 D. Louther has the following assets and liabilities at 1 January 19x5:

	£
Plant at cost	30,000
Stocks of materials	14,000
Debtors	8,000
Creditors	12,500
Heat and light owing	500
Bank balance	24,000

He has the following details of receipts and payments from the bank paying-in and cheque books:

	£
Paying-in book:	
Cash sales	2,000
Cash and cheques from debtors	80,000
Cheque book:	
Suppliers of materials	40,000
Drawings	12,000
Purchase of premises	50,000
Heat and light	3,800
Insurance	1,200
General expenses	2,400

At 31 December 19x5, he owes £9,000 to suppliers of materials and £700 for

heat and light. Insurance paid during the year includes £250 for 19x6. Debtors at 31 December 19x5 amount to £13,000 and stocks of materials are £8,500. Depreciation of 10 per cent on cost is to be provided on plant, and 5 per cent on premises.

Prepare final accounts with complete supporting workings for 19x5.

14.7x K. Ingram has not kept proper records of his business transactions. His assets and liabilities at the beginning and end of 19x5 were as follows:

	£	£
Stocks of materials	5,800	4,800
Debtors	3,200	3,900
Creditors	2,900	2,400
Rent prepaid	250	150
Electricity owing	350	400
Plant at net book value	3,700	6,500

His bank account for 19x5 is summarized as follows:

	£		£
Balance at 1 January 19x5	640	Creditors	9,700
Receipts from debtors	12,250	Plant purchased	3,500
Cash sales banked	220	Motor expenses	300
Loan from relative	6,000	Office expenses	290
		Electricity	900
		Rent of premises	500
		Loan interest	300

The closing bank balance at 31 December 19x5 was £2,200. Any shortfall is assumed to be drawings. In addition, cash sales used for wages amounted to £380. The loan was held throughout the year, and bears interest at 10 per cent per annum.

Prepare final accounts.

15 Accounting for not-for-profit organizations

Aims of the chapter

The aims of this chapter are to:

- examine the special financial transactions of not-for-profit organizations
- demonstrate the calculation and recording of subscriptions and fees
- demonstrate the preparation of accounts for not-for-profit organizations.

Clubs, associations, societies and other not-for-profit organizations produce final accounts which are slightly different from those prepared by businesses. The main differences are that such organizations do not exist primarily to make profits, and do not have owners; thus they do not produce a profit and loss account, and they do not have capital in their balance sheets.

Types of transactions in non-profit-making organizations

The types of income and expenditure vary according to the needs of the organization. Typical transactions include the following:

- *Income* — subscriptions, entrance fees and joining fees to members
  - hire of equipment
  - fund-raising events, such as sales, raffles, competitions, dances
  - profit from running a bar, café or shop
  - grants and donations
- *Expenditure* — premises upkeep, insurance, repairs
  - wages to caretakers, cleaners and grounds staff
  - raffle prizes
  - refreshments and bar stocks

In addition, the organization might buy fixed assets, on which depreciation must be charged.

Surpluses and deficits and the income and expenditure account

Because they do not exist primarily to make profits, but rather to provide facilities and services to their members or clients, these organizations do not calculate a 'profit' or 'loss'. Instead, they produce an *income and expenditure account* for the period, which results in the calculation of a *surplus* or a *deficit*. The principles for the preparation of this account are identical to those used in a profit and loss account – i.e. adjustments must be made for accruals and prepayments, provisions must be made against assets, and the account must not contain capital items.

The accumulated fund

Because a club or society does not have owners, then it does not have owner's capital or drawings. Instead, it has an *accumulated fund* to which surpluses are added and deficits deducted.

Trading activities

Although profit-making is not the prime objective, some organizations do trade in a similar way to a business, by buying and selling items for a profit. Examples include running a bar, a café, or a shop selling new and second-hand equipment. If this is the case, then a trading account is prepared in exactly the same way as for a business, for that trading activity, and its profit is taken to the income and expenditure account.

Records maintained by not-for-profit organizations

Many of these organizations maintain incomplete records, and so the figures required to prepare the final accounts may need to be ascertained in the same way as those for businesses who maintain incomplete records. This subject was covered in the previous chapter.

Special transactions in not-for-profit organizations

Subscriptions received

The income and expenditure account must show the income earned during the period. Under the accruals concept this means that the subscription income must be that to which the organization was entitled during the period, irrespective of whether the subscriptions were received in that period or not. Adjustment must therefore be made to the subscriptions received figure to allow for the following:

- Subscriptions received in earlier periods, but in respect of the current period
- Subscriptions received in later periods, but in respect of the current period
- Subscriptions received in the current period, but in respect of an earlier period
- Subscriptions received in the current period, but in respect of a later period.

The simplest method of making these adjustments is to draw up a *subscriptions received ledger account*.

Example

Subscriptions received by a club during 19x6 amounted to £8,450. £100 of this was in respect of 19x5 and £180 in respect of 19x7. At the end of 19x5, £350 had already been received in respect of 19x6, and at the end of 19x6, subscriptions of £400 were still owing.

The subscriptions received ledger account would appear as follows:

Subscriptions received

19x6	£	19x6	£
1 Jan Arrears b/fwd	100	1 Jan In advance b/fwd	350
31 Dec In advance c/d	180	1 Jan–31 Dec Received	8,450
Income & expenditure a/c	8,920	31 Dec Arrears c/d	400
	9,200		9,200
19x7		19x7	
1 Jan Arrears b/d	400	1 Jan In advance b/d	180

The arrears are shown on the balance sheet as current assets; the receipts in advance are shown as current liabilities.

Under the prudence concept, we should not adjust for subscriptions in arrears at the end of the period, as in many clubs and societies members leave without notice and no attempt is made to chase up their outstanding subscriptions. However, if you are given figures for subscriptions in arrears in an examination, include them in your calculations unless the question is asking for you to adopt the prudence concept.

If adjustment has been made for subscriptions in arrears, and it is later discovered that those subscriptions were never received, then the opening debit balance must be reduced by crediting the subscriptions received account and debiting a subscriptions written off account, which is later debited to the income and expenditure account. Alternatively, the unpaid subscriptions can be ignored and adjusted when the arrears to be carried forward at the end of the year are calculated.

Gifts, donations and legacies received

These are often received from members who have enjoyed the facilities of the organization, or non-members who have admired the work of the organization over some time. They increase the accumulated fund.

Joining fees and life membership

These represent a charge for the use of the organization's facilities over several accounting periods. They should not therefore be taken to the income and expenditure account in full in the period in which they are received. Instead, they are credited to a separate *joining fees or life memberships account*, and a proportion transferred to the income and expenditure account each year.

The proportion to be transferred depends on the type of organization and its members. A religious organization whose members join when young might spread this income over twenty years; an over-70s' club might prefer five or ten years.

Example

A sports club charges a joining fee during 19x5 of £2,000. The average time which a member remains with the club is five years. The fee is credited to a joining fees account, and a fifth transferred out to the income and expenditure account each year. The joining fees account would be as follows:

		Joining fees		
19x5	£		*19x5*	£
31 Dec Income &				
expenditure a/c	400		1 Jan–31 Dec	
Balance c/d	1,600		Bank	2,000
	2,000			2,000
19x6			*19x6*	
31 Dec Income &				
expenditure a/c	400		1 Jan Balance b/d	1,600
Balance c/d	1,200			
	1,600			1,600
19x7			*19x7*	
			Balance b/d	1,200

The balance at the end of each year will be shown on the balance sheet as a long-term liability.

Receipts and payments accounts

Some organizations produce a summary of monies received and paid out during the period. This is sometimes a useful additional statement, but it should not be produced on its own unless the organization has few or no assets and liabilities. It is really only a summary of cash and bank transactions, and it makes no adjustments for accruals and prepayments, it does not account for depreciation or other provisions, and it includes capital expenditure. It does not show previously acquired fixed assets; nor does it show stocks, debtors or liabilities. The account is really only suitable for small fund-raising groups such as parent–teacher associations, whose only assets are bank and cash balances.

However, examination questions often commence with a *Receipts and payments account*, or ask candidates to prepare one. Even if one is not requested, it is often useful to prepare one as part of your workings.

A worked example

The Whaley Widows' Tennis Club has the following receipts and payments account for the year ended 31 May 19x5:

Whaley Widows' Tennis Club
Receipts and payments account, year ended 31 May 19x5

	£		£
Bank balance 1 June 19x4	300	*Payments*	
Receipts		Equipment	2,000
Subscriptions	900	Bar staff wages	1,200
Bank interest received	200	Repairs to equipment	800
Sale of dance tickets	1,200	Dance expenses	400
Jumble sale takings	170	Post and stationery	810
Hire of courts to school	700	Bar suppliers	1,400
Bar sales	6,800	Bank balance 31 May 19x5	3,660
	10,270		10,270

Its balance sheet at 31 May 19x4 is as follows:

	£	£	£
Fixed assets at valuation			
Land and Buildings		20,000	
Equipment		1,100	
			21,100
Current assets			
Bar stocks	650		
Stock of stamps and stationery	140		
Subscriptions in arrears	100		
Bank balance	300		
		1,190	
less Current liabilities			
Creditors – bar supplies	400		
Subscriptions in advance	200		
Owing for equipment repairs	250		
		850	
			340
			21,440
less Long-term liabilities			
Loan from A. Member (interest-free)			1,000
Accumulated fund			20,440

At 31 May 19x5 bar stocks were £570; creditors for bar supplies were £190; £450 was owing for equipment repairs; £50 was owing for dance expenses; and there was a stock of stationery of £160. Subscriptions in advance were £140 and subscriptions in arrears were £150.

You are also told that bar purchases during the year were £1,190, and that depreciation is to be charged at 5 per cent per annum on the value of land and buildings, and at 10 per cent per annum on equipment, with a full year's depreciation in the year of purchase.

Workings:

(a) The subscriptions received account needs to be compiled as follows:

Subscriptions received

19x4	£	19x4	£
1 June In arrears b/d	100	1 June In advance b/d	200
19x5		1 June–31 May	
31 May Income &		Received	900
expenditure a/c	1,010	19x5	
In advance c/d	140	31 May In arrears c/d	150
	1,250		1,250

(b) Dance expenses
	– paid	£400
	– *add* Accrued 31 May 19x5	£ 50
		£450

(c) Equipment repairs
	– paid	£800
	– *less* Accrued 1 June 19x4	£250
		£550
	– *add* Accrued 31 May 19x5	£450
		£1,000

(d) Post and stationery
	– paid	810
	– *add* Stock 1 June 19x4	140
		950
	– *less* Stock 31 May 19x5	160
		790

The final accounts will appear as follows:

Whaley Widows' Tennis Club
Bar trading and profit and loss account for the year ending 31 May 19x5

	£	£
Bar sales		6,800
less Cost of goods sold:		
Opening stocks	650	
Purchases	1,190	
	1,840	
less Closing stocks	570	
		1,270
Gross profit		5,530
less Bar expenses:		
Bar staff wages		1,200
Net profit		4,330

Whaley Widows' Tennis Club
Income and expenditure account for the year ending 31 May 19x5

Income	£	£	£
Subscriptions		1,010	
Bank interest received		200	
Net profit from bar		4,330	
Profit on dance:			
Sale of tickets	1,200		
Expenses	450		
		750	
Jumble sale takings		170	
Hire of courts to school		700	
			7,160
Expenditure			
Equipment repairs		1,000	
Post and stationery		790	
Depreciation of land and buildings		1,000	
Depreciation of equipment		310	
			3,100
Surplus for the year			4,060

Whaley Widows' Tennis Club balance sheet as at 31 May 19x5

Fixed assets	Valuation	Depreciation	Net book value	
	£	£	£	£
Land and Buildings	20,000	1,000	19,000	
Equipment	3,100	310	2,790	
	23,100	1,310		21,790
Current assets				
Stocks – bar		570		
– stationery		160		
Subscriptions in arrears		150		
Bank		3,660		
			4,540	
less Current liabilities				
Creditors – bar		190		
– equipment repairs		450		
– dance expenses		50		
Subscriptions in advance		140		
			830	
				3,710
				25,500
less Long-term liabilities				
Loan from A. Member				1,000
				24,500
Financed by:				
Accumulated fund at 1 June 19x4				20,440
Surplus for the year to 31 May 19x5				4,060
				24,500

Summary

By the end of this chapter you should be able to understand the special transactions of not-for-profit organizations and how to record them in the ledger. You

should be able to prepare income and expenditure accounts and balance sheets for such organizations.

15.1 From the following information, prepare a subscriptions received account for 19x5:

At 1 January 19x5	– subscriptions re 19x5 received in 19x4	£120
During 19x5	– subscriptions received re 19x4	£140
	– subscriptions received re 19x5	£975
	– subscriptions received re 19x6	£135
At 31 December 19x5	– subscriptions due, paid in 19x6	£ 40

15.2 The treasurer of the Lower Parkstone Cricket Club has prepared a receipts and payments account for the members for the past eight years, but members have been complaining that the information which it contains is inadequate. The account for 19x5 is as follows:

Lower Parkstone Cricket Club
Receipts and payments account for the year ended 31 December 19x5

Receipts	£	Payments	£
Opening balance	524	Bar supplies	3,962
Subscriptions	1,331	Groundsman's wages	939
Donations	120	Bar staff wages	624
Raffle tickets sold	100	Bar expenses	234
Bar sales	5,628	Pavilion repairs	348
		Purchase of equipment	500
		Raffle prizes	60
		Closing balance	1,036
	7,703		7,703

In addition, there were the following assets and liabilities at the start and end of the year:

	at 1 January 19x5	at 31 December 19x5
	£	£
Bar stocks	496	558
Bar expenses owing	100	200
Fixed assets – pavilion	6,000	
– equipment	1,200	
Creditors for bar supplies	420	380
Subscriptions in advance	100	110
Subscriptions in arrears	80	25
Raffle prizes purchased in advance	10	–

The pavilion is to be depreciated at 10 per cent per annum on the reducing balance basis. It cost £10,000 when new. The equipment is to be depreciated at 20 per cent per annum straight-line on cost. The equipment at 1 January 19x5 cost £2,000 when new.

Prepare an income and expenditure account for 19x5 and a balance sheet at 31 December 19x5.

15.3x The Midtown Mother-and-Toddler Club has the following receipts and payments account for the year ending 31 March 19x6:

Receipts	£	*Payments*	£
Balance b/fwd	450	Room rental	520
Entrance fees	560	Entertainers' expenses	100
Commission from book sale	600	New toys	1,060
Grant from local council	750	Refreshments	340
Sale of clothes	1,350	Clothing suppliers	1,120
Tickets for zoo trip	220	Christmas party costs	260
		Zoo entrance fees	120
		Balance c/fwd	410
	3,930		3,930

The following information is also available:

	1 April 19x5 £	*31 March 19x6* £
Room rental in advance	40	45
Book commission owing	50	80
Stock of clothes for sale	275	175
Owing to clothing suppliers	340	420
Owing for coach to zoo	nil	80
Toys at valuation	120	

Toys are to be depreciated at 25 per cent per annum on the reducing balance basis. The toys at 1 April 19x5 cost £750 when new.

Prepare an income and expenditure account for the year ending 31 March 19x6, and a balance sheet as at that date.

15.4 The Marcham Badminton Club was established in 1985. At a meeting held on 31 December 1990, the following details were presented to the members by the treasurer as she made her financial report.

Marcham Badminton Club
Review of the 1990 season (1 January–31 December 1990)
Financial position at 31 December 1989

	£
Cost of equipment	4,000
Depreciation of equipment	800
Subscriptions owing	800
Subscriptions in advance	600
Life membership fund	4,500
Accumulated fund	1,070
Bank	2,170

Membership
The rate for ordinary subscriptions had been set by the committee at £40 per season for the 1989 and 1990 season and at £50 per person for the 1991 season. Alternatively, members can take out life membership by making a single payment of £500. The club then makes transfers from this sum into the Income and Expenditure account over a 10-year period, starting in the year when the money is received. Up until 31 December 1989, 10 members had paid a life membership fee, all of those members having joined during the 1989 season.

The 1990 season
During 1990, £2,340 was received in ordinary subscriptions. This sum included 10 members' payments for the 1991 season. 8 members have still not paid for the 1990 season, but they have promised their cheques within the next few days. In addition to the money received from ordinary subscriptions, 4 new members have paid the life membership fee. £250 of new equipment was purchased during the year and £473 was paid out as miscellaneous expenses. A surplus of income over expenditure of £1,762 has been made.

Depreciation policy
Equipment is depreciated at 10% per annum on cost, with a full year's depreciation charged in the year of purchase and no depreciation in the year of disposal.

Prepare the following:

(a) The club's Receipts and Payments Account for the year ended 31 December 1990
(b) The club's Subscriptions Account (ordinary subscriptions only) for the year ended 31 December 1990
(c) The club's Balance Sheet as at 31 December 1990.

(AAT, June 1991)

Aims of the chapter

The aims of this chapter are to:

- explain the purpose of manufacturing accounts
- explain the nature of costs and cost classification
- explain the treatment of work-in-progress
- explain the component parts of 'prime cost'
- demonstrate the preparation of a manufacturing account.

Organizations which make their own goods to sell incur different kinds of expenses to those which buy in goods ready-made to sell. Manufacturers need to prepare a *manufacturing account* to bring together all the costs of making goods, which must be differentiated from the costs of selling and delivering goods and providing administrative support.

The manufacturing account collects together the factory or production expenses, in order to arrive at the factory cost of goods completed during the period. This figure is then passed to the trading account to form part of the calculation of gross profit.

Classification of costs

There are many different ways of classifying costs.

Direct and indirect costs

A *direct cost* is one which can be identified with an individual unit of production. A unit of production might be a single product, but could also be a batch of similar products manufactured together.

An *indirect cost* is one which cannot be identified with an individual unit of production, but is incurred on behalf of a number of dissimilar units together.

Materials, labour and overheads

These are known as the *elements* of cost.

Materials costs are those incurred in buying raw materials and component parts, including the costs of delivery. They are often direct costs, as they are measurable and traceable to units of production. Packing and cleaning materials and stationery are more likely to be classed as indirect costs.

Labour costs are the gross wages and salaries paid, plus employer's National Insurance contributions. Direct labour is the labour cost of machine operators, craftworkers or labourers who work on manufacturing the units. Indirect labour would include the costs of factory supervisors, who oversee the production of different units, engineers and administrative staff.

Overheads are those costs which cannot be classed as materials or labour. Some organizations put all indirect costs into this category, including indirect materials and labour. Some organizations also consider that all overheads are indirect (sometimes called *indirect expenses*), but there are a few examples of direct overheads, such as the hire of equipment, power costs, insurance, special security precautions or royalties paid on production, where the unit of production affected can be identified.

The total of direct materials, labour and overheads is known as *prime cost*.

Manufacturing, trading and administrative costs

Manufacturing costs are those incurred in production, whether direct or indirect. They are sometimes referred to as *factory costs* and *production costs*. As well as the items mentioned above, factory indirect costs include expenses such as factory rent and rates, depreciation of factory machinery, and factory insurance. These expenses are often debited in total to the ledger accounts when they are incurred, and a proportion is taken to be a factory cost, with the remainder taken to be an administrative cost.

Manufacturing costs are brought together in the Manufacturing Account.

Work-in-progress (WIP)

Many manufacturers start and end the period with stocks of goods which are only partly completed. These are known as *work-in-progress* or *semi-finished goods*. During the period, part of the production costs will be incurred in the completion of the opening WIP and part will be incurred in producing closing WIP. The production cost incurred during the period will need to be adjusted by adding in the opening WIP and deducting the closing WIP.

Trading costs are those incurred in bringing the goods which are sold to a saleable condition. In a manufacturing organization, most of these costs are taken to the manufacturing account and the cost of completed or 'finished' goods is taken to the trading account. Of course, not all finished goods are sold, so there will be opening and closing stocks to be added and deducted from the factory cost of goods completed.

There are very few occasions when any other costs would be included in the trading account. Remember that gross profit is the difference between the revenue from sales and the cost of making those goods saleable. It does not include the cost of selling or delivering goods to the customer.

Sometimes organizations buy in ready-made goods as well as making their own. These appear in the trading account in the usual way.

Administrative costs are all other costs incurred by the organization, which are brought together in the profit and loss account to calculate net profit. Larger organizations sometimes group them together as follows:

- selling and distribution costs
- administrative costs
- research and development costs
- financing costs.

There is no need to adhere to these groupings at this stage in your studies. A straightforward list of administrative costs is acceptable in examinations.

A worked example

Patricia gives you the following extract of balances from her ledgers at 30 June 19x5:

	DR £000	CR £000
Sales		288
Returns inwards	8	
Purchases of raw materials	111	
Opening stock – raw materials	50	
– WIP	39	
– finished goods	45	
Carriage inwards	2	
Returns outwards		5
Labour costs – direct	12	
– factory supervisors	6	
– administrators	4	
Heat and light	10	
Rates	5	
Insurance – buildings	6	
– delivery vans	1	
Buildings at cost	400	
Factory plant and machinery at cost	60	
Delivery vans at cost	20	

She gives you the following additional information at 30 June 19x5

(i)   Closing stocks were:

Raw materials	£40,000
Work-in-progress	£26,000
Finished goods	£53,000

(ii)   Heat and light accrued was £2,000. Heat and light is to be apportioned ⅔ to the factory and ⅓ to the offices

(iii)   Rates prepaid amounted to £1,000

(iv)   Buildings are to be depreciated at 2½ per cent per annum on cost

(v)   Delivery vans are to be depreciated at 25 per cent per annum on cost

(vi)   Plant and machinery is to be depreciated at 10 per cent per annum on cost

(vii) Rates, buildings insurance and buildings depreciation are to be apportioned 50 per cent each to the factory and offices.

She asks you to produce a manufacturing account and a trading and profit and loss account for the year ending 30 June 19x5.

Workings:

(a) *Heat and light*		(b) *Rates*	
Per ledger accounts	£10,000	Per ledger accounts	£5,000
Accrued	£ 2,000	Prepaid	£1,000
Total	£12,000	Total	£4,000

Apportioned:		*Apportioned:*	
Manufacturing a/c 2/3	£8,000	Manufacturing a/c 50%	£2,000
Profit and loss a/c 1/3	£4,000	Profit and loss a/c 50%	£2,000

(c) *Buildings insurance*		(d) *Depreciation on buildings*	
Total	£6,000	Total 2½% of £400,000	£10,000

Apportioned:		*Apportioned:*	
Manufacturing a/c 50%	£3,000	Manufacturing a/c 50%	£5,000
Profit and loss a/c 50%	£3,000	Profit and loss a/c 50%	£5,000

(e) *Depreciation on delivery vans*		(f) *Depreciation on plant and machinery*	
25% of £20,000	£5,000	10% of £60,000	£6,000

The accounts can now be prepared as follows:

Patricia – Manufacturing account for the year ending 30 June 19x5

	£000	£000
Raw materials:		
Opening stocks		50
Purchases	111	
Carriage inwards	2	
	113	
less Returns outwards	5	
		108
		158
less Closing stocks		40
Direct materials consumed		118
Direct labour		12
Prime cost		130
Indirect factory expenses:		
Factory supervisors	6	
Heat and light	8	
Rates	2	
Buildings insurance	3	
Buildings depreciation	5	
Plant depreciation	6	
		30
Total factory cost of production		160
add Opening work in progress	39	
less Closing work in progress	26	
		13
Factory cost of goods completed		173

Patricia – Trading and profit and loss account for the year ending 30 June 19x5

	£000	£000
Sales		288
less Returns inwards		8
Net sales		280
less Cost of goods sold:		
Opening stocks of finished goods	45	
Factory cost of goods completed	173	
	218	
less Closing stocks of finished goods	53	
		165
Gross profit		115
Less Expenses:		
Administrators' salaries	4	
Heat and light	4	
Rates	2	
Buildings insurance	3	
Buildings depreciation	5	
Delivery vans depreciation	5	
		23
Net profit for the year		92

The balance sheet at 30 June 19x5 will contain three categories of stocks which should be shown as follows:

	£000	£000
Current assets		
Stocks – raw materials	40	
– work in progress	26	
– finished goods	53	
		119

Manufacturing accounts are usually regarded as 'internal' accounts which are not passed to users outside the organization.

Summary

By the end of this chapter you should understand the purpose of manufacturing accounts, and the different types of costs contained within them. You should be able to distinguish between costs which are connected with manufacturing, as opposed to those connected with trading or administration. You should be able to prepare a manufacturing account with appropriate sub-headings and adjustment for work-in-progress.

Exercises

16.1 From the following information regarding the year to 30 June 19x6, prepare a manufacturing account and a trading and profit and loss account:

	£000
Sales	15,700
Opening stocks – raw materials	6,700
– work-in-progress	3,600
– finished goods	7,100
Purchases – raw materials	8,000
Closing stocks – raw materials	4,600
– work-in-progress	4,800
– finished goods	11,600
Office salaries	100
Direct production wages	1,600
Factory supervisors' wages	5,200
Rent of factory	400
Rent of offices	150
Depreciation of production machinery	300
Production power costs	1,300
Heating and lighting costs (40% factory)	250
Depreciation of office machinery	200
Rates (80% factory)	1,000
Delivery costs on sales	120
Delivery costs on purchases	150
General office expenses	180

16.2x From the following information, prepare a manufacturing account and a trading and profit and loss account:

	£
Opening stocks – raw materials	25,000
– work-in-progress	17,000
– finished goods	10,000
Closing stocks – raw materials	65,000
– work-in-progress	33,000
– finished goods	13,000
Sales	110,000
Purchases – raw materials	125,000
Factory wages – production workers	18,000
– supervisors	1,500
Office salaries	3,500
Depreciation – factory machinery	1,000
Depreciation – motor vehicles (10% factory)	1,700
Rates (40% factory)	2,000
Insurance (factory)	800
Light and heat (⅓ factory)	1,500
Carriage inwards	1,900
Printing and stationery	700
Sundry factory expenses	300
Bank interest payable	200

17 Partnership accounts

Aims of the chapter

The aims of this chapter are to:

- explain the nature and legal implications of a partnership
- explain the financial implications of a partnership, including the appropriation of profits
- describe the special ledger accounts required by partnerships
- demonstrate the calculation of interest on partners' drawings
- demonstrate the preparation of a partnership appropriation account, partners' current accounts and the capital section of the balance sheet
- explain the various changes in partnerships which can occur
- explain and demonstrate the effects on partners of revalued assets and their treatment in the accounts
- explain the nature of goodwill
- explain and demonstrate the effects on partners of goodwill and its treatment in the accounts.

A *partnership* exists where two or more people join together to form a business. They need not be 'equal' partners – they can each contribute different amounts of capital, perform different amounts of work, be allocated different amounts of profit and so on. These points should be agreed at the beginning of the partnership to avoid arguments later on, although there is no legal requirement that this should be done.

Most partnerships are restricted to a maximum of twenty partners. The advantage of a partnership over a sole trader is that more people are available to provide capital for the business; in addition, banks and other lenders are more willing to lend where there are more owners to call upon if the debt is not repaid by the business.

The partnership agreement

The agreement should consider the following for each partner:

- How much capital is to be provided
- How much work is to be done
- How profits (and losses) are to be divided (appropriated)
- Whether partners are to be allowed to withdraw profits, when, and how much is to be withdrawn
- Whether partners are to be allocated interest on their capitals, or charged interest on their drawings, and if so, how much
- Whether partners can lend money to the business, and whether this is to be regarded as additional capital or as a straightforward loan
- What is to happen to the partnership if a partner dies or retires or a new partner is admitted.

The Partnership Act 1890	This states that if there is no partnership agreement, and the partners cannot agree, then all profits and losses since the beginning of the partnership are to be shared equally between the partners, no interest is to be given on capitals or charged on drawings, no partner is to receive a salary or other kind of appropriation, and loans from partners are to receive interest at 5 per cent per annum.

You can see that if one partner has provided most of the capital and performed most of the work, this could produce a very inequitable result.

Liability of partners	Each partner is liable for the debts of the partnership in full. If the partnership itself has debts which it cannot pay, then any or all of the partners can be called upon to pay the debts from their own private funds. This is known as *unlimited liability*. The exception to this is if a partner is a *limited* or *sleeping* partner. Under the Limited Partnership Act of 1907 a limited partner is only liable for the amount of capital which he has contributed or earned. However, a limited partner cannot take part in the management of the business, and at least one partner must have unlimited liability.

Appropriating the profits (or losses)	'Appropriating' means dividing the profits between the partners. It is important to realize that this appropriation does not mean that partners will, or can, withdraw their shares from the business. It is simply a way of dividing up the net profit which, in a sole trader's business, goes in its entirety into his single capital account; in a partnership the net profit goes into several partners' capital accounts. The capitals are then reduced by drawings if there are any.

The appropriation might be a simple split of net profit between the partners, or it might include some or all of the following:

- *Salaries* – useful where partners do differing amounts of work
- *Commissions* – useful where a partner obtains new business
- *Interest on capital* – useful where partners contribute different amounts.

These amounts are all taken out of net profit and increase partners' capitals.

If partners are charged interest on their drawings, this is added back to net profit and decreases partners' capitals.

Any remaining balance of profit (or loss) is then shared out in an agreed *profit-sharing ratio*, which need not be equal. The ratio might be expressed as a percentage, e.g. four partners might each receive 25 per cent; or it might be expressed as a straight ratio, e.g. three partners might share profits in the ratio 3:2:1, which means that the first partner receives 3/6 of the profits, the second partner receives 2/6 and the third partner 1/6.

It is important to realize that the appropriation of profits is *not* a business expense, and none of the above appropriations, whatever their title, should appear as expenses in the profit and loss account.

The appropriation is shown in an *appropriation account*, which follows the profit and loss account.

Drawings	*Drawings* are withdrawals of capital. They are not business expenses, so do not appear in the profit and loss account. Nor are they appropriations of profit, so do not appear in the appropriation account either. Each partner will have a drawings account in the ledger, to which his drawings will be debited. At the end of the period, the balance will be transferred to his capital account, to reduce his investment in the business.

Capital and current accounts

In a sole trader's business, a single account is all that is necessary to record his transactions with the business – the *capital account*. In a partnership, each partner will have a capital account in which introductions of capital, appropriations of profit and drawings are recorded. This is known as a *fluctuating capital account*. It might be preferable to keep the capital account for major introductions and withdrawals of capital only, and to keep a separate current account for each partner, to which the profit shares are appropriated each year and from which drawings are deducted. If this is the case, the capital account is known as a *fixed capital account*.

The total investment by each partner will be found by adding together the capital and current account balances, which should normally be credit balances. If, however, a partner has withdrawn more than the balance on his capital and/or current account, then it will show a debit balance and will be classed as 'overdrawn'. Some partnerships allow this, some do not and may charge interest on the overdrawn balance if it is not repaid.

Loan accounts

Any partner who lends money to the business will have a separate *loan account*. The interest on partners' loans is treated as a normal business expense and will therefore appear in the profit and loss account rather than the appropriation account. In theory, it should be credited to the partner's loan account and added to the loan, but in most cases it is credited to the partner's current (or fluctuating capital) account.

Ledger accounts for partners

Where there are only a few partners, the capital, current and drawings accounts can be maintained in columnar format, rather like a cash book, with a column on each side for each partner. If there are several partners, then separate accounts are probably more convenient.

Calculation of interest on drawings

Ideally, partners should wait until the profit share is calculated at the end of the year before withdrawing amounts for themselves. They should also withdraw the same amount as each other in order to maintain equity between the partners. In practice, this rarely happens, so some partnerships charge *interest* on drawings. In examination questions you might be given this figure, but sometimes you are asked to calculate it for yourself.

The interest is charged on each withdrawal from the date of withdrawal until the end of the accounting year, probably on a monthly basis.

Example

Cathy and Vicki are in partnership and have agreed to charge interest on drawings of 5 per cent per annum. Their year end is 31 December. During 19x5 the following drawings and calculations of interest took place:

	Amount	Date	Interest calculation	
Cathy	£720	31 January	£720 x 5% × 11 months	£33
	£400	31 March	£400 x 5% × 9 months	£15
	£240	30 June	£240 x 5% × 6 months	£6
	£480	31 October	£480 x 5% × 2 months	£4
	£1,840			£58
Vicki	£1,200	30 September	£1,200 x 5% × 3 months	£15
	£2,400	30 November	£2,400 x 5% × 1 month	£10
	£3,600			£25

Note that although Vicki's drawings are much greater than Cathy's, they were made later in the year and hence she was using the business profits for a shorter period, thereby incurring less interest.

A worked example

Cathy and Vicki have been in partnership for many years. Their capital and current account balances at 1 January 19x5 are:

	Cathy	Vicki
Capital accounts	£40,000	£60,000
Current accounts	£15,000	£ 5,000

Their net profit for the year to 31 December 19x5 was £20,917, before charging interest on partners' loans.

The partnership agreement stated that:

1 Salaries were to be allocated of £7,000 to Cathy and £3,000 to Vicki.
2 Interest on capital at the start of the year is to be allocated, at 7 per cent per annum.
3 Cathy has loaned the business £10,000, on which interest at 10 per cent per annum is to be given.
4 Remaining profits and losses are to be shared in the proportion of Cathy ⅓ and Vicki ⅔.

The appropriation account would appear as follows:

	£	£	£
Net profit per the profit and loss account			20,917
Interest on partner's loan			1,000
Adjusted net profit			19,917
add Interest on drawings – Cathy		58	
– Vicki		25	
			83
			20,000
Less:			
Salaries – Cathy	7,000		
– Vicki	3,000		
		10,000	
Interest on capital – Cathy	2,800		
– Vicki	4,200		
		7,000	
			17,000
			3,000
Balance of profits – Cathy ⅓		1,000	
– Vicki ⅔		2,000	
			3,000

Their capital and current accounts would appear as follows:

Capital accounts

Date	Details	Cathy	Vicki	Date	Details	Cathy	Vicki
				19x5		£	£
				Jan 1	Balances	40,000	60,000

Current accounts

Date	Details	Cathy £	Vicki £	Date	Details	Cathy £	Vicki £
19x5				*19x5*			
31 Dec	Drawings	1,840	3,600	1 Jan	Balances b/d	15,000	5,000
	Interest on drawings	58	25	31 Dec	Salaries	7,000	3,000
					Interest on capital	2,800	4,200
					Interest on loan	1,000	
	Balances c/d	24,902	11,575		Profit share	1,000	2,000
		26,800	14,200			26,800	14,200

The balance sheet of Cathy and Vicki will show the balances of their capital and current accounts as follows:

	£	£
Capital accounts – Cathy	40,000	
– Vicki	60,000	
		100,000
Current accounts – Cathy	24,902	
– Vicki	10,575	
		35,477
		135,477

If any partner's current account shows a debit balance, this is deducted from the other's credit balances on the balance sheet.

The loan account will be shown as a long-term liability, unless it is repayable in the next twelve months.

Changes in the profit-sharing ratios of partners

Any change in a partnership requires the value of each partner's share before and after the change to be calculated. Changes include retirement of a partner, admission of a new partner, and changes in the profit-sharing ratios of existing partners.

Revaluation of assets

If the balance sheet accurately reflects the true value of the assets, then the partners' capital and current accounts will also reflect the value of their shares in the business. However, it is unlikely that this is the case, and the assets will probably need to be revalued.

These new values must be substituted for the present values, and a new balance for each partner calculated. This is done by debiting or crediting the appropriate asset account with the opposite entry to a *revaluation account*. When all assets have been revalued, the resulting balance on the revaluation account is distributed to the partners' capital accounts in their old profit-sharing ratio.

Suppose that A, B and C are in partnership, sharing profits in the ratio of 3:2:1. Their balance sheet at 31 December 19x5 shows the following figures:

	£
Land and buildings	60,000
Plant and machinery	20,000
Stocks	10,000
Debtors	15,000
Bank	5,000
	110,000
less Creditors and loans	10,000
Net assets	100,000

Capital and current accounts:	
A	45,000
B	25,000
C	30,000
	100,000

They decide to share profits equally from 1 January 19x6. An examination of asset values at that date reveals that land and buildings are worth £92,000, plant and machinery is worth £15,000, stocks to be written off amount to £2,000, and bad debts of £1,000 are discovered.

Journal entries to record the revaluations and resulting adjustment to partners' capital accounts are as follows:

	DR £	CR £
Land and buildings	32,000	
Plant and machinery		5,000
Stocks		2,000
Debtors		1,000
Revaluation account		24,000

being adjustment to balances following revaluation.

Revaluation account	24,000	
Partners' capital accounts:		
A – ³⁄₆		12,000
B – ²⁄₆		8,000
C – ¹⁄₆		4,000

being net profit on revaluation of assets divided between partners in their agreed profit-sharing ratios prior to amendment.

The partnership would then commence the next period with the new capital account and asset account balances.

Goodwill on revaluation

If the business has generated goodwill in the past, then it is only fair that the partners are given credit for that goodwill in their old profit-sharing ratios. Suppose that, in the example above, goodwill was valued at £12,000. The journal entries would be as follows:

	DR £	CR £
Goodwill	12,000	
Partners' capital accounts:		
A – ⅗		6,000
B – ⅖		4,000
C – ⅙		2,000

being introduction of goodwill into the partnership.

<table>
<tr><td>Eliminating goodwill
from the books</td><td>Once goodwill has been introduced, a decision needs to be made as to whether to retain it in the books of the partnership. As discussed in Chapter 5, it is modern practice not to retain goodwill in the books, but to write it off as soon as possible. This is done by debiting the partners in their new profit-sharing ratio, with the amount written off. The journal entries would be as follows:</td></tr>
</table>

	DR £	CR £
Partners' capital accounts:		
A – ⅓	4,000	
B – ⅓	4,000	
C – ⅓	4,000	
Goodwill account		12,000

being the elimination of goodwill from the accounts.

A partnership might decide to eliminate the revaluation reserve in the same way.

Restatement of partners' capital accounts

The partners' capital accounts will now appear as follows, after the above revaluations:

Capital accounts

	A £	B £	C £		A £	B £	C £
				Balance b/d	45,000	25,000	30,000
Write-off of goodwill	4,000	4,000	4,000	Revaluation of assets	12,000	8,000	4,000
Balances c/d	59,000	33,000	32,000	Valuation of goodwill	6,000	4,000	2,000
	63,000	37,000	36,000		63,000	37,000	36,000

Note that the new balances on the partners' capital accounts equal the revised net asset values, *without* the value of goodwill, i.e. original net asset value of £100,000, plus revaluation of assets of £24,000.

Retirement or death of a partner

The retirement or death of a partner will also mean a change in the profit-sharing ratios. When a partner leaves, his share of the partnership assets must be calculated and he, or his estate, will receive that value from the partnership. The procedure is very similar to that when there is a change in the profit-sharing ratios. The stages are as follows:

- Revalue the assets
- Introduce goodwill
- Recalculate the capital account balances
- Eliminate goodwill.

Example

P, Q and R are in partnership, sharing profits in the ratio of 40 per cent, 40 per cent and 20 per cent. Their capital account balances at 31 December 19x5 were as follows:

	£
P	45,000
Q	25,000
R	20,000
	90,000

P decided to retire at 31 December 19x5. The net assets at that date are revalued at £120,000, and goodwill of £20,000 is created. Q and R agree to share profits equally thereafter, and not to retain either goodwill or the revaluation of assets in the books.

The journal entries to record this are as follows:

	Dr £	Cr £
Net assets	30,000	
Goodwill	20,000	
Partners' capital accounts:		
P – 40%		20,000
Q – 40%		20,000
R – 20%		10,000
being the revaluation of assets and goodwill		
Partners' capital accounts:		
Q – 50%	25,000	
R – 50%	25,000	
Goodwill		20,000
Net assets		30,000
being goodwill and revaluation of net assets written off		

P would be paid out £65,000, representing the original balance sheet value of his capital account, plus £20,000 to represent the increase in net asset values and goodwill.

Admission of a new partner

When a new partner is admitted, he may agree to bring in an amount of capital and an allowance for the existing goodwill of the business. The capital is credited to his capital account as normal. The contribution towards goodwill is credited to his capital account also. The total goodwill of the business is then shared out between all the partners in their new profit-sharing ratios.

Example

X and Y are in business, sharing profits in the ratio of 2:1. Their capital accounts at 31 December 19x5 are X £50,000 and Y £30,000. The net assets are revalued upwards by £18,000, and goodwill is valued at £24,000. Z is admitted, and contributes £20,000 capital plus £8,000 for his share of the goodwill. Profits are to be shared equally thereafter. Goodwill is not retained in the books.

The journal entries required to record the above are as follows:

	DR £	CR £
Net assets	18,000	
Goodwill	24,000	
Partners' capital accounts:		
X		28,000
Y		14,000
being revaluation of assets and introduction of goodwill		
Partners' capital accounts:		
X	8,000	
Y	8,000	
Z	8,000	
Goodwill		24,000
being elimination of goodwill from the accounts		

The partners' capital accounts after the above transactions will appear as follows:

Capital accounts

	X £	Y £	Z £		X £	Y £	Z £
Elimination of goodwill	8,000	8,000	8,000	Balances	50,000	30,000	
Balances c/d	70,000	36,000	20,000	Revaluation and goodwill	28,000	14,000	
				Cash introduced			28,000
	78,000	44,000	18,000		78,000	44,000	28,000

The closing balances represent the revised net assets total of £98,000, plus the additional cash injected by Z of £28,000.

Formation of a partnership from two or more sole traders

As with the other forms of reorganization, the net assets require revaluation, goodwill is introduced, and the new business is set up with revised capital accounts for each partner.

Example
Nylan and Abigail were two sole traders who decided to form a partnership on 1 January 19x5, sharing profits in the ratio of 3:1. Their balance sheets at that date were as follows:

	Nylan £	Abigail £
Freehold property	nil	40,000
Equipment	25,000	nil
Stocks	8,000	4,000
Debtors	12,000	8,000
Bank	5,000	2,000
	60,000	54,000
less Creditors	10,000	14,000
Net assets	50,000	40,000
Capital	50,000	40,000

The freehold property is valued at £50,000 and the equipment at £22,000, and goodwill is introduced at a valuation of £5,000 for Nylan and £7,000 for Abigail. The goodwill is to be written off immediately the new partnership is formed.

The ledger accounts would appear as follows:

(a) In the old sole traders' books:

Capital account – Nylan

	£		£
Revaluation	3,000	Balance b/d	50,000
To partnership accounts	52,000	Goodwill	5,000
	55,000		55,000

Capital account – Abigail

	£		£
		Balance b/d	40,000
		Revaluation	10,000
To partnership accounts	57,000	Goodwill	7,000
	57,000		57,000

(b) In the new partnership books:

Capital accounts

	Nylan	Abigail		Nylan	Abigail
	£	£		£	£
Goodwill			Transfer		
written off	9,000	3,000	old businesses	52,000	57,000
Balances c/d	43,000	54,000			
	52,000	57,000		52,000	57,000

The revised capital account balances equal the revised net asset total, ignoring goodwill, i.e.:

Original net assets – Nylan	50,000
– Abigail	40,000
Revaluation of freehold property	10,000
Revaluation of equipment	(3,000)
Total net assets	97,000

Summary

By the end of this chapter you should understand the nature of partnerships and the legal and financial implications of operating as a partnership. You should be able to prepare partnership ledger accounts, appropriation accounts and balance sheets. You should be able to deal with the revaluation of assets and the introduction of goodwill which arise when there are changes in the profit-sharing ratio or the structure of a partnership, and their subsequent elimination from the books of account.

Exercises

17.1 The net profit of Bert and Sid for the year ended 31 December 19x5 was £120,000. The partnership agreement stated that:

(a) salaries were to be allocated of £17,000 per annum to Bert and £8,000 to Sid
(b) interest on capital at the start of the year is to be given, at 7 per cent per annum
(c) drawings of £500 per month each are to be allowed
(d) interest on drawings of £150 each is to be charged
(e) remaining profits and losses are to be shared in the proportion of Bert ⅓ and Sid ⅔
(f) loans are to carry interest at 10 per cent per annum.

Partners' capital account balances at 1 January 19x5 were Bert, £40,000 credit, and Sid, £60,000 credit. Partners' current account balances at the same date were Bert, £25,000 credit, and Sid, £5,000 credit. Bert has an outstanding loan to the partnership of £10,000.

Prepare the appropriation account for the year, and show the partners' current and capital accounts.

17.2x Ann, Barbara and Carol are in partnership, sharing profits in the ratio of 3:2:1 respectively. Their capital and current accounts at 1 January 19x5 were as follows:

	Capital a/c	Current a/c
	£	£
Ann	20,000	3,000
Barbara	40,000	4,000
Carol	17,000	5,000

Ann receives a salary of £10,000 per annum, Barbara and Carol each receive £5,000. Each partner has drawings of £6,000 per annum. Interest is payable on capital account balances at the start of the year, of 5 per cent per annum.

Net profit for the year ended 31 December 19x5 was £43,000, after deducting partners' salaries in the profit and loss account.

Prepare the appropriation account for the year ended 31 December 19x5, and the partners' capital and current accounts for the year. Show how the capital section of the balance sheet at 31 December 19x5 would appear.

17.3 Dog, Cat and Mouse are in partnership, sharing profits equally, after allocating a salary of £4,000 to Dog. Their capital and current accounts at 1 January 19x5 were as follows:

	Capital a/c	Current a/c
	£	£
Dog	8,000	5,000
Cat	5,000	6,000
Mouse	4,000	500

The net profit for the year ended 31 December 19x5 was £1,000, and drawings amounted to £2,000 each.

Prepare the appropriation account and the partners' capital and current accounts for the year.

17.4 X, Y and Z have shared profits in the ratios of 3:3:2 respectively for many years. This is to be changed to 3:2:1 from 1 January 19x6. At 31 December 19x5 the net assets of the partnership amounted to £280,000, and the capitals of the partners were:

X   £120,000
Y   £ 96,000
Z   £ 64,000

Goodwill at 1 January 19x6 is valued at £240,000. The net assets include land and buildings, which is to be revalued upwards by £48,000.

(a) Show the journal entries to record the revaluation of assets and the introduction of goodwill, and the adjustments to the partners' capital accounts.
(b) State the net assets figure and show the partners' capital accounts at 1 January 19x6, assuming:
    (i)   that goodwill is retained in the business
    (ii) that goodwill is not retained in the business.

17.5 Peter and Paul are in partnership, sharing profits equally. They decide to admit Pamela. Goodwill at the point of admission is valued at £30,000. Pamela is asked to provide £35,000 in cash for her share. The new profit-sharing ratio is to be 4:3:3 respectively for Peter, Paul and Pamela.
    Net assets prior to the admission of Pamela amounted to £60,000, and the partners' capital accounts were Peter, £40,000, and Paul, £20,000.

(a) Show the journal entries for the admission of Pamela
(b) Show the journal entries for the elimination of goodwill immediately
(c) Show the opening balance sheet of the new business.

17.6 Brown, Green and Black are in partnership, sharing profits in the ratio 4:4:2. Black decides to retire. At that date, the net assets of £240,000 are revalued upwards by £40,000, and goodwill is valued at £50,000. Black is to be paid in cash on retirement, after which Brown and Green will share profits equally.

Show the journal entries dealing with the above, on the assumption that goodwill is to be written off immediately. Show the position of the balance sheet after the retirement of Black.

17.7 David and Dawn decide to amalgamate their two businesses into a partnership. Their balance sheets at that date were as follows:

	David £	Dawn £
Plant and machinery	80,000	40,000
Stocks	12,000	13,000
Debtors	18,000	14,000
	110,000	67,000
Creditors	15,000	9,000
	95,000	58,000

David's plant is revalued at £100,000 and Dawn's at £35,000. Goodwill is valued at £20,000 for David and £30,000 for Dawn, and is to be retained in the books of account after amalgamation of the two businesses.

Show the journal entries required for the amalgamation and the opening balance sheet of the new partnership.

18   Limited company accounts

Aims of the chapter

The aims of this chapter are to:

- explain the distinction between a limited company and an unincorporated organization
- explain the meaning of share capital and the different values which can be attributed to shares
- explain how the profits of a limited company are appropriated, after deducting expenses
- explain the meaning and composition of shareholders' funds
- explain the content of limited company published accounts
- demonstrate the preparation of limited company accounts in a format not for publication
- explain the scope and purpose of auditing a limited company's accounts.

A *limited company* is an organization in which the liability of its owners for the debts incurred by the organization is limited in some way. An unincorporated organization, such as a sole trader, or the partners in a partnership (apart from limited partners), all have unlimited liability for the debts of the organization. Their personal assets can be seized in order to pay the creditors.

In a limited company, the owners buy 'shares' in the company. A *share* is a fixed portion of the company's capital. The liability of the owners is limited to the purchase price of the shares which are still unpaid – if the shares have already been paid for, then that sum is lost, but there will be no more to pay.

A limited company has the advantage of being able to divide its capital into many shares and hence encourage many owners to contribute to the capital of the company. A person owning shares is called a *shareholder* or a *member*, and is a part-owner of the company. Many shareholders are entitled to vote at general meetings of the company, and although they are not involved in the day-to-day running of the company they can still exert their influence at meetings.

Setting up a limited company

A limited company is governed by legislation. The Companies Act 1985 (amended 1989) provides many of the regulations with which companies must comply. A company must submit a Memorandum and Articles of Association to the Registrar of Companies which lay down the way in which the company is to be organized, its financing structure and the areas in which it will operate.

Public and private limited companies

A *private company* is one which restricts the issue of its shares. It often issues shares only to family and friends. A *public company* is one which opens up the ownership of its shares to anyone who wants to buy them. A public limited company contains the designation 'plc' in its name.

Share capital

The capital of the company is divided into shares. When the company wants to raise money it does so by issuing (selling) shares to the shareholders. The share capital which a company is allowed to issue or raise is called the *authorized share capital*. It is divided up into groups or classes of shares, each with a 'par' or 'face' value. For example, if a company decides to divide its share capital of £1 million into £10 shares, there will be 100,000 shares with a par value of £10 each. If a company wants to exceed this authorized amount it must refer back to the Registrar of Companies for permission.

The capital which it actually issues is called the *issued share capital*. It is always the issued share capital which appears on the balance sheet and which is used in any calculations of dividends. There can be several different categories and types of shares, which are considered later in the chapter.

Share values

A share in a company can have many different values.

Par value

This is the 'face' or basic value of a share, also called the *nominal value.* It is the original value of the share as agreed with the Company Registrar. Thus in a company with a £1 million share capital, divided into 100,000 shares, each share will have a par value of £10.

Issue price

When shares are *issued* (sold by the company), they are often issued for more than their par value. The additional amount is called the *share premium*. For example, if a £1 share is sold for £1.20, then a share premium of 20p is raised. The par value is credited to an account entitled 'Shares issued at par' and the premium is credited to an account entitled 'Share premium account'. It is regarded as a *capital reserve,* which means that it is not usually available to be distributed as dividends to the shareholders.

Market value

Once shares have been issued to shareholders or members, those shareholders are free to sell them in the open market (except for shares in private limited companies where permission to sell is granted only by the other shareholders). These dealings by shareholders have no effect at all on the company – they are the private transactions of shareholders. Thus, the *market value* of a share is not recorded in the accounts of the company at all.

Dividends

Shareholders expect something in return for their investment. A sole trader receives all of the profit his business makes; a partner receives his share of the profit. A shareholder receives whatever the directors decide upon; this is called a *dividend*, and is usually expressed as a number of pence per share. Only shares issued qualify for dividends, and the dividend is based on the par value, never on the issue price or the market value.

There is no guarantee that a dividend will be paid; some businesses retain their profits in order to expand.

If a dividend is paid out halfway through the year it is called an *interim dividend*. The balance is paid at the end of the year, and is known as a *final dividend*.

Types of shares

Preference shares

These are shares which are entitled to receive their dividend before other shares receive theirs. Thus, if profits are low, they have more chance of receiving their dividend than have other classes of share. They have a fixed rate of dividend attached to them. The rate is usually fairly small, and the shareholders often have no entitlement to vote at general meetings. Although there is a fixed rate of dividend, there is no guarantee that it will be paid if the directors do not 'declare' a dividend on those shares. Some preference shares are *cumulative,* in that any unpaid dividends are carried forward to future periods. Even so, this does not guarantee payment if the directors do not declare a dividend.

If the company is wound up (ceases to exist), then provided that there are sufficient funds, the preference shareholders would receive the issue price of their shares as repayment, prior to any other shareholders receiving a payment.

Ordinary shares (equity shares)	These shares have no preference at all above others. However, if profits are good, then the rate of dividend which ordinary shareholders receive is unlimited. If the company is wound up, the ordinary shareholders would share out the remainder of the assets of the company, after paying off the preference shareholders first. Ordinary shareholders are usually entitled to vote at general meetings, and hence are regarded as controlling the company.
Reserves	Reserves are of two types, according to how they have arisen.
Revenue reserves	These arise where *profits* have been set aside for particular or general purposes, such as to replace fixed assets, or to provide for unforeseen events. They are available to pay dividends, in most circumstances.
Capital reserves	These arise as a result of capital transactions, such as the issue of shares at a premium, or the revaluation of fixed assets to a higher value. They are not generally available to pay dividends. Capital reserves are described in more detail in Chapter 19.
Debentures	These are loans to the company, usually long-term and secured on some of the assets of the company. Debenture-holders receive interest on their loans, which is a normal business expense, and which is unavoidable. Debenture-holders are not shareholders and therefore are not owners of the business.
Directors	A company is run by its directors. They are people appointed by the shareholders. In a private limited company, the directors are often the major shareholders of the company, or friends and family of major shareholders. A director is an employee of the company. His wages, salaries and fees are normal business expenses and appear in the profit and loss account.
Auditors' fees	A limited company is required by law to have its books and records examined by an independent registered auditor, who states that the accounts prepared show a true and fair view of the affairs of the company. The fees paid to the auditors are a normal business expense.
Appropriating the profits	The profit of a limited company is calculated as for any other type of organization. Remember that directors' fees and debenture interest are normal business

expenses and are taken out of the profit and loss account before arriving at net profit.

The net profit is then *appropriated* in an *appropriation account* in various ways.

Corporation tax

This is not really an appropriation of profits, but is a business expense. You will not have to calculate the corporation tax in examinations – the figure will be given to you. In a sole trader's or partnership's business, tax is a personal expense and therefore does not appear in the firm's accounts. In a limited company, tax is a company expense, and so it does appear.

The normal situation is that tax is estimated at the end of the year and is entered in the accounts; during the next year, it is paid. Any amounts unpaid at the end of the year are shown in the firm's balance sheet as current liabilities.

Transfers to reserves (revenue reserves)

Some firms transfer part of their profits to a separate ledger account called a *Reserve account*. There may be more than one such account for particular purposes. For example, there may be a fixed asset replacement reserve account, which is intended to set aside profits to replace fixed assets when the need arises. There may be a general reserve account, which acts as a 'contingency' reserve in case expenses occur which were not forecast. The balance on the reserve accounts is shown on the balance sheet as part of the capital employed.

It is important to realize that reserve accounts are only ledger accounts; they do not necessarily represent cash funds in a bank or other account. Their purpose is to make users of the accounts aware that the profits are not all available for distribution to the members if the company is to be able to replace its assets in the future and provide for unforeseen events.

If cash funds are to be set aside for these purposes, then that is a separate issue, to be reflected on the balance sheet in the breakdown of cash and bank balances.

Dividends proposed

Strictly speaking, the directors 'propose' or 'declare' dividends and the members in annual general meeting approve or otherwise that proposal. However, it is expected that the members will approve the proposal, so it is assumed that the dividends will eventually be paid in the following accounting year. Dividends are also known as *distributions of profit*. The amount unpaid at the end of the year is shown on the balance sheet as a current liability.

It is the law that a business cannot distribute more in profits than it has made. In many companies, previous years' profits (or losses) are added to (or subtracted from) the current year's profits or losses to produce a distributable profit. This means that a company can distribute previous years' profits at a later date.

The unappropriated and undistributed amount of profits each year is added to previous profits and carried forward in a profit and loss ledger account.

Shareholders' funds

In the case of a company ceasing to exist, the preference shareholders have entitlement only to the repayment of the issue price of their shares. The remainder of the capital of the company belongs to the ordinary shareholders, and might consist of:

- par value of ordinary shares issued
- share premium
- reserves of any kind
- the balance on the profit and loss ledger account.

The total of these items is the total of ordinary shareholders' funds. If the company were to close down, and assuming the net assets would all realize their book values, this is the total which the ordinary shareholders would receive.

Shareholders' funds are often referred to as *equity funds*.

Published accounts

A limited company must 'publish' its accounts each year by lodging a copy with the Registrar of Companies. A set of published accounts must conform to the layout prescribed by the Companies Acts, and is normally accompanied by a comprehensive set of notes containing additional information on the figures in the accounts. Items in the accounts which require further clarification are said to require *disclosure* in the notes to the accounts.

The Companies Act 1985 lays down several alternative formats for the profit and loss account and balance sheet. An example is shown at Appendix A.

Companies must also disclose their accounting policies (see Chapter 7) and the bases of valuation of assets. For depreciation, the following must be disclosed, for each major class of asset:

● the methods of depreciation used
● the useful lives of assets, or the depreciation rates applied
● the total depreciation charged for the period
● the gross amount of depreciable assets and the related accumulated depreciation.

In addition, if there have been any changes in the methods or rates used, this must be disclosed, together with the effect of the changes or of revaluation of assets.

A worked example

MJA Limited has, among others, the following balances at 31 October 19x5:

	DR £000	CR £000
Ordinary shares of £1 each		1,000
6% preference shares of £1 each		100
Share premium account		200
General reserves		300
Profit and loss account at 1 November 19x4		880
Administrative expenses	400	
Debtors	350	
Creditors		300
Directors' fees and salaries	200	
Office machinery – net book value	3,000	
Bank and cash	600	
10% debentures, repayable 2000		500

You are told that:

(i)   gross profit for the year ending 31 October 19x5 amounted to £2,100,000
(ii) stock of materials at 31 October 19x5 amounted to £200,000
(iii) directors' salaries of £150,000 have yet to be accounted for
(iv) corporation tax of £130,000 is due on the profits for the year
(v)   £500,000 is to be transferred into general reserves
(vi) a dividend of 8p per ordinary share is to be declared

(vii) authorized share capital is £1,200,000 ordinary and £200,000 preference shares.

Before commencing the profit and loss appropriation account and balance sheet, consider the following comments:

1 Limited companies' transactions often run into millions of pounds, so be prepared for some very large figures to appear in such examples. Note that the trial balance is headed with the notation '£000'. This means that the figures are all in thousands of pounds; thus a figure in the trial balance of £5,000 really represents £5,000,000.
2 The list of balances already shows a figure for general reserves of £300,000. The notes below the list tell you that a further £500,000 is to be transferred into general reserves. This comes out of the current year's appropriation account. The balance sheet at 31 October 19x5 will show the revised total, i.e. £800,000.
3 The list of balances shows a balance on the profit and loss account at 1 November 19x4. This represents previous years' unappropriated and undistributed profits, to which the current year's will be added.
4 Dividends are calculated on the par value of the shares issued.

The profit and loss account would appear as follows:

MJA Limited – Profit and loss account for the year ended 31 October 1995

	£000	£000
Gross profit		2,100
less Expenses:		
Administrative expenses	400	
Debenture interest	50	
Directors' fees and salaries	350	
		800
Net profit before tax		1,300
Corporation tax		130
Net profit after tax		1,170
Transfer to general reserves		500
		670
Dividends proposed:		
Preference	6	
Ordinary	80	
		86
Profit and loss balance for the year		584
Profit and loss balance b/fwd		880
Profit and loss balance c/fwd		1,464

MJA Limited – Balance sheet at 31 October 19x5

	£000	£000	£000
Fixed assets			
Net book value			3,000
Current assets			
Stocks	200		
Debtors	350		
Bank and cash	600		
		1,150	

less Creditors: amounts due in less than one year

Creditors	300	
Directors' fees accrued	150	
Debenture interest accrued	50	
Dividends proposed	86	
	586	

Net current assets   564

3,564

less Creditors: amounts due beyond one year:

10% debentures, repayable 2000	500
	3,064

Financed by:

Ordinary shares of £1	1,000
Preference shares of £1	100
Share premium account	200
General reserves	300
Profit and loss account balance	1,464
	3,064

Note the headings for Current and Long-term liabilities – these are named 'Creditors: amounts due in less than one year' and 'Creditors: amounts due beyond one year', which is common practice in published accounts.

Auditing the limited company

A Limited Company is obliged by law to have its accounts audited. This means that they are examined by an independent registered auditor and a report is issued by the auditor that the accounts have been prepared in accordance with the Companies Acts and with standard accounting practice and that they show a true and fair view of the company's results for the year and of its financial position at the end of the year.

If the auditor is unable to make this statement, then he must 'qualify' the audit report, which means he must state the matters on which he disagrees with the accounts. This will only be done after he has consulted with the directors and tried to persuade them to alter the accounts.

Because the auditor is an independent person, he is an *external* auditor. He is appointed by the shareholders in the annual general meeting, and reports to them. He is not involved in the day-to-day running of the company and is not an employee of the company. He might provide additional services above and beyond the external audit, but these are the subject of a separate contract between himself and the company. For the purposes of the external audit, he is acting on behalf of the shareholders.

Some companies also have *internal* auditors. These are employees of the company and are therefore not independent. They report to management. However, if they are properly qualified, then the external auditors are allowed to place some reliance on the audit work which the internal auditors carry out.

It is not the responsibility of the auditor to detect fraud. He is obliged to conduct his audit in such a way that there is a *reasonable expectation* of detecting any fraud.

Summary

By the end of this chapter you should understand the financial structure of a limited company, including common types of shares and share valuations. You should be able to prepare final accounts for a limited company (in a format not for publication), distinguishing between expenses and appropriations of profit, and should appreciate the scope and purpose of the external audit of a limited company.

Exercises

18.1 RJA Limited has the following trial balance at 31 December 19x5:

	Debit £000	Credit £000
Ordinary shares of £1 each		1,000
Preference shares of £1 each		100
Share premium account		200
General reserves		300
Profit and loss account 1 January 19x5		380
Sales turnover		10,000
Stock at 1 January 19x5	600	
Purchases of materials	7,700	
Carriage outwards	50	
Auditors' fees	30	
General expenses	260	
Debtors	1,000	
Creditors		300
Office machinery		
– cost	3,000	
– depreciation at 1 January 19x5	460	
Bank and cash	600	
10% debentures, payable 2000		500
	13,240	13,240

You are told that:

(i)   closing stock at 31 December 19x5 is £400,000
(ii)   directors' salaries of £150,000 have yet to be paid
(iii)   a dividend of 8p per ordinary share is proposed
(iv)   depreciation of 5 per cent on cost is to be provided on office machinery
(v)   corporation tax of £130,000 is due on the profits for the year
(vi)   £500,000 is to be transferred into general reserves
(vii)   authorized share capital is 1.2 million ordinary and 200,000 preference shares, of £1 each.

Prepare a trading and profit and loss account for the year ending 31 December 19x5, and a balance sheet as at that date.

18.2x Sandstone Co Ltd has the following trial balance at 31 December 19x5:

	Debit £000	Credit £000
Sales and purchases	150	300
Stock at 1 January 19x5	80	
General expenses	30	
Plant and machinery – cost	400	
– depreciation		70
Ordinary shares of £1 each		150
Share premium account		20
Debtors and creditors	65	25
8% preference shares of £1 each		100
Motor vehicles at cost	130	
General reserves		180
12% debentures, repayable 2005		100
Bank and cash	135	
Profit and loss account b/fwd		45
	990	990

You are also told that, at 31 December 19x5:

(i)   closing stock is £100,000
(ii) a dividend of 10p per ordinary share is proposed
(iii) depreciation is to be provided at 10 per cent on plant and £70,000 on motor vehicles
(iv) £50,000 is to be transferred to general reserves
(v)   authorized share capital is 150,000 ordinary and 150,000 preference shares of £1 each.

Prepare final accounts.

18.3 The trial balance of Zed Limited at 1 January 1993 contains the following items:

	£000
Bank overdraft	7
Building – cost	80
– depreciation	5
Creditors – trade	28
– operating expenses	2
16% Debentures	50
Debtors	24
Land at valuation	125
Machinery – cost	90
– depreciation	43
Ordinary shares, £1 each	100
10% preference shares, £1 each	40
Profit and loss account	34
Revaluation reserve	45
Stocks	35

Summarized transactions and events for the year to 31 December 1993 are as follows:

(i)	£000
Sales	920
Purchases	500
Bad debts written off	5
Contras between debtors' and creditors' accounts	8
Operating expenses paid	360

(ii) 30,000 £1 ordinary shares were issued at £2.00 per share on 1 January 1993; this transaction was not reflected in the trial balance above.
(iii) Debenture interest and the preference dividend for the year were all paid on 31 December 1993. An ordinary dividend of 20p per share was paid on 31 December.
(iv) The land is revalued at 31 December 1993, at £130,000. The machinery is to be depreciated at 10 per cent on cost and the buildings are to be depreciated on the straight-line basis over eighty years.

(v)   At 31 December 1993:

	£000
additional operating expenses owing are	10
closing stock is	40
closing debtors are	35
closing trade creditors are	25

Prepare the balance sheet as at 31 December 1993 and the profit and loss account for the year ended 31 December 1993. These statements do not need to comply with the Companies Act disclosure requirements, but should be presented in a format which is generally accepted and which presents the information helpful to the reader. Submit all workings. Ignore taxation.

(ACCA, June 1994)

18.4x DWS Ltd. prepares its accounts to 30 September each year. At 30 September 1994 its trial balance was as follows:

	Dr £	Cr £
Plant and machinery – cost	125,000	
– depreciation at 1 October 1993	1993	28,000
Office equipment – cost	45,000	
– depreciation at 1 October 1993		15,000
Stocks at 1 October 1993	31,000	
Purchases and sales	115,000	188,000
Returns inwards and outwards	8,000	6,000
Selling expenses	12,000	
Heat and light	8,000	
Wages and salaries	14,000	
Directors' fees	5,000	
Printing and stationery	6,000	
Telephone and fax	6,000	
Rent, rates and insurances	4,000	
Trade debtors and creditors	35,000	33,000
Provision for doubtful debts at 1 October 1993		4,000
Bank	3,000	
Petty cash	1,000	
Interim dividend paid	2,000	
Ordinary shares of 50p each		100,000
Share premium account		8,000
General reserve		7,000
Profit and loss account balance at 1 October 1993		34,000
Suspense account	3,000	
	423,000	423,000

The following additional information at 30 September 1994 is available:

(i)	Closing stocks of goods for resale	£53,000
(ii)	Prepayments:	
	– telephone and fax rental	£1,000
	– rates and insurance	£1,000
(iii)	Accruals:	
	– wages and salaries	£1,500
	– directors' fees	2% of net turnover
	– auditor's fees	£3,500

(iv)   Specific bad debts to be written off amount to £3,000

(v)   Provision for doubtful debts is to be amended to 5% of debtors, after adjusting for bad debts written off

(vi)   The following book-keeping errors are discovered:
- the purchase of an item of stock has been debited to the office equipment account, cost £1,200
- the payment of £1,300 to a creditor has been recorded by debiting the bank account and crediting the creditors' account

Any remaining balance on the suspense account is to be added to prepayments or accruals, as appropriate, on the balance sheet

(vii)   The figure in the trial balance for the bank balance is the balance appearing in the cash book prior to the reconciliation with the bank statement. Upon reconciliation, it is discovered that:
- unpresented cheques amount to £3,000
- bank charges not entered in the ledgers amount to £4,000

(viii)   Depreciation of fixed assets is to be provided as follows:
- plant and machinery 10% on cost
- office equipment 33⅓% on the reducing balance at the end of the year

(ix)   A final dividend of 1.5p per share is to be proposed

(x)   £10,000 is to be transferred to general reserves

(xi)   Provision of £1,000 for corporation tax is to be made.

(a)   Prepare a trading and profit and loss account for the year ended 30 September 1994.

(b)   Prepare a balance sheet at 30 September 1994.

(CIMA, May 1995, amended)

19   Post-balance sheet events, contingencies, reserves

Aims of the chapter

The aims of this chapter are to:

- explain the nature and treatment of post-balance sheet events and contingencies
- explain the nature and treatment of reserves.

Post-balance sheet events

The final accounts of a business are prepared at a fixed point in time. As discussed previously, all transactions which have occurred have a bearing on those accounts, even if the cash has not changed hands. Final accounts in a limited company often take several weeks to compile, and by the time the auditors arrive to check the accounts, various other transactions may have taken place, and items of information may have come to light.

SSAP 17 deals with accounting events which occur after the date of the balance sheet, but before the date at which the financial accounts are approved. Some of those events provide evidence of situations which occurred at the date of the balance sheet, but which were not known until later. These events should be taken into consideration when preparing the accounts. For example, it may become known that, at the balance sheet date, stocks were in existence which were later sold for less than their cost. This means that they should have been written down to their net realizable value. This is known as an *adjusting event*.

SSAP17 defines adjusting events as being 'post balance sheet events which provide additional evidence of conditions existing at the balance sheet date'.

Some events are known as *non-adjusting events*. This means that the accounts themselves are not amended as a result of the event, but a note should be provided to give the users of accounts additional information about events which did not exist at the balance sheet date, but nevertheless are material to the user of accounts. Examples include labour disputes, a plan to close down part of the business activities and further issues of shares and/or debentures.

Disclosure of post-balance sheet

An *adjusting event* need not be disclosed to the users of the accounts, as it is already adjusted in the figures presented to them.

Non-adjusting events are not adjusted in the accounts of the business, but should be disclosed in the notes to the accounts.

Contingencies

SSAP 18 defines a contingency as 'a condition which exists at the balance sheet date where the outcome will be confirmed only on the occurrence or non-occurrence of one or more uncertain future events. A contingent gain or loss is a gain or loss dependent on a contingency'.

A contingency is different from a post-balance sheet event in that it exists at the balance sheet date, whereas a post-balance sheet event is one which occurs later.

In line with the prudence concept, a contingent gain is not disclosed unless it is probable that it will occur. On the other hand, a contingent loss is treated in the following ways:

- as a provision in the accounts, if it is probable that it will occur
- as a disclosure in the accounts if it is possible that it will occur
- with no provision or disclosure if its occurrence is considered to be remote.

Examples of a contingency include:

- the gain or loss from a pending legal action
- guarantees given to customers, which have not yet expired.

The company is required to disclose the nature of the contingency, what circumstances are likely to affect it, and a prudent estimate of the eventual effect of the contingency.

Reserves

Reserves are gains or profits which have been retained in the company, apart from the nominal value of the shares. Together with the nominal share value, they form the shareholders' funds, and equate to the net assets of the company.

There are two categories of reserves:

- revenue reserves
- capital reserves.

Revenue reserves are undistributed trading profits. They are calculated each period in the profit and loss account, and after taking out amounts for distribution to the shareholders (dividends) the remainder is retained in the company and added to previous retained profits. The balance is kept in the profit and loss ledger account, and carried forward each period.

Some companies like to separate some of the profits into a 'general reserve' account, but this is a paper exercise only – there is no legal distinction between the revenue reserves held in this account and the revenue reserves held in the profit and loss account.

Capital reserves are profits and gains which have accrued from some activity other than a normal trading activity. Examples include:

(a) *Share premium account*, which is the excess over par value paid by shareholders on the purchase of their shares, as discussed in Chapter 18.
(b) *Revaluation reserve account*, which is the excess which arises when fixed assets are revalued to a figure which is higher than the current net book value. The asset account is debited by this excess and the reserve account is credited.

Neither of these two reserve accounts can be regarded as available to pay dividends to shareholders except in very unusual circumstances. They represent gains which are *unrealized*, which means there is uncertainty as to their reliability.

(c) *Capital redemption reserve account*, which arises when a company purchases its own shares, or buys back its shares from existing shareholders who have purchased *redeemable preference shares*. The reserve is used to fund this reduction of capital.

Summary

By the end of this chapter you should be able to account correctly for transactions which arise after the year end. You should appreciate the distinction between post-balance sheet events and contingencies, and should be able to determine which should be adjusted for in the accounts, which require disclosure in the notes to the accounts, and which do not require any special treatment at all. You should also understand how reserves arise, and the different applications of revenue and capital reserves.

Exercises

19.1 With reference to SSAP 17 (Accounting for post-balance sheet events) and SSAP 18 (Accounting for contingencies):

(a) define the following terms:
   (i)   post-balance sheet events
   (ii) adjusting events
   (iii) non-adjusting events
   (iv) contingent gain/loss

(b) give FOUR examples of adjusting events and FOUR examples of non-adjusting events.
(c) state how
   (i) a material contingent loss, and
   (ii) material contingent gains

should be accounted for in financial statements.

(AAT, December 1990)

Aims of the chapter

The aims of this chapter are to:

- consider the connection between profit and cash and to explain why an organization's cash resources are not wholly dependent on the profit or loss which is made
- demonstrate the preparation of a cash flow statement in accordance with FRS 1.

If a business makes a profit, it is reasonable to assume that its cash and bank balances will improve, and if a business makes a loss, its cash and bank balances might suffer. However, there are many reasons why the obvious might not occur, the main one being that funds do not necessarily flow into a business at the same time as profits are made.

Profits are calculated using the *accruals concept* – profit equals revenue earned less expenses consumed in earning that revenue. Cash and bank balances do not come into this equation. Revenue is earned and expenses are consumed irrespective of the cash changing hands. Cash might change hands before or after the profit is made, and funds are flowing in and out of the business at all times irrespective of whether or not a profit is being made.

Profits are affected by a variety of provisions (and, in limited companies, by reserves), such as depreciation of fixed assets and doubtful debts. Neither of these involve money changing hands and yet they reduce profit; on the other hand, the purchase of fixed assets affects funds but not profits, except by depreciation. Raising capital, for example by an issue of shares, brings cash into the business, but has no effect on profits.

It is obvious, therefore, that cash flows and profits are not necessarily dependent on each other. In the 1980s many small businesses failed – not because they were not profitable, but because they did not manage their cash resources effectively. Selling goods is a prime example. The sales value is a starting point in the calculation of profit; deducting expenses gives a net profit – and yet the debtor may not have paid up. Profit is made, but no cash is received from the customer – and it may be that the supplier, the wages and all the other expenses have already been paid. So a profitable business may suffer from shortage of cash.

Format of the cash flow statement

Most limited companies are now required to submit a *cash flow statement* along with their published accounts. The format is dictated by Financial Reporting Standard (FRS 1), which includes the following sections:

	£
Net cash inflow/outflow from operating activities	xxx
Returns on investments and servicing of finance	xxx
Taxation	xxx
Investing activities	xxx
Net cash inflow/outflow before financing	xxx
Financing	xxx
Net cash flow	xxx

We will now look at each section in turn.

Net cash inflow/outflow from operating activities

This is the cash flowing in from trading and normal business activities. It can be calculated in one of two ways.

(a) The indirect method

The net operating profit (before tax) is the starting point, as cash flows in if profits are made, but this needs to be adjusted for items in the profit calculation which do not affect cash, which affect cash by a different amount, or which affect cash at a different point in time. For example, the profit will have been reduced by depreciation and other provisions which do not affect cash; it will include all sales revenue even though some debtors have yet to pay up, and conversely it will exclude receipts from debtors whose revenue was included in the previous period's profits; it will include the cost of all goods sold even though some purchases have not yet been paid for or were already in stock.

The net operating profit therefore needs to be adjusted as follows to determine the net cash inflow or outflow from operating activities:

	£	£
Net operating profit		xxx
Add: – depreciation	xxx	
– loss on disposal of fixed assets	xxx	
– decrease in stocks	xxx	
– decrease in debtors	xxx	
– increase in creditors	xxx	
		xxx
Less: – profit on disposal of fixed assets	xxx	
– increase in stocks	xxx	
– increase in debtors	xxx	
– decrease in creditors	xxx	
		(xxx)
Net cash flow from operating activities		xxx

We also need to add back any interest charges in the profit and loss account, and deduct any interest receivable, as these are not considered to be flows from operating activities, but returns from investments and servicing of finance.

(b) The direct method

This is an alternative approach to the indirect method, giving the same result. It is prepared by analysing the cash and bank accounts of the company, as follows:

	£	£
Cash sales	xxx	
Cash received from debtors	xxx	
		xxx
Less: – cash purchases	xxx	
– cash paid to creditors	xxx	
– cash expenses	xxx	
		(xxx)
Net cash flow from operating activities		xxx

FRS 1 recommends that companies use the direct method, but it also insists that they prepare a reconciliation of the net operating profit with the cash flow from operating activities, so the indirect method must be applied anyway.

| Returns on investments and servicing of finance | This heading includes dividends and interest received and paid. Dividends are shown net of tax and interest is shown gross. The dividends figure should be the amount paid during the year (which will be last year's proposed dividends) and not the amount proposed in the accounts for the current year. |

| Taxation | This heading includes corporation tax, but not VAT which is included with the creditors figure. The figure should be the amount paid during the year (based on last year's profits) and not the amount provided for against the current year's profits. |

| Investing activities | This heading includes cash flows from the purchase or sale of tangible or intangible fixed assets and other investments. |

| Financing | This heading includes the raising or repayment of loans, debentures and share capital, unless these are included in the creditors figure. Note that only the capital element of loan repayments is included – the interest charges are part of returns on investments and servicing of finance. |

A worked example
BVA plc has the following balance sheets:

	31.12.x5		31.12.x6	
	£m	£m	£m	£m
Fixed assets				
Plant at cost	100		120	
Plant depreciation	20		22	
		80		98
Current assets				
Stocks	35		25	
Debtors	24		28	
Bank and cash	63		101	
	122		154	
less Creditors: amounts falling due within one year				
Trade creditors	31		33	
Taxation	12		16	
Dividends	20		30	
	63		79	
		59		75
		139		173
less Creditors: amounts due after more than one year				
Debenture		30		21
		109		152
Financed by:				
Share capital		100		120
Reserves		9		32
		109		152

Its profit and loss account for the year ended 31 December 19x6 was as follows:

	£m	£m
Sales		120
less Cost of goods sold		30
Gross profit		90
add Interest receivable		13
		103
Less:		
General expenses	17	
Interest payable	3	
Depreciation on plant	10	
Loss on disposal of plant	4	
		34
Net profit before tax		69
Taxation		16
Net profit after taxation		53
Dividends proposed		30
Net profit retained		23

You are told that during the year plant was sold for £3m, which had cost £15m and on which £8m depreciation had been charged.

Solution:

Cash flow from operating activities:

	£m	£m
Net operating profit		69
Add: – interest payable	3	
– depreciation	10	
– loss on disposal of fixed assets	4	
– decrease in stocks	10	
– increase in creditors	2	
		29
Less: – interest receivable	13	
– increase in debtors	4	
		(17)
Net cash flow from operating activities		81

Cash flow statement for the year ending 31 December 19x6

	£m	
Net cash inflow from operating activities	81	
Returns on investments and servicing of finance	(10)	(see note (i) below)
Taxation	(12)	
Investing activities	(32)	(see note (ii) below)
Net cash inflow/outflow before financing	27	
Financing	11	(see note (iii) below)
Net cash inflow	38	(see note (iv) below)

Note (i) *Returns on investments and servicing of finance consists of:*

	£m
Cash inflow from interest receivable	13
Cash outflow from interest payable	(3)
Cash outflow from dividends paid	(20)
	(10)

Note (ii) *Investing activities requires a calculation of plant purchases:*

	£m
Plant at cost at 31.12.x5	100
less Cost of plant disposed of during year	15
	85
Plant at cost at 31.12.x6	120
Plant purchased during year	35

and therefore Investing activities is made up of:

	£m
Cash outflow for plant purchased	(35)
Cash inflow from plant sold	3
	(32)

Note (iii) *Financing activities consists of:*

	£m
Cash inflow from shares issued	20
Cash outflow from debenture repaid	(9)
	11

Note (iv) *The net cash inflow or outflow should agree with the change in the balance sheet for cash and cash equivalents (e.g. deposits and short-term investments).*

The cash flow statement can be used to see where cash has come from and gone to during the period, rather than simply giving a closing cash figure in the balance sheet. It enables the user to see why the profit for the year and the closing cash balance are not necessarily the same.

Examination note

Some examining bodies do not yet expect students to be able to prepare a cash flow statement in accordance with FRS 1, but will accept any reasonably prepared statement which commences with profit, and shows the cash inflows and outflow, to reconcile with the change in cash and cash equivalents. If the question does not specifically ask for the FRS 1 format, then you can choose whether to attempt that format or to use another, easier-to-prepare format.

Summary

By the end of this chapter you should appreciate that profit or loss is not the only factor affecting the cash position of an organization. You should be able to recognize those transactions which do or do not affect cash, and those which affect cash at different times to their effect on profits. You should be able to prepare a statement which reconciles the profit or loss with the change in cash and cash equivalents, in accordance with the format prescribed by FRS 1.

20.1 TA Ltd has the following profit and loss account for the year ended 30 April 19x6:

	£000	£000
Gross profit		90
Add: interest receivable	10	
profit on disposal of plant	7	
		17
		107
Less:		
General expenses	5	
Interest payable	2	
Depreciation on plant	22	
		29
Net profit before tax		78
Taxation		16
Net profit after taxation		62
Dividends proposed	2	
Transfer to reserves	5	
		7
		55
Profit and loss account balance b/fwd		135
Profit and loss account balance c/fwd		190

Its balance sheets at 30 April 19x5 and 19x6 were as follows:

TA Ltd balance sheets as at 30 April

	19x5		19x6	
	£000	£000	£000	£000
Fixed assets				
Plant – cost	180		260	
– depreciation	48		65	
		132		195
Current assets				
Stocks	54		62	
Debtors	22		21	
Bank and cash	10		–	
	86		83	
less Current liabilities:				
Creditors	10		6	
Taxation	13		16	
Dividends	3		2	
Bank	–		1	
	26		25	
Net current assets		60		58
		192		253
Less Long-term liabilities:				
Debenture		12		–
		180		253
Financed by:				
Ordinary shares of £1 each		30		40
Share premium account		5		8
General reserves		10		15
Profit and loss account		135		190
		180		253

You are also told that the plant which was sold had cost £25,000 and had been depreciated by £5,000, the proceeds of sale being £27,000.

Prepare a cash flow statement for the year ended 30 April 19x6.

20.2x YPY plc had the following profit and loss account for the year ended 31 March 19x6:

YPY plc profit and loss account for the year ended 31 March 19x6

	£000	£000
Gross profit		132
Add: Interest receivable		23
		155
Less:		
General expenses	29	
Interest payable	3	
Depreciation on plant	10	
Loss on disposal of plant	9	
		51
Net profit before tax		104
Taxation		24
Net profit after taxation		80
Dividends proposed		40
Net profit for the year		40
Profit and loss account b/fwd		110
Profit and loss account c/fwd		150

You are also given the following balance sheets at 30 April 19x5 and 19x6:

	19x5		19x6	
	£000	£000	£000	£000
Fixed assets				
Plant – at cost	400		600	
– depreciation	120		150	
		280		450
Current assets				
Stocks	280		340	
Debtors	270		260	
Bank	90		180	
	640		780	
less Current liabilities:				
Creditors	70		66	
Taxation	10		24	
Dividends	20		40	
	100		130	
Net current assets		540		650
		820		1,100
less: Long-term liabilities		–		100
		820		1,000
Financed by:				
Share capital:				
Ordinary shares of £1 each		450		500
Share premium		200		250
General reserves		60		100
Profit and loss account		110		150
		820		1,000

You are told that the plant which was sold had cost £80,000 and had been depreciated by £20,000. Sale proceeds were £51,000.

Prepare a cash flow statement for the year ended 31 March 19x6.

20.3 From the following balance sheets, prepare a cash flow statement for 19x6:

	19x5		19x6	
	£000	£000	£000	£000
Fixed assets				
Freehold premises		220		235
Plant – cost	189		218	
– depreciation	75		91	
		114		127
Motor vehicles – cost	45		69	
– depreciation	29		37	
		16		32
Investments at cost		115		167
		465		561
Current assets				
Stocks	65		114	
Debtors	114		195	
Bank and cash	119		2	
	298		311	
less Current liabilities				
Creditors	206		109	
Proposed dividend	21		18	
	227		127	
Net current assets		71		184
		536		745
less Long-term liabilities:				
Debentures		50		–
		486		745
Shareholders' funds				
Ordinary share capital	300		450	
General reserves	120		140	
Profit and loss account	66		155	
	486		745	

20.4x GH has the following balance sheet at 30 April 1995, with corresponding figures for the previous year:

	19x5		19x6	
	£000	£000	£000	£000
Fixed assets		277		206
Current assets				
Stocks	46		42	
Debtors	37		36	
Cash and bank	13		54	
	96		132	
less Current liabilities:				
Creditors	16		23	
		80		109
		357		315
less Long-term liabilities		10		50
Net assets		347		265
Financed by:				
Capital at start		265		214
Capital introduced		20		–
Net profit for the year		92		78
		377		292
Drawings		30		27
		347		265

(a) Prepare a cash flow statement for the year ended 30 April 1995 in a format which shows the increase or decrease in cash balances. State any assumptions which you make.

(b) Briefly describe the accounting information requirements of FOUR different user groups.

(CIMA, May 1995)

21   Interpretation of accounts

The aims of this chapter are to:

- explain the importance of the comparison of financial results
- demonstrate the calculation of, and explain the usefulness of, the main accounting comparisons.

The figures contained in the final accounts produced by an organization provide a great deal of information about the financial activities of the organization over the past year, and of its position at the time at which the final accounts are drawn up. However, on their own they do not give a full picture without comparison with other figures.

Consider the following example of a company's results for the last two years:

	19x5	19x6
	£	£
Sales	100,000	120,000
Net profit	10,000	11,500

At first sight, 19x6 seems the best year, because net profit was higher than in 19x5. But then, so was the sales total, so we might expect net profit to be higher. Is it as high as we might have expected? In percentage terms, the net profit in 19x5 was 10 per cent of the sales turnover; in 19x6 the net profit was only 9.58 per cent of the sales turnover. So although the actual profit figure was higher in 19x6, as a percentage of sales turnover it was lower. In other words, the business was less efficient in utilizing its sales to make a profit in 19x6.

We only realize that by making the comparison of net profit with sales in each year, and then comparing the two percentages of 10 per cent and 9.58 per cent.

We cannot say which year was best, as this depends on the objectives of the company for that year. If the objective was to increase turnover, then that objective has been fulfilled. Turnover rose by £20,000 from its 19x5 level of £100,000 – an increase of 20 per cent (yet another comparison).

Both the use of percentages and the comparison with others enable us to see the performance of the organization in a different light. They do not give us answers as to why the results have improved or diminished, or as to what needs to be done to improve them. But they are useful measurements with which to identify financial results which need further investigation.

There are several financial results of a business which can usefully be measured using comparisons. In theory, any comparison is relevant if it holds some meaning to the user, but there are some common comparisons which are regularly used. These are grouped according to the type of comparison which is being made. These comparisons are generally referred to as *ratios*, as they attempt to calculate the relationship between one figure and another.

The main groupings are:

- performance (profitability) ratios
- solvency (liquidity) ratios

- use of assets (efficiency) ratios
- capital structure (gearing) ratios
- investors' (security) ratios.

In all cases, the figures concerned must be compared with other figures from any or all of the following:

- previous periods
- other organizations (usually in the same line of business)
- plans and budgets.

The next section uses the following financial accounts to illustrate the calculation and interpretation of accounting ratios:

CRW Limited – Trading and profit and loss account for the year ending 31 October 19x5

	£000
Sales	100,000
less Cost of sales	60,000
Gross profit	40,000
less Expenses (including interest of £1,000)	30,000
Net profit before tax	10,000
Taxation	2,000
Net profit after tax	8,000
Dividends	1,000
Retained profit for the year	7,000

CRW Limited – Balance sheet as at 31 October 19x5

	£000	£000
Fixed assets		50,000
Current assets		
Stocks	15,000	
Debtors	12,000	
Bank and cash	8,000	
	35,000	
less Current liabilities		
Creditors	22,000	
Net current assets		13,000
		37,000
less Long-term liabilities		13,000
Net assets		24,000
Financed by:		
15m ordinary shares of £1 each		15,000
Reserves		9,000
		24,000

Additional information will be needed for some of the ratios which follow.

Performance (profitability) ratios

These measure the level of profitability of the business. The following comparisons are common:

Gross profit
percentage

This measures the *gross profit* as a percentage of sales revenue.

$$Gross\ profit\ percentage\ = \frac{Gross\ profit}{Sales} \times 100$$

and from the above accounts, the gross profit percentage is:

$$\frac{40,000}{100,000} \times 100 = 40\%$$

If last year's percentage was, say, only 30 per cent, then you could consider whether or not cost of goods sold had increased to diminish the gross profit; or whether selling prices had been reduced in order to retain market share. There are other possibilities, such as an alteration to the sales mix or exceptional wastage of materials.

This percentage is also called the *margin percentage*. It is often used to compare with previous periods and budgets. There is no standard 'good' or 'bad' level of gross profit margin – every type and size of business will have its own acceptable range of percentages. A business with high manufacturing costs but low distribution and administrative costs will have a low gross profit margin in comparison to a business with minimal manufacturing costs but high distribution and administrative costs.

The gross profit margin is used by internal management to aid the control of costs and profitability.

Mark-up percentage

This is very similar to the gross profit percentage, but is gross profit calculated as a percentage of the cost of sales:

$$Mark\text{-}up\ percentage\ = \frac{Gross\ profit}{Cost\ of\ sales} \times 100$$

and from the above accounts, the mark-up percentage is:

$$\frac{40,000}{60,000} \times 100\ =\ 66\tfrac{2}{3}\%$$

Like the margin percentage, it is used to compare with previous periods and budgets, and is used by internal management.

Net profit
percentage

This expresses the net profit as a percentage of sales. It is the figure most often used by companies to compare their profits with those of other companies. It can also be compared to the margin percentage to establish the proportion of gross profit which has been consumed by general running costs:

$$Net\ profit\ percentage\ =\ \frac{Net\ profit\ before\ tax}{Sales} \times 100$$

and from the above accounts, the net profit percentage is:

$$\frac{10,000}{100,000} \times 100\ =\ 10\%$$

The net profit figure is taken before tax, as the amount of tax is not always related to the level of profit, and therefore comparison with other firms and periods would be distorted if the profit after tax figure were to be used.

Return on capital employed

This expresses the net profit as a percentage of the capital invested in the business. It is of interest to shareholders and long-term lenders as it shows the amount of profit being made by their funds. The ratio needs careful definition as there are different opinions as to what constitutes 'capital employed'. One opinion is that it should include only ordinary shareholders' funds (including reserves); another opinion is that it should include all shareholders' funds and long-term loans.

If we include long-term loans as 'capital', then we should use the net profit before charging interest on those loans, as this then gives a figure of profit which is available to provide a return to those providers of capital:

Return on Capital Employed (ROCE) =

$$\frac{\text{Net profit before interest and tax (PBIT)}}{\text{Shareholders' funds + long-term loans}} \times 100$$

and from the above accounts, the ROCE is:

$$\frac{10{,}000 + 1{,}000 \text{ (interest)}}{24{,}000 + 13{,}000} \times 100 = 29.7\%$$

However, if we include only shareholders' funds in the calculation, then the return on capital employed is:

$$\frac{\text{Net profit before tax}}{\text{Net assets}} \times 100$$

and from the above accounts, the return is:

$$\frac{10{,}000}{24{,}000} \times 100 = 41.7\%$$

This latter calculation is sometimes referred to as the *return on net assets*.

It is compared with returns from previous periods, and with other companies, although a high return is not the only measure which investors use – a company with a lower return might be more steady and command higher share prices.

Solvency (liquidity) ratios

These measure the ability of the company to pay its debts as they fall due. As mentioned previously, many profitable businesses have failed because of their inability to control cash and have fallen short of money. A company's liquid funds obviously include cash and bank balances, but it is common to also consider debtors as liquid funds, as it is expected that payment will be received in time to pay the creditors. There are two main ratios which measure solvency.

The current ratio or working capital ratio

This compares current assets with current liabilities:

The current ratio = current assets:current liabilities

(*Note:* the ':' sign in between current assets and current liabilities means 'compared to', i.e. current assets compared to current liabilities)

and from the above accounts, the current ratio = 35,000:22,000 = 1.6:1

The ratio is calculated by dividing the current assets by the current liabilities, so that current liabilities is always brought down to 1. This means that for every £1 which is owed to creditors (and which will need to be paid out shortly), there is £1.60 in current assets which could be made available to pay those debts. A standard ratio is around 2:1, but in recent years it has become increasingly difficult for businesses to maintain this level of comfort, and a ratio of 1.6:1 is common.

Some industries have much lower ratios, particularly those with very fast turnovers and a high proportion of cash transactions, such as supermarkets.

The ratio must be compared to previous periods, as a slowing down of the ratio could warn of a cash shortage. An increase in the ratio is not necessarily welcome either – too high a ratio might indicate that the business has too much money tied up in current assets which are not immediately required and which are not earning profits for the business whilst they are in existence. However, a high ratio does give reassurance to creditors. If the ratio is too low, and creditors are not paid, they have the power to close a business down.

To keep control of the ratio, excess cash should be invested, debtors should be encouraged to pay more promptly, stocks should be sold as quickly as possible and creditors should not be paid earlier than is necessary. New businesses commonly struggle to maintain a safe ratio if they are spending funds to equip themselves with fixed assets.

The acid test (quick) ratio

This ratio removes stock from the current assets figure where the stocks are not likely to be sold very quickly, otherwise a false impression of true liquidity can be given:

The acid test ratio = Current assets less stock:current liabilities

and from the above accounts, the acid test ratio is:

20,000:22,000 = 0.91:1

This means that for every £1 which is owed to creditors, there is only 91p in liquid funds. The standard for this ratio is 1:1, but a slightly lower ratio is not unacceptable. If the ratio falls, it might be of concern to creditors; if it rises, it might indicate an excess of cash or debtors.

Use of assets (efficiency) ratios

There are several types of ratio which come into this category, covering both current assets and fixed assets. Those involving current assets attempt to measure the speed with which current assets are moved through the business in order to improve cash flow. They are sometimes included with the liquidity ratios in the previous section. Those involving fixed assets attempt to measure the efficiency of the business in using its fixed assets to achieve the level of turnover.

The stock turnover ratio

This shows how quickly the business sells its stock – how many times the stock 'turns over' in a year:

$$\textit{Rate of stock turnover} = \frac{\text{Cost of sales}}{\text{Average stock held throughout the year}}$$

and the average stock held $= \dfrac{\text{opening stock + closing stock}}{2}$

Using the accounts above, and assuming that the previous year's stock was £13,000, the rate of stock turnover is:

$$\frac{60,000}{(13,000+15,000)/2} = \frac{60,000}{14,000} = 4.3 \text{ times}$$

This shows that stock turns over 4.3 times during the year, which is relatively slow. Every type of business is different – a heavy engineering firm will have a slow stock turnover, whilst a greengrocer will expect a very fast stock turnover. The ratio should be compared with previous periods, as a deterioration in the rate of stock turnover indicates that stock is not selling as quickly, which could eventually lead to a cash flow problem. Generally speaking, a fast stock turnover is not detrimental, providing it is sold profitably.

The ratio can also be used to calculate the number of days stock on hand at the end of the period:

$$\textit{Number of days' stock on hand} = \frac{365}{\text{Rate of stock turnover}}$$

and from the above accounts, the number of days' stock on hand is:

$$\frac{36}{4.3} = 85 \text{ days}$$

Debtors' turnover ratio (also called debtors' collection period)

This shows how long it is taking to collect debts from customers. As with the stock turnover ratio, the faster cash is collected from debtors, the better the cash flow of the business:

$$\textit{Debtors' collection period} = \frac{\text{Debtors}}{\text{Credit sales}} \times 365$$

and from the above accounts (assuming all sales are on credit), the debtors' collection period is:

$$\frac{12,000}{100,000} \times 365 = 44 \text{ days}$$

Again, every business is different. A supermarket has virtually no debtors, and therefore the number of days is extremely low. It is important to compare the rate with previous periods.

Creditors' turnover ratio (also called creditors' payment period)

This shows how quickly the business pays its creditors:

$$\textit{Creditors' payment period} = \frac{\text{Creditors}}{\text{Credit purchases}} \times 365$$

and from the above accounts (assuming credit purchases of £62,000), the creditors' payment period is:

$$\frac{22,000}{62,000} \times 365 = 129 \text{ days}$$

Again, this should be compared with previous periods. A longer period indicates that the business is taking longer to pay its creditors and hence is holding onto its cash. This might please the bank manager and aid cash flow, but it might antagonize creditors, who may refuse to sell to the business, or close the business down.

It is also important to compare the creditors' payment period with the debtors' payment period – it should take longer to pay creditors than to collect monies from debtors.

Asset turnover

This measures the efficiency of use of different groups of assets to produce turnover. It is commonly calculated using fixed assets, but can be calculated using any other asset group:

$$Fixed\ asset\ turnover = \frac{\text{Turnover}}{\text{Fixed assets}}$$

and from the above accounts, the fixed asset turnover is:

$$\frac{100,000}{50,000} = 2$$

This means that each £1 invested in fixed assets produces £2 in turnover. Businesses with a large investment in fixed assets will experience a lower ratio than those with, say, a high proportion of labour costs.

Capital structure (gearing) ratios

Gearing is a measure of the ratio of capital provided by lenders and fixed-dividend shareholders compared to capital provided by equity shareholders.

$$The\ gearing\ ratio = \frac{\text{Debt and fixed-rate capital}}{\text{Equity capital}} \times 100$$

and from the above accounts, the gearing ratio is:

$$\frac{13,000}{24,000} \times 100 = 54\%$$

This indicates that the fixed-rate lenders and shareholders provide over 50 per cent of the amount provided by the equity shareholders. A ratio of over 50 per cent is regarded as 'high gearing' and a highly-geared company will have to pay out a larger proportion of its profits to these investors before it can pay dividends to the ordinary shareholders. In times when profits are falling, this could turn an otherwise reasonable profit into a loss, which would be avoided if the capital had been raised from the ordinary shareholders. If there is insufficient cash to pay the interest on loans, the business could be forced to sell any assets used as security for the loans, or even be forced to close.

On the other hand, when profits are rising there will be fewer shareholders to share out the surplus.

A highly-geared company might find it difficult to raise additional capital, as new lenders will be concerned about the ability to pay interest and new shareholders will be concerned that there will be insufficient profit remaining to pay dividends or to reinvest in the growth of the business.

Investors' (security) ratios

Investors are those who put their money into a business on a long-term basis. They expect to get something in return for that investment.

Lenders are particularly interested in the ability of the company to pay interest, while shareholders are interested both in the ability to pay dividends periodically and the likely rise in share prices if the company is successful in making profits and has potential growth.

Interest cover

This shows how comfortably the interest to lenders is covered by the profits:

$$Interest\ cover = \frac{Profit\ before\ interest\ and\ tax}{Annual\ interest\ payable}$$

and from the above accounts, interest cover is:

$$\frac{11,000}{1,000} = 11\ times$$

This means that the interest could be paid 11 times over from the profits made by the company. If the rate of coverage is falling, lenders could feel uneasy.

Dividend cover

This is a similar calculation for shareholders. It shows the number of times which the available profits could cover the dividend proposed for the year:

$$Dividend\ cover = \frac{Profit\ before\ tax}{Gross\ dividends\ paid}$$

The dividend figure which appears in the profit and loss account is after the deduction of tax at 20 per cent. To gross up this figure, it needs to be multiplied by 10/8; thus from the accounts above, the gross dividends will be:

$$1,000 \times \frac{10}{8} = £1,250$$

and the dividend cover is then:

$$\frac{10,000}{1,250} = 8\ times$$

Dividends per share

This shows the amount declared as dividends for each share. Again, the dividend is the gross amount, which is £1,250,000 in total (remember, the figures in the above accounts are in thousands of pounds):

$$Dividends\ per\ share = \frac{Gross\ dividend}{Number\ of\ ordinary\ shares}$$

and for the accounts above, the dividend per share is:

$$\frac{1,250,000}{15,000,000} = 8.33p\ per\ share$$

Investors will look for an increase in this dividend from year to year, or will compare it with other companies.

Dividend yield

Shareholders rarely pay the par value for their shares, but some higher or lower figure, and it is that figure which truly represents their investment in the business, and with which they will compare the dividend which they receive. We cannot calculate the yield for every shareholder, as they will all have paid different amounts for their shares, but we can calculate the yield based on the current market price:

$$Dividend\ yield = \frac{Gross\ dividend\ paid\ per\ share}{Market\ price\ per\ ordinary\ share} \times 100$$

and from the accounts above, given a market price of £3 per ordinary share, the dividend yield is:

$$\frac{8.33p}{300p} = 2.8\%$$

The yield can be compared to the yield from other companies, and with previous years' yields.

Earnings per share

This shows the profits available per share with which to pay dividends. That is not to say that the shareholder will receive that sum in dividends, but the amount which is not paid out is retained in the business for the future:

$$Earnings\ per\ share = \frac{Profit\ after\ tax\ and\ preference\ dividends}{Number\ of\ ordinary\ shares\ issued}$$

and from the accounts above, the earnings per share is:

$$\frac{8,000,000}{15,000,000} = 53.33p$$

Price/Earnings (P/E) ratio

This shows the ratio of the market price to the earnings per share. It attempts to measure the number of years which it would take for the earnings to recoup the market price of the share:

$$The\ price\ earnings\ ratio = \frac{Market\ price\ per\ ordinary\ share}{Earnings\ per\ share}$$

and from the accounts above, the price earnings ratio is:

$$\frac{300p}{53.33p} = 5.6$$

This indicates that it would take 5.6 years to recoup the market price of a share. A high ratio also indicates that the shares are in demand, as investors are prepared to pay a high multiple of earnings to acquire them. This could be because of an expectation of high profits in the future or because of a proposed take-over bid.

Questions involving ratios are popular examination questions. You need to be able to calculate them accurately, but also to be able to comment on their purpose and the results which you obtain.

Summary

By the end of this chapter you should be familiar with the reasons for comparison between years, budget periods, or other companies in the same line of business, and you should be able to calculate and interpret a range of ratios.

Exercises

21.1 (a) If sales are £4,000 and gross margin is 30 per cent, calculate the amount of gross profit.
  (b) If cost of sales is £6,000 and mark-up is 40 per cent, calculate gross profit and sales.
  (c) Given that:
    – opening stock is £400
    – closing stock is £600
    – purchases are £5,200, and
    – mark-up is 20 per cent
    calculate gross profit and sales.
  (d) Given that:
    – opening stock is £500
    – closing stock is £800
    – Sales are £6,400, and
    – gross margin is 25 per cent
    calculate gross profit and purchases.
  (e) If cost of sales is £6,000 and gross margin is 40 per cent, calculate sales and gross profit.
  (f) If sales are £4,000 and mark-up is 25 per cent, calculate cost of sales and gross profit.

21.2 J. Burgess has the following final accounts for 19x5 and 19x6:

Trading and profit and loss account

	19x5		19x6	
	£000	£000	£000	£000
Sales		2,800		3,000
less Cost of sales:				
Opening stock	420		300	
Purchases	2,400		2,600	
	2,820		2,900	
less Closing stock	300		350	
		2,520		2,550
Gross profit		280		450
less Expenses		144		350
Net profit		136		100

Balance sheets as at 31 December

	19x5		19x6	
	£000	£000	£000	£000
Fixed assets		1,200		1,300
Current assets				
Stocks	300		350	
Debtors	240		400	
Bank and cash	40		–	
	580		750	
less Current liabilities				
Creditors	280		150	
Overdraft	–		300	
	280		450	
Net current assets		300		300
		1,500		1,600
Financed by:				
Capital at 1 January		1,364		1,500
Net profit		136		100
		1,500		1,600

In addition, you are told that at 1 January 19x5 debtors and creditors amounted to £160,000 and £250,000 respectively.

Calculate suitable ratios to analyse the business and comment on your results.

21.3x P. Goodwin has the following final accounts for 19x5 and 19x6:

Trading and profit and loss account

	19x5		19x6	
	£000	£000	£000	£000
Sales		800		1,200
less Cost of sales:				
Opening stock	320		300	
Purchases	540		650	
	860		950	
less Closing stock	300		200	
		560		750
Gross profit		240		450
less Expenses		144		320
Net profit		96		130

Balance sheets as at 31 December

	19x5		19x6	
	£000	£000	£000	£000
Fixed assets		450		650
Current assets				
Stocks	300		200	
Debtors	80		300	
Bank and cash	150		–	
	530		500	
less Current liabilities				
Creditors	280		180	
Overdraft	–		140	
	280		320	
Net current assets		250		180
		700		830

In addition, you are told that at 1 January 19x5 debtors and creditors amounted to £160,000 and £250,000 respectively.

Calculate suitable ratios to analyse the business and comment on your results.

21.4 The following figures have been extracted from the published accounts of MBC plc, at 31 October 1995:

	£m
Ordinary share capital	30
Share premium	3
Reserves	5
	38
6% debentures	10
	48

The net profit (after tax of £1m) for the year to 31 October 1995 was £4m, and dividends amounted to £0.5m. The company is considering raising a further £10m in the next financial year to finance research and development.

(a) State the formula for, and calculate, the company's gearing ratio.
(b) State the formula for, and calculate, the company's return on capital employed (ROCE).
(c) Discuss the different effects on gearing and ROCE of raising the additional £10m by the issue of shares or by the issue of debentures.
(d) Briefly describe the various kinds of research and development, and explain the accounting concepts which govern the treatment of such expenditure in the accounts.

(CIMA, November 1995)

21.5 The following information relates to Lamp plc:

Profit and loss accounts for the two years to 31 December 1990 and 1991

	1990 £000	1991 £000
Credit sales	175	400
Cost of sales	105	250
	70	150
Expenses	25	50
	45	100
Taxation	15	25
	30	75
Dividends	20	50
Retained profits	10	25

Balance sheets at 31 December 1990 and 1991

	1990 £000	1991 £000
Fixed assets (net book value)	1,035	960
Current assets		
Stocks	40	50
Debtors	90	180
Cash	380	30
	510	260
less Current liabilities:		
Trade creditors	115	50
Taxation	15	25
Proposed dividends	20	25
	150	100
Net current assets	360	160
	1,395	1,120
less Long-term liabilities:		
Loans (15% debenture stock)	500	200
Total net assets	895	920
Capital and reserves:		
Ordinary shares £1 each	600	600
Share premium account	100	100
Retained profits	195	220
	895	920

Additional information:
(i)   The stock at 1 January 1990 was £30,000
(ii) Purchases for the year to 31 December 1990 amounted to £200,000 and for the year to 31 December 1991, £245,000
(iii) The market price of the company's shares at 31 December 1990 was 50p per share and at 31 December 1991, 60p per share.

Required:
Using the above information, calculate, for each of the two years to 31 December 1990 and 1991 respectively, the following ratios commonly used by accountants in interpreting financial accounting information:

(a) TWO liquidity (or solvency) ratios, THREE profitability ratios, and FOUR efficiency (or utilization) ratios
(b) the following investment ratios:
    (i)   gearing
    (ii) dividend cover
    (iii) price/earnings ratio.

(AAT, June 1992)

Aims of the chapter

The aims of this chapter are to:

- describe the ways in which computers can be useful in accounting operations
- explain the difference between hardware and software
- describe the use of different types of software used by accountants
- explain the input, processing and output operations of a basic accounting system
- explain the usefulness of codes in a computerized accounting system
- explain some of the basic controls over the use of computers in accounting.

Computers are now widely used in most business areas, but are particularly useful in the accounting operation, for a variety of purposes. They can be used to:

- maintain ledger accounts
- maintain books of original entry
- produce trading, profit and loss accounts and balance sheets
- maintain stock records
- prepare the payroll and produce cheques or automatic bank transfers, payslips and forms
- maintain the fixed asset register
- produce budgets and forecasts, in particular a cash budget
- calculate ratios
- produce invoices and statements
- produce cheques to pay creditors
- raise purchase orders.

They can also be used to maintain reference files, such as names and addresses of customers, employee details and lists of outstanding sales orders.

Computerized v manual systems

The principles involved in the preparation of ledger accounts in a computerized system are identical to those of a manual system. The system still requires books of original entry and ledger accounts maintained using the double-entry system. The difference is that some or all of these records might be maintained on the computer rather than on handwritten records or by mechanical means.

Hardware and software

Computer *hardware* is the machinery used to run the computer system. It includes the computer itself, its memory and processor, the keyboard and screen, and peripheral equipment such as printers, scanners, external disks and cassettes.

The *software* is the package of instructions which the computer uses to carry out its tasks. These instructions are written by programmers, and can be written specially for the business or bought 'off the shelf' from software suppliers.

The instructions which cause the computer to work are known as the *operating system*, and this is also a piece of software. It is particularly useful in the accounting system to prevent unauthorized personnel from obtaining access to sensitive or confidential data or files, perhaps by means of a 'password' system.

Types of software of use to accountants

The two main types of software used by accountants are:

● general-purpose packages and
● application packages.

General-purpose packages include word-processors, spreadsheets, databases and graphics software, which can be used for a variety of purposes as determined by the user. *Application packages* are designed for a particular accounting purpose and will not perform other tasks.

Accounting packages

These might be acquired as individual modules to perform particular tasks. For example, a sales ledger module will maintain the sales ledger, but no other ledger.

An accounting 'suite' will consist of several modules to cover the whole accounting system, including perhaps the production of invoices, payroll, fixed asset register and maybe costing systems.

Some packages are available as *integrated packages,* which means that they contain a number of modules for different areas of the accounting system, which interlink with one another. The particular advantage which integrated packages have is that a transaction need only be input once and the system automatically updates the relevant ledgers and accounting records. For example, inputting details of the sale of goods to a customer might initiate the following actions:

● the production of an invoice
● the updating of the sales ledger
● the updating of the nominal ledger sales account and VAT account
● the updating of the stock file to remove the item from stock
● the raising of a purchase order to replace the stock
● the updating of relevant control accounts
● the production of reports on monthly sales by region or agent.

Accounting modules: the sales ledger

As stated above, an accounting module performs a particular accounting task. The sales ledger is a comprehensive accounting module, so we will use that to illustrate the mode of operation and features of an accounting module.

Files The sales ledger will probably consist of a *master file* of ledger accounts with all the transactions which have occurred, together with a calculated balance. In addition, there will be a *reference file* of debtors' names, addresses, telephone numbers, contact names and so on. Whenever data is input to the system, another file called a *transaction file* might be used to gather together all the transactions to be input, such as invoices, change of address reports or cheques received. The transaction file is used to update the reference or master file, depending on the type of transaction.

Records The sales ledger master file will contain a *record* for each debtor. So will the sales ledger reference file.

Fields Each record will consist of a number of *fields of data*. For example, the sales ledger reference file might contain fields for the customer's name, address, telephone number and so on.

Inputs and outputs

The files will be updated by data input to the system and they will produce various outputs.

Inputs will include invoices, credit notes, cash and cheques received, discounts, bad debts written off and other transactions.

Outputs might include some or all of the following:

- monthly statements
- aged debt reports
- analyses of sales by region
- totals for the sales ledger control account
- reconciliations with the control account
- debtors' reminder letters
- day book listings
- ad hoc reports on individual debtors or groups of debtors.

Output need not be printed. It can be output on screen, or be passed to another module on disk, cassette or automatically.

Batch v real-time systems

Transactions can be input in batches or groups of like items. The advantages are that greater speed of input is obtained when like items are input together, and there is a facility to total up the transactions included in the batch, to be checked by the computer after entry. These are known as *batch totals* and might include totals of invoices, account numbers, or values. They are an important part of the system of keeping control over the use of computers in accounting.

Segregation of duties

In any accounting system, it is safer if different people are responsible for different areas of the system. This applies even more in a computerized system where it is relatively easy for mistakes to go unnoticed or be untraceable. For example, the person who maintains the purchase ledger should not be involved in the issue of cheques, otherwise they could issue cheques to fictitious suppliers (i.e. themselves). In addition, there should be proper authorization for the setting up of suppliers' accounts to avoid such a situation arising. Transactions which are input singly and update the files immediately are processed in *real time*.

Other security precautions

A computer system should only allow access to those who are authorized to use it. Passwords are a simple way of ensuring this, by allowing only certain passwords to have access to parts of the system.

Keeping computers locked up safely when not in use is also important. It is vital that no equipment, including disks, is taken off the premises without authorization and that files of data are not left in a position where they can be viewed by unauthorized persons.

Full use of control accounts and reconciliations should be made, to check on the accuracy of the system.

From an auditing point of view, it should be possible to trace every transaction through the system, and therefore adequate records of input, processing and output should be maintained.

Accounting codes

In any large system, and particularly in computerized systems, it is difficult to locate the large number of accounts unless there is a system of coding each account. There are many different coding systems and structures, but the basic principle is that the various accounts are grouped together and the codes are related to each group.

The coding system might start by allocating a code to each major category of asset, liability, capital, revenue and expense as appears in the final accounts. An extract from such a system might be as follows:

Code 01 Sales revenue
Code 02 Cost of sales
Code 03 Selling expenses
Code 04 Distribution expenses
Code 05 Administration expenses
Code 06 Research and development expenses
Code 07 Other revenues
Code 08 Other expenses
Code 09 Fixed assets
Code 10 Stocks
Code 11 Debtors
and so on.

Within each major category code there will be subsidiary codes. Debtors might be further broken down into sales region, for example:

Code 114 Debtors in Scotland
Code 115 Debtors in London
Code 116 Debtors in the Midlands

and within each sales region there might be sales representatives, so the code is extended. For example, Scottish debtors might be covered by twenty sales representatives, so the codes would become:

11401
11402
11403, etc.

Then the individual debtors will be identified by a unique code which is added to the end of the above code. Assuming there are no more than 999 Scottish debtors, the code for debtor number 456 covered by sales representative number 15 would be 11415456, broken down as follows:

11	4	15	456
Debtors	Region	Representative	Debtor

In this way, each debtor is given a unique code.

Features of a good code

A good code should offer the following basic features:

- It should be unique to the item concerned.
- It should be expandable for new items to be inserted.
- It should be meaningful if possible – i.e. logical in its sequence, or including letters which give a clue to the item, e.g. SC12 might refer to Scotland, representative number 12.

- It should be as concise as possible.
- It should be sufficiently different from other codes to avoid confusion.
- It should contain a self-checking facility to ensure that the code is valid. The use of 'check digits' assists here, whereby an additional digit is added to the code which is meaningless but is calculated by applying some formula to the other digits in the code. If the code is input incorrectly, the check digit will identify the error because the formula applied will fail to agree with the check digit.

Spreadsheets

The *spreadsheet* is probably the most useful general purpose package to the accountant. It is designed to manipulate figures, and is ideal for many accounting purposes. It consists of rows and columns in a matrix format.

Where each row and column intersect, a *cell* is created. A cell can contain any of the following:

- numerical data
- text
- formulae
- instructions
- the results of calculations performed on other cells.

Cells can be moved around, copied to other locations, cut out, revised, added to other cells and so on.

The spreadsheet can be used to create accounting reports such as trading and profit and loss accounts, balance sheets and cash budgets. It can also be used for 'what if?' analyses where a number of different alternatives produce different results. For example, a spreadsheet might be designed to calculate the profit from a particular product, given a certain quantity and selling price. The spreadsheet can easily calculate the profit for a range of quantities and selling prices to enable the accountant to compare the possibilities and make a decision.

An example of a spreadsheet used to prepare a cash budget is as follows:

	A	B	C	D	E
		January	*February*	*March*	*Total*
1		£	£	£	£
2	**Receipts:**				
3	Sales income	10,000	10,000	12,000	32,000
4	Rent received	50	100	50	200
5	**Total receipts**	10,050	10,100	12,050	32,200
6					
7	**Payments:**				
8	Purchases	6,000	5,000	5,000	16,000
9	Rent and rates	500	500	500	1,500
10	Wages	1,000	1,000	1,000	3,000
11	Fixed assets	5,000	2,000		7,000
12	**Total payments**	12,500	8,500	6,500	27,500
13					
14	**Opening balance**	2,000	−450	1,150	2,000
15	**Add receipts**	10,050	10,100	12,050	32,200
16	**Less payments**	12,500	8,500	6,500	27,500
17	**Closing balance**	−450	1,150	6,700	6,700

The individual receipts and payments, e.g. sales income, wages, might be input from manual records or transferred from other spreadsheets or accounting systems. The total of receipts and payments, and the bottom section which calculates the closing balance, will all be based on formulas of some kind. Some examples are as follows:

Total receipts for January (cell B5) is found by the formula (=B3+B4). This total is then taken to cell B15 (Add Receipts), by inserting the formula (=B5).

Closing balance at the end of January (cell B17) is found by inserting the formula (=B14+B15−B16), and this is then taken to cell C14 to commence February.

Databases

A *database* is a file of data organized in such a way that a number of different applications can use it with the same degree of efficiency. It can be likened to a telephone directory which can only be accessed if the name of the person is known, and preferably the address as well. From these two pieces of data, the telephone number can be obtained. But if all you have is the address, you cannot find the number or the name. So a telephone directory is a file, not a database. In order for it to be a database, it must be capable of accessing all the data held there whether the enquirer knows the name, the address or the telephone number.

Advantages and disadvantages of computer systems

There are many advantages of computer systems. Some of these are as follows:

- The computer works many times faster than the human brain.
- The computer is very accurate – it does not make mistakes if programmed correctly. If non-human methods of input are used, such as barcodes, then even fewer errors occur.
- The computer can process large volumes of data.
- Large volumes of data can be stored on a single disk which could equate to several drawers in a filing cabinet.
- Production of reports and analyses can be automatic.

There are also disadvantages, as follows:

- Computer hardware and software is expensive.
- Computer files may be open to access from unauthorized personnel.
- The inability to 'see into' the computer can lead to lack of audit trail – i.e. it is not possible to see what has happened to a transaction without additional investigation.
- Staff may be reluctant to use the computer.

Characteristics of good information

Whatever the computer system does, the information it produces must be 'good'. In order to fulfil this role, the following characteristics should exist. Information should be:

- *Accurate*. Inaccurate information may lead to incorrect decision-making.
- *Timely*. Information should be provided at the right time. If it is required for a meeting, then it is no use if the information is not provided until after the meeting is over.
- *To the right level of precision*. A sales report for the previous year can be rounded to the nearest thousand pounds, but the calculation of VAT must be to the nearest penny.
- *Concise*. A report on wages costs should be summarized, rather than listing individual employees' wages.

- *Economical to produce.* It should not cost more to produce than the value which is obtained from it.
- *Communicated to the right person and in the right manner.* A telephone conversation in an open room to discuss a member of staff's salary is the wrong manner of communication.

Summary

By the end of this chapter you should appreciate how computers can assist in the production of financial information. You should understand the differences between hardware and software, and the types of general and application software which can be used. You should be able to explain the basic operations of a computerized accounting system, together with the controls necessary to ensure accuracy and security of the information processed.

Exercises

22.1 XW Limited is a medium-sized company which is considering improvements to its methods of recording accounting transactions; one of the improvements will be the implementation of a coding system for stock records.

(a) Explain the purpose of financial accounting records.
(b) Briefly describe FIVE characteristics of a good coding system.
(c) Explain THREE accounting concepts which govern the valuation of stock.

(CIMA, November 1995)

22.2x Your company maintains a computerized purchase ledger system, which automatically produces cheques at the end of the month. Invoices and credit notes arrive in the post, and are passed immediately to the purchase ledger clerk who inputs them to the computer. The system displays a warning message if an invoice is input for which there is no supplier record already on file, and the clerk sets one up and re-enters the invoice.

On several occasions, the system has produced cheques for suppliers who were not entitled to payment, or the amount of the payment was incorrect.

(a) Identify six areas of the system in which errors or fraud could occur.
(b) For each area, describe controls which could be used to prevent their occurrence.

22.3 Microcomputers are being used by many organizations of varying sizes either to prepare their accounts or to assist the managers of an organization to control its activities.

(a) Describe how a microcomputer accounting package may be used to deal with accounting transactions.
(b) What are the advantages of using such accounting packages instead of a manual system?

(CIMA, November 1990)

Appendix

Consolidated profit and loss account for the year ended 1 July 1995 – Regent Inns plc

	Note	Year ended 1 July 1995 £'000	Year ended 2 July 1994 (Restated) £'000
Turnover			
Continuing operations		18,335	12,825
Acquisitions		3,132	–
Discontinued operations		535	2,468
	2	22.002	15,293
Cost of sales	3	(6,856)	(4,821)
Gross profit		15,146	10,472
Branch and head office administrative expenses	3	(10,318)	(7,931)
Other operating income	3	239	27
Operating profit			
Continuing operations		4,231	2,071
Acquisitions		708	–
Discontinued operations		128	497
		5,067	2,568
Loss on sale of fixed assets in continuing operations		(3)	(2)
Profit on sale of fixed assets in discontinued operations	29	45	12
		5,109	2,578
Interest receivable		21	23
Interest payable	4	(697)	(288)
Profit on ordinary activities before taxation	5	4,433	2,313
Tax on profit on ordinary activities	8	(636)	(249)
Profit on ordinary activities after taxation		3,797	2,064
Dividends – equity	10	(1,080)	(795)
Retained profit for the year	20	2,717	1,269
Earnings per ordinary share	11	25.6 pence	14.0 pence

Consolidated balance sheet at 1 July 1995 – Regent Inns plc

	Note	Year ended 1 July 1995 £'000	Year ended 2 July 1994 (Restated) £'000
Fixed assets			
Tangible assets	12	34,856	26,753
Investments	13	707	272
		35,563	27,025
Current assets			
Stocks	14	418	313
Debtors	15	4,952	1,758
Cash at bank and in hand		1,244	381
		6,614	2,452
Creditors: Amounts falling due within one year	16	(7,584)	(5,669)
Net current liabilities		(970)	(3,217)
Total assets less current liabilities		34,593	23,808
Creditors: Amounts falling due after more than one year	17	(8,471)	(5,711)
Provision for liabilities and charges			
Deferred taxation	18	–	(7)
		26,122	18,090
Capital and reserves			
Called up share capital	19	3,924	3,685
Share premium account	20	12,384	9,147
Revaluation reserve	20	4,300	2,245
Profit and loss account	20	5,514	3,013
Equity shareholders' funds		26,122	18,090

Solutions to exercises

Chapter 2 2.1

Profit and loss account

	£	
Sales		400
less Cost of stock sold		180
Gross profit		220
less Expenses:		
Heat and light	50	
Wages	30	
		80
Net profit		140

Balance sheet

Assets	£	Capital	£	£
Premises	700	Capital at the start	830	
Equipment	100	Profit for the period	140	
Stocks	20			970
Debtors	60	*Liabilities*		
Cash	250	Loans	120	
		Creditors	40	
				160
	1,130			1,130

2.2

Assets – office machinery, debtors, bank, premises, stock remaining
Liabilities – creditors, loans
Revenues – rent receivable, bank interest receivable
Expenses – electricity, gas, rent and rates payable, wages and salaries, cost of stock sold

2.3

	Type of account	*Side of ledger*
Increase in cash	Asset	Debit
Decrease in creditor	Liability	Debit
Increase in electricity	Expense	Debit
Increase in bank balance	Asset	Debit
Decrease in debtors	Asset	Credit
Increase in sales	Revenue	Credit
Increase in capital	Capital	Credit
Decrease in electricity	Expense	Credit
Increase in purchases	Expense	Debit
Increase in rent payable	Expense	Debit
Decrease in rent receivable	Revenue	Debit
Increase in machinery	Asset	Debit
Decrease in bank balance	Asset	Credit
Increase in bank loan	Liability	Credit

2.4

Date	Titles of accounts	Types of accounts	Increase/ decrease	Debit/ credit
1 Jan	Cash	Asset	Increase	Debit
	Capital	Capital	Increase	Credit
2 Jan	P. Smith	Liability	Increase	Credit
	Cash	Asset	Increase	Debit
3 Jan	Telephone	Expense	Increase	Debit
	Cash	Asset	Decrease	Credit
4 Jan	Cash	Asset	Decrease	Credit
	P. Smith	Liability	Decrease	Debit
5 Jan	Equipment	Asset	Increase	Debit
	Cash	Asset	Decrease	Credit
6 Jan	Purchases	Expense	Increase	Debit
	Cash	Asset	Decrease	Credit.
7 Jan	Equipment	Asset	Increase	Debit
	L. Peters	Liability	Increase	Credit
8 Jan	Sales	Revenue	Increase	Credit
	L. Samson	Asset	Increase	Debit
9 Jan	Rent receivable	Revenue	Increase	Credit
	Cash	Asset	Increase	Debit
10 Jan	L. Peters	Liability	Decrease	Debit
	Cash	Asset	Decrease	Credit

Capital

			1 Jan	Cash	1,000

Cash

1 Jan	Capital	1,000	3 Jan	Telephone	100
2 Jan	P. Smith	500	4 Jan	P. Smith	100
9 Jan	Rent receivable	10	5 Jan	Equipment	400
			6 Jan	Purchases	150
			10 Jan	L. Peters	50

P. Smith

4 Jan	Cash	100	2 Jan	Cash	500

Telephone

3 Jan	Cash	100		

Equipment

5 Jan	Cash	400		
7 Jan	L Peters	200		

Purchases

6 Jan	Cash	150		

L. Peters

10 Jan	Cash	50	7 Jan	Equipment	400

Sales

			8 Jan	L. Samson	270

L. Samson

8 Jan	Sales	270		

Rent Receivable

			9 Jan	Cash	10

2.7

Capital

			1 Jan	Bank	2,500
				Cash	500

Bank

1 Jan	Capital	2,500	12 Jan	Equipment	3,000
30 Jan	Cash	200	20 Jan	Purchases	350
			28 Jan	J. Martin	250

Cash

1 Jan	Capital	500	30 Jan	Bank	200
23 Jan	Equipment	100			

Purchases

2 Jan	Martin	700			
20 Jan	Bank	350			

J. Martin

17 Jan	Purchase returns	150	2 Jan	Purchases	700
28 Jan	Bank	250			

Sales

			3 Jan	G. Goddard	300
			7 Jan	K. Lemon	1,100

G. Goddard

3 Jan	Sales	300	29 Jan	Bad debts written off	150

K .Lemon

7 Jan	Sales	1,100	18 Jan	Sales returns	240

Equipment

12 Jan	Bank	3,000	23 Jan	Cash	100

Purchase returns

			17 Jan	J. Martin	150

Sales returns

18 Jan	K. Lemon	240			

Bad debts written off

29 Jan	G. Goddard	150			

2.8

Capital

			1 Jan	Bank	5,000
				Cash	500

Bank

1 Jan	Capital	5,000	3 Jan	Fixtures and fittings	2,000
26 Jan	Interest receivable	10	17 Jan	D. Hill	1,500
			28 Jan	Cash	100

Cash

1 Jan	Capital	500	10 Jan	Drawings	30
28 Jan	Bank	100	11 Jan	Carriage inwards	20
29 Jan	L. Harwood	300	12 Jan	Carriage outwards	50
			23 Jan	Rent and rates	60
			24 Jan	Gas	40

Fixtures and fittings

3 Jan	Bank	2,000	

Purchases

4 Jan	D. Hill	3,000	
1 Jan	D. Hill	1,200	

D. Hill

6 Jan	Purchase returns	800	4 Jan	Purchases	3,000
17 Jan	Bank	1,500	11 Jan	Purchases	1,200

Purchase returns

		6 Jan	D. Hill	800

Sales

		9 Jan	A. Clark	1,700
		14 Jan	H. Fielding	80
		23 Jan	A. Clark	1,900

A. Clark

9 Jan	Sales	1,700	19 Jan	Sales returns	200
23 Jan	Sales	1,900			

Drawings

10 Jan	Cash	30	

Carriage inwards

11 Jan	Cash	20	

Carriage outwards

12 Jan	Cash	50	

H. Fielding

14 Jan	Sales	80	24 Jan	Bad debts written off	80

Sales returns

19 Jan	A. Clark	200	

Rent and rates

23 Jan	Cash	60	

Gas

23 Jan	Cash	40	

Bad debts written off

24 Jan	H. Fielding	80	

Bank interest receivable

	26 Jan Bank	10

L. Harwood

	29 Jan Cash	300

2.10

Capital

	1 May Bank	5,000

Bank

1 May Capital	5,000	5 May Electricity	50
29 May Interest receivable	15	7 May Carriage inwards	25
		27 May Carriage outwards	35

Machinery

3 May J. Lomas	1,400	18 May Cash	300
		23 May J. Lomas	200

J. Lomas

23 May Machinery	200	3 May Machinery	1,400

Electricity

5 May Bank	50	

Purchases

7 May R. Fisher	800	

R. Fisher

10 May Purchase Returns	40	7 May Purchases	800

Carriage inwards

7 May Bank	25	

Sales

		9 May Cash	70
		14 May E. Wishbone	450
		25 May N. Capstick	85

Cash

9 May Sales	70	12 May Office wages	25
18 May Machinery	300		
21 May Commission receivable	170		

Purchase returns

		10 May R. Fisher	40

Office wages

12 May Cash	25	

E. Wishbone

14 May Sales	450	24 May Sales returns	80

Commission receivable

		21 May Cash	170

	Sales returns		
24 May E. Wishbone	80		

	N. Capstick		
25 May Sales	85		

	Carriage outwards		
27 May Bank	35		

	Interest receivable		
		29 May Bank	15

Chapter 3 3.1

P. Roberts – Trial balance at 31 January 19x6 (from Exercise 2.7)

	DR	CR
	£	£
Capital		3,000
Bank		900
Cash	400	
Purchases	1,050	
Creditors		300
Sales		1,400
Debtors	1,010	
Equipment	2,900	
Purchase returns		150
Sales returns	240	
Bad debts written off	150	
	5,750	5,750

3.2

R. Moss – Trial balance at 31 January 19x6 (from Exercise 2.8)

	DR	CR
	£	£
Capital		5,500
Bank	1,410	
Cash	700	
Fixtures and fittings	2,000	
Purchases	4,200	
Creditors		2,200
Purchase returns		800
Sales		3,680
Debtors	3,400	
Drawings	30	
Carriage inwards	20	
Carriage outwards	50	
Sales returns	200	
Rent and rates	60	
Gas	40	
Bad debts written off	80	
Bank interest receivable		10
	12,190	12,190

3.4

T. Wood – Trial balance at 31 May 19x6 (from Exercise 2.10)

	DR £	CR £
Capital		5,000
Bank	4,905	
Machinery	900	
Creditors		1,960
Electricity	50	
Purchases	800	
Carriage inwards	25	
Sales		605
Cash	515	
Purchase returns		40
Office Wages	25	
Debtors	455	
Commission receivable		170
Sales returns	80	
Carriage outwards	35	
Interest receivable		15
	7,790	7,790

3.6

P. Roberts – trading and profit and loss account for the month ending 31 January 19x6 (from Exercise 2.7)

	£	£
Sales	1,400	
less Sales returns		240
Net sales		1,160
less Cost of goods sold:		
Purchases	1,050	
less Purchase returns	150	
Net purchases	900	
less Closing stock	200	
		700
Gross profit		460
less Expenses:		
Bad debts written off		150
Net profit		310

3.7

R. Moss – trading and profit and loss account for the month ending 31 January 19x6 (from Exercise 2.8)

	£	£
Sales		3,680
less Sales returns		200
Net sales		3,480
less Cost of goods sold:		
Purchases	4,200	
Carriage inwards	20	
	4,220	
less Purchase returns	800	
Net purchases	3,420	
less Closing stock	660	
		2,760
Gross profit		720
add Other revenues:		
Bank interest receivable		10
		730
less Expenses:		
Carriage outwards	50	
Rent and rates	60	
Gas	40	
Bad debts written off	80	
		230
Net profit		500

3.7

T. Wood – trading and profit and loss account for the month ending 31 May 19x6 (from Exercise 2.10)

	£	£
Sales		605
less Sales returns		80
Net sales		525
less Cost of goods sold:		
Purchases	800	
Carriage inwards	25	
	825	
less Purchase returns	40	
Net purchases	785	
less Closing stock	460	
		325
Gross profit		200
add Other revenues:		
Commission receivable	170	
Bank interest receivable	15	
		185
		385
less Expenses:		
Wages	25	
Carriage outwards	35	
Electricity	50	
		110
Net profit		275

3.11   (From Exercise 2.7). Entries required are:

Dr Sales £1,400; Cr Sales returns £240; Cr Purchases £1,050;
Dr Purchase returns £150; Dr Stock £200; Credit Bad debts written off £150;
Debit Capital £310 (Net profit)

3.12   (From Exercise 2.8). Entries required are:

Dr Sales £3,680; Cr Sales returns £200; Cr Purchases £4,200;
Cr. Carriage inwards £20; Dr Purchase returns £800; Dr Stock £660;
Dr Bank interest receivable £10; Cr Carriage outwards £50; Cr Rent and rates £60;
Cr Gas £40; Cr Bad debts written off £80; Cr Capital £500 (Net profit);
Cr Drawings £30; Dr Capital £30

3.14   (From Exercise 2.10). Entries required are:

Dr Sales £605; Cr Sales returns £80; Cr Purchases £800; Cr Carriage inwards £25;
Dr Purchase returns £40; Dr Stock £460; Dr Commission receivable £170;
Dr Bank interest receivable £15; Cr Wages £25; Cr Carriage outwards £35;
Cr Electricity £50; Cr Capital £275 (Net profit)

3.16   (From exercise 2.7)

P. Roberts – balance sheet at 31 January 19x6

	£	£	£
Fixed assets			
Equipment			2,900
Current assets			
Stocks	200		
Debtors	1,010		
Cash	400		
		1,610	
less Current liabilities			
Creditors	300		
Bank overdraft	900		
		1,200	
Net current assets			410
			3,310
Financed by:			
Opening capital		3,000	
add Net profit		310	
			3,310

3.17

(From exercise 2.8)

R. Moss – balance sheet at 31 January 19x6

	£	£	£
Fixed assets			
Fixtures and fittings			2,000
Current assets			
Stocks	660		
Debtors	3,400		
Bank	1,410		
Cash	700		
		6,170	
less Current liabilities			
Creditors	2,200		
		2,200	
Net current assets			3,970
			5,970
Financed by:			
Opening capital		5,500	
add Net profit		500	
		6,000	
less Drawings		30	
			5,970

3.19

(From Exercise 2.10)

T. Wood – Balance Sheet at 31 May 19x6

	£	£	£
Fixed assets			
Machinery			900
Current assets			
Stocks	460		
Debtors	455		
Bank	4,905		
Cash	515		
		6,335	
less Current liabilities			
Creditors	1,960		
		1,960	
Net current assets			4,375
			5,275
Financed by:			
Opening capital		5,000	
Add net profit		275	
			5,275

3.21

Capital – purchase of plant; delivery costs of plant purchased; income from the sale of plant; insurance claim for stolen motor vehicle
Revenue – repairs to plant; income from the sale of stocks; income from the sale of stationery; expenditure on stationery; insurance claim for stock destroyed by fire; commission receivable

Chapter 4 4.1   (From Exercise 2.7)

Capital

			1 Jan	Bank		2,500
						500
31 Jan	Balance c/d	3,310	31 Jan	Net profit		310
		3,310				3,310
			1 Feb	Balance b/d		3,310

Bank

1 Jan	Capital	2,500	12 Jan	Equipment	3,000
30 Jan	Cash	200	20 Jan	Purchases	350
31 Jan	Balance c/d	900	28 Jan	J. Martin	250
		3,600			3,600
			1 Feb	Balance b/d	900

Cash

1 Jan	Capital	500	30 Jan	Bank	200
23 Jan	Equipment	100	31 Jan	Balance c/d	400
		600			600
1 Feb	Balance c/d	400			

J. Martin

17 Jan	Purchase returns	150	2 Jan	Purchases	700
28 Jan	Bank	250			
31 Jan	Balance c/d	300			
		700			700
			Feb 1	Balance b/d	300

G. Goddard

3 Jan	Sales	300	29 Jan	Bad debts written off	150
			31 Jan	Balance c/d	150
		300			300
1 Feb	Balance b/d	150			

K. Lemon

7 Jan	Sales	1,100	18 Jan	Sales returns	240
			31 Jan	Balance c/d	860
		1,100			1,100
1 Feb	Balance b/d	860			

4.2

Capital

31 Jan	Drawings	30	1 Jan	Bank	5,000
				Cash	500
	Balance c/d	5,970	31 Jan	Net profit	500
		6,000			6,000
			1 Feb	Balance b/d	5,970

Bank

1 Jan	Capital	5,000	3 Jan	Fixtures and fittings	2,000
26 Jan	Interest receivable	10	17 Jan	D. Hill	1,500
			28 Jan	Cash	100
			31 Jan	Balance c/d	1,410
		5,010			5,010
1 Feb	Balance b/d	1,410			

Cash

1 Jan	Capital	500	10 Jan	Drawings	30
28 Jan	Bank	100	11 Jan	Carriage inwards	20
29 Jan	L. Harwood	300	12 Jan	Carriage outwards	50
			23 Jan	Rent and rates	60
			24 Jan	Gas	40
			31 Jan	Balance c/d	700
		900			900
1 Feb	Balance b/d	700			

Fixtures and Fittings

3 Jan	Bank	2,000	31 Jan	Balance c/d	2,000
1 Feb	Balance b/d	2,000			

D. Hill

6 Jan	Purchase returns	800	4 Jan	Purchases	3,000
17 Jan	Bank	1,500	11 Jan	Purchases	1,200
31 Jan	Balance c/d	1,900			
		4,200			4,200
			1 Feb	Balance b/d	1,900

A. Clark

9 Jan	Sales	1,700	19 Jan	Sales returns	200
2 Jan	Sales	1,900	31 Jan	Balance c/d	3,400
		3,600			3,600
Feb 1	Balance b/d	3,400			

H. Fielding

14 Jan	Sales	80	24 Jan	Bad debts written off	80

L. Harwood

31 Jan	Balance c/d	300	29 Jan	Cash	300
			1 Feb	Balance b/d	300

4.4

Capital

			1 May	Bank	5,000
31 May	Balance c/d	5,275	31 May	Net profit	275
		5,275			5,275
			1 Jun	Balance b/d	5,275

Bank

1 May	Capital	5,000	5 May	Electricity	50
29 May	Interest Receivable	15	7 May	Carriage inwards	25
			27 May	Carriage outwards	35
			31 May	Balance c/d	4,905
		5,015			5,015
1 Jun	Balance b/d	4,905			

Machinery

3 May	J. Lomas	1,400	18 May	Cash	300
			23 May	J. Lomas	200
			31 May	Balance c/d	900
		1,400			1,400
1 Jun	Balance b/d	900			

J. Lomas

23 May	Machinery	200	3 May	Machinery	1,400
31 May	Balance c/d	1,200			
		1,400			1,400
			1 Jun	Balance b/d	1,200

R. Fisher

10 May	Purchase returns	40	7 May	Purchases	800
31 May	Balance c/d	760			
		800			800

Cash

9 May	Sales	70	12 May	Office wages	25
18 May	Machinery	300			
21 May	Commission Receivable	170	31 May	Balance c/d	515
		540			540
1 Jun	Balance c/d	515			

E. Wishbone

14 May	Sales	450	24 May	Sales returns	80
			31 May	Balance c/d	370
		450			450
1 Jun	Balance b/d	370			

N. Capstick

25 May	Sales	85	31 May	Balance c/d	85
1 Jun	Balance b/d	85			

4.6

Rent payable

19x5			*19x5*		
1 Jan	Balance b/fwd	150	31 Dec	Profit and loss account	650
28 Feb	Bank	150		Prepaid c/d	100
31 May	Bank	150			
31 Aug	Bank	150			
30 Nov	Bank	150			
		750			750
19x6					
1 Jan	Prepaid b/d	100			

Electricity

19x5			*19x5*		
5 Feb	Bank	100	1 Jan	Balance b/fwd	80
10 May	Bank	130			
8 Aug	Bank	150			
7 Nov	Bank	110			
31 Dec	Accrued c/d	90	31 Dec	Profit and loss account	500
		580			580
			19x6		
			1 Jan	Accrued b/d	90

Stationery

19x5			19x5		
1 Jan	Balance b/fwd	50	31 Dec	Profit and loss account	270
31 Jul	Cash	300		Balance c/d	80
		350			350
19x6					
1 Jan	Balance b/d	80			

Interest receivable

19x5			19x5		
1 Jan	Balance b/fwd	30	2 Jan	Bank	25
			3 Jul	Bank	60
31 Dec	Profit and loss account	85	31 Dec	Accrued c/d	30
		115			115
19x6					
1 Jan	Accrued b/d	30			

Balance sheet (extracts) Current assets, Prepayments – Rent payable   £100
                                                  – Stationery stock   £ 80
                                                  – Interest receivable £ 30
                         Current Liabilities, Accruals – Electricity   £ 90

Meaning of the balances at 31 December 19x5:
Rent payable – £100 has been paid in 19x5 in respect of 19x6
Electricity – £90 is owing for electricity consumed in 19x5 but not paid for until 19x6
Stationery – there is an unused stock of stationery of £80
Interest receivable – £30 is owing for interest earned during 19x5, not received until 19x6

4.8

Rent Payable

19x5			19x5		
8 Feb	Bank	3,600	31 Dec	Profit and loss account	2,400
				Prepaid c/d	1,200
		3,600			3,600
19x6			19x6		
1 Jan	Prepaid b/d	1,200			
3 Jul	Bank	2,400	31 Dec	Profit and loss account	2,640
8 Nov	Bank	480		Prepaid c/d	1,440
		4,080			4,080
19x7					
1 Jan	Prepaid b/d	1,440			

4.9

Debit side:
1 Jan Balance – there is a stock of oil worth £100 at the start of the year
5 Jan – £80 was paid for oil
6 Jul – £300 was paid for oil
10 Nov – £450 was paid for oil
31 Dec Balance accrued – £120 is owing for oil bought during 19x5 not yet paid for
Credit side:
1 Jan Balance – £80 is owing for oil bought during 19x4, not paid for until 19x5
31 Dec Profit and loss a/c – £880 is the value of oil consumed during the year to

be transferred to the profit and loss account for 19x5
31 Dec Balance c/d – there is a stock of oil worth £90 at the end of the year

Chapter 5 5.1

(a) Machine A depreciation p.a. = £1,200 – £200 = £50 per annum, straight-line
20 years

Machine B	Cost 1 July 19x7	£2,000
	Depreciation 19x7	200
	Net book value	1,800
	Depreciation 19x8	180
	Net book value	1,620
	Depreciation 19x9	162
	Net book value	1,458

Machinery at cost

19x6				19x6			
1 Jul	Cash		1,200	31 Dec	Balance c/d		1,200
19x7				19x7			
1 Jan	Balance b/d		1,200				
1 Jul	Cash		2,000	31 Dec	Balance c/d		3,200
			3,200				3,200
19x8				19x8			
1 Jan	Balance b/d		3,200	31 Dec	Balance c/d		3,200
19x9				19x9			
1 Jan	Balance b/d		3,200	31 Dec	Balance c/d		3,200

Machinery – provision for depreciation

19x6				19x6			
31 Dec	Balance c/d		50	31 Dec	Profit and loss account		50
19x7				19x7			
				1 Jan	Balance b/d		50
31 Dec	Balance c/d		300	31 Dec	Profit and loss account		250
			300				300
19x8				19x8			
				1 Jan	Balance b/d		300
31 Dec	Balance c/d		530	31 Dec	Profit and loss account		230
			530				530
19x9				19x9			
				1 Jan	Balance b/d		530
31 Dec	balance c/d		742	31 Dec	Profit and loss account		212
			742				742

(b)   Balance Sheet (extracts)

	19x6	19x7	19x8	19x9
Machinery – cost	1,200	3,200	3,200	3,200
– depreciation	50	300	530	742
– net book value	1,150	2,900	2,670	2,458

5.3

Furniture at cost

19x5			19x5		
1 Oct	Cash	4,000	31 Dec	Balance c/d	4,000
19x6			19x6		
1 Jan	Balance b/d	4,000	31 Dec	Balance c/d	4,000
19x7			19x7		
1 Jan	Balance b/d	4,000	31 Dec	Balance c/d	4,000
19x8			19x8		
1 Jan	Balance b/d	4,000	31 Dec	Balance c/d	4,000
19x9			19x9		
1 Jan	Balance b/d	4,000	31 Mar	Disposals account	4,000

Furniture – provision for depreciation

19x5			19x5		
31 Dec	Balance c/d	100	31 Dec	Profit and loss account	100
19x6			19x6		
31 Dec	Balance c/d	500	1 Jan	Balance b/d	100
			31 Dec	Profit and loss account	400
		500			500
19x7			19x7		
			1 Jan	Balance b/d	500
31 Dec	Balance c/d	900	31 Dec	Profit and loss account	400
		900			900
19x8			19x8		
			1 Jan	Balance b/d	900
31 Dec	Balance c/d	1,300	31 Dec	Profit and loss account	400
		1,300			1,300
19x9			19x9		
31 Mar	Disposals account	1,300	1 Jan	Balance b/d	1,300

Disposal of fixed assets

19x9			19x9		
31 Mar	Furniture at cost	4,000	31 Mar	Depreciation	1,300
				Cash	2,500
			31 Dec	Profit and loss account	200
		4,000			4,000

5.4

Machinery at cost

19x1			19x1		
1 Jul	Cash	2,000	31 Dec	Balance c/d	2,000
19x2			19x2		
1 Jan	Balance b/d	2,000			
1 Jun	Cash	1,000	31 Dec	Balance c/d	3,000
		3,000			3,000
19x3			19x3		
1 Jan	Balance b/d	3,000			
29 Apr	Cash	1,000	31 Dec	Balance c/d	4,000
		4,000			4,000

Machinery at cost

19x4			19x4		
1 Jan	Balance b/d	4,000	18 May	Disposals	2,000
			31 Dec	Balance c/d	2,000
		4,000			4,000
19x5			19x5		
1 Jan	Balance b/d	2,000	5 Aug	Disposals	1,000
			31 Dec	Balance c/d	1,000
		2,000			2,000

Machinery – provision for depreciation

19x1			19x1		
31 Dec	Balance c/d	400	31 Dec	Profit and loss account	400
19x2			19x2		
			1 Jan	Balance b/d	400
31 Dec	Balance c/d	900	31 Dec	Profit and loss account	500
		900			900
19x3			19x3		
			1 Jan	Balance b/d	900
31 Dec	Balance c/d	1,500	31 Dec	Profit and loss account	600
		1,500			1,500
19x4			19x4		
18 May	Disposals	1,200	1 Jan	Balance b/d	1,500
31 Dec	Balance c/d	500	31 Dec	Profit and loss account	200
		1,700			1,700
19x5			19x5		
5 Aug	Disposals	300	1 Jan	Balance b/d	500
31 Dec	Balance c/d	300	31 Dec	Profit and loss account	100
		600			600

Machinery disposals

19x4			19x4		
18 May	Machinery at cost	2,000	18 May	Depreciation	1,200
31 Dec	Profit and loss account	200		Cash	1,000
		2,200			2,200
19x5			19x5		
Aug 5	Machinery at cost	1,000	Aug 5	Depreciation	300
				Cash	500
			31 Dec	Profit and loss account	200
		1,000			1,000

5.6

Provision for doubtful debts

19x1			19x1		
31 Dec	Balance c/d	550	31 Dec	Profit and loss account	550
19x2			19x2		
			1 Jan	Balance b/d	550
31 Dec	Balance c/d	640	31 Dec	Profit and loss account	90
		640			640

Provision for doubtful debts

19x3			*19x3*		
31 Dec	Profit and loss account	90	1 Jan	Balance b/d	640
	Balance c/d	550			
		640			640
19x4			*19x4*		
			1 Jan	Balance b/d	550
31 Dec	Balance c/d	780	31 Dec	Profit and loss account	230
		780			780

Balance sheet (extracts)

	19x1	*19x2*	*19x3*	*19x4*
Debtors	11,000	12,800	11,000	13,000
less Provision for doubtful debts				
	550	640	550	780
	10,450	12,160	10,450	12,220

Chapter 6 6.1

*T. Topley – Trading and profit and loss account
for the year ending 31 December 19x5*

	£	£
Sales		10,600
less Cost of goods sold:		
Opening stock	2,970	
Purchases	5,930	
	8,900	
less Closing stock	1,780	
		7,120
Gross profit		3,480
less Expenses:		
Wages and salaries	1,560	
Rent and rates	1,240	
Bad debts written off	110	
Depreciation:		
Motor vehicles	300	
Fixtures and fittings	100	
General expenses	190	
Provision for doubtful debts	54	
		3,554
Net loss		74

T. Topley – Balance sheet at 31 December 19x5

	£ Cost	£ Dep'n	£ NBV
Fixed assets			
Motor vehicles	1,500	900	600
Fixtures and fittings	1,400	500	900
	2,900	1,400	1,500
Current assets			
Stocks		1,780	
Debtors	3,350		
less Provisions	134		
		3,216	
Prepayments		40	
Bank		520	
		5,556	
less Current liabilities			
Creditors	1,680		
Accrued expenses	40		
		1,720	
Net current assets			3,836
			5,336
Financed by:			
Opening capital		6,850	
less Net loss		74	
		6,776	
less Drawings		1,440	
			5,336

6.3

*K. Overthorpe – Trading and profit and loss account
for the year ending 31 October 19x6*

	£	£	£
Sales			19,350
less Sales returns			1,020
Net sales			18,330
less Cost of goods sold:			
Opening stock		1,630	
Purchases	14,500		
Carriage inwards	125		
	14,625		
less Purchase returns	825		
		13,800	
		15,430	
less Closing stock		5,370	
			10,060
Gross profit			8,270
Commission receivable			1,290
			9,560
less Expenses:			
Carriage outwards		160	
Wages		3,215	
Rent and rates		2,570	
Heat and light		465	
Telephone		270	
Bad debts written off		180	
Provision for doubtful debts		94	
Loan interest		350	
Depreciation – premises		500	
– equipment		500	
			8,304
Net profit			1,256

K. Overthorpe – Balance Sheet at 31 October 19x6

	£ Cost	£ Dep'n	£ NBV
Fixed assets			
Premises	10,000	2,500	7,500
Equipment	4,000	1,000	3,000
	14,000	3,500	10,500
Current assets			
Stocks		5,370	
Debtors	3,670		
less Provisions	294		
		3,376	
Prepayments		180	
Bank		1,770	
		10,646	
less Current liabilities			
Creditors	2,740		
Accrued expenses	95		
		2,835	
Net current assets			7,811
			18,311
less Long-term liabilities			
Loan			3,500
			14,811
Financed by:			
Opening capital		13,555	
Net profit		1,256	
			14,811

Chapter 7 7.1

Report to the Managing Director

The following addresses the problem of determining the true value of the following items in the company accounts:

- goodwill
- fixed assets and
- research costs

Goodwill

Goodwill exists where a business is able to generate higher profits than would otherwise be the case if goodwill did not exist. It might stem from the reputation of the company to provide high-quality tried and tested products; or it might stem from the company being in an advantageous geographical position; the loyalty and experience of the workforce might be a contributory factor, as might the strength of the management of the company.

The valuation of goodwill is highly subjective, and therefore it should only be included in the accounts as an asset when it can be measured with any degree of accuracy. This only applies where the goodwill has been purchased as part of the acquisition of a business, where the price paid is greater than the fair value of the assets taken over. The amount should be written off (amortized) over the early years following acquisition.

All other goodwill should be written off immediately against reserves, and therefore the balance sheet should not include any figure for non-purchased goodwill.

The main accounting concept which governs the treatment of goodwill is the prudence concept, which states that provision should be made for all known expenses and liabilities and assets and revenues should not be overstated.

Fixed assets

Fixed assets are normally valued at their original cost less accumulated depreciation. As depreciation is an estimated figure, it is unlikely that the net book value arising will equal the true value of the assets. If inflation exists and/or the value of fixed assets is falling at a slower rate than the depreciation being charged, then the valuation might well be lower than the replacement cost of the assets. It is possible to revalue assets upwards, providing that an expert valuation is obtained, but this is reserved only for larger, more expensive assets such as land and buildings. For other assets, the historical cost less accumulated depreciation is used, in order to be consistent.

The prudence concept also applies here, as does the matching or accruals concept which states that expenses should be matched with the revenue earned from the use of those expenses; therefore depreciation represents an expense incurred in earning revenue and should be written off against the revenue of the period.

Research costs

These are normally written off against the profits of the period in which they are incurred unless it can be shown that there will be a commercial benefit arising from the research, and that benefit exceeds the costs incurred. The prudence concept is the main consideration here also.

7.2

(a) Motor Vehicles added to fixed asset register:

	£
List price	£24,000
less 20%	4,800
	19,200
add VAT at 17.5%	3,360
	22,560
add cost of name	100
	22,660

Plant and machinery

	Cost £	Accumulated depreciation £
Balance per ledger	120,000	30,000
less disposal	30,000	5,700
	90,000	24,300

Calculation of office equipment:

	Cost £	accumulated depreciation £	net book value £
Motor vehicles	48,000	12,000	36,000
Plant and machinery	90,000	24,300	65,700
Office equipment	27,500	7,500	20,000
	165,500	43,800	121,700

Revised fixed asset register
(£147,500 + £22,660) — 170,160
Therefore purchase of office equipment was — 48,460

(b)   Depreciation calculations:

Motor vehicles	25% × £48,000	£12,000
	25% × £22,600 × 3/12	£ 1,416
		£13,416
Plant and machinery	10% × £90,000	£ 9,000
Office equipment	10% × £68,460	£ 6,846

(c) An organization charges depreciation on fixed assets so as to comply with SSAP 2, which states that depreciation is the reduction in value of an asset due to usage, wear and tear or obsolescence. The aim is to spread the cost of the fixed assets over their expected useful life, and to charge a proportion of the cost against profits each year in which the asset is in use. The concepts involved are the prudence concept, which states that provision should be made for all known expenses and liabilities, and the matching concept, which states that expenses should be matched with the revenues which they have earned. If depreciation is charged, this avoids the danger of overstating profits which might then be taken out of the business unwisely.

7.4

(a)   (i) An asset is something which an organization controls and which will be of future benefit to the organization, either in the long term (fixed asset) or in the short term (current asset).
  (ii) A revenue is an amount of income received or earned, providing that the amount is reasonably certain of being received.
 (iii) An expense is an amount used up or consumed, perhaps in the earning of revenue, or with no benefit in the past and/or in the future.
 (iv) Matching is the allocation of revenues against the expenses incurred in earning those revenues.

(b) A balance sheet is a statement of the position of an organization at a point in time. It consists of the assets, liabilities and capital of the organization, i.e. the resources which the organization has, and the claims against those resources.
  The figures included in the balance sheet are taken from the ledger accounting system of the organization, and are based primarily on using the original cost for the valuation of most items, except where the cost is known to be too high. Assets such as fixed assets and stocks may not be represented in the balance sheet at their true value. Debtors may include debts not likely to be recovered, and stocks may be obsolete.
  The balance sheet attempts to portray a picture of an organization as a whole, but in fact it is nothing more than a list of ledger balances and it excludes relevant items such as the loyalty of the workforce, the market share, the reliability of its products, etc.

(c) Freehold buildings have tended to rise in value in recent years, and therefore many organizations have felt justified in ceasing to charge depreciation. The main argument is that as the asset has not fallen in value, then it should not be depreciated. Against this is the concept of matching, which states that revenues should be matched with the expenses incurred in earning them, and thus depreciation should be charged against profits, even if the asset value does not diminish. Buildings do wear out, and therefore have a finite life.
  Another argument is that to charge depreciation is artificial because it does not set aside funds for the replacement of those assets. Against this is the fact that the charging of depreciation is not intended to set aside funds, but the

charge does reduce profits and hence reduces the amount which can be withdrawn from the business by the owners. This helps to preserve the capital base of the organization.

An argument in favour of charging depreciation on buildings is that it is consistent with the treatment of other assets used in earning revenue.

Chapter 8 8.1

Purchases

2 Jan T. Gosling	4,800		

T. Gosling

20 Jan Bank	4,704	2 Jan Purchases	4,800
Discount received	96		

Bank

	20 Jan T. Gosling	4,704

Cash discount received

	20 Jan T. Gosling	96

8.2

		Net value	VAT	Amount paid
Purchases	1 Jan	£80	£13.65	£91.65
	2 Jan	£100	£17.50	£117.50
	3 Jan	£450	£74.81	£524.81
Sales	1 Jan	£300	£47.25	£317.25
	2 Jan	£800	£133	£933
	3 Jan	£170	£29.75	£199.75

(a) Debit purchases £630   Credit sales £1,270
(b) VAT £104.04 to be paid over
(c) Discounts received £2; Discounts allowed £30

8.3

Balance per supplier's statement	£5,950
less Discount (13 Jan)	(200)
less Cash in transit	(1,400)
less Debit note 65	(300)
Revised statement balance	4,050
Balance per ledger	3,350
add Invoice 026 not received	800
less Credit note 0070 not received	(100)
Revised ledger balance	4,050

Chapter 9 9.1

(a) 60 toasters at £50 each	£3,000
less 20% trade discount	600
	2,400
less 5% cash discount	120
	2,280
(i) Payment within 14 days	£2,280
(ii) Payment not within 14 days	£2,400

(iii)	Double entry for sale	Debit Drayton Electrical	£2,400
		Credit Sales	£2,400
	Double entry for receipt	Debit Bank	£2,280
		Debit Discounts allowed	£ 120
		Credit Drayton Electrical	£2,400

(b) (i) Sales ledger
    (ii) Credit note
    (iii) Returns inwards journal
    (iv) £1,763 debit

(c) Invoice number, invoice date, name of seller, address of seller, name of purchaser, address of purchaser, quantity of items sold, description of items sold, price per unit sold, total price before discounts, trade discount, total of invoice, cash discount offered, order number, delivery address (any ten of these).

Chapter 10 10.1

Cash Book

Date	Details	Disc	Cash	Bank	Date	Details	Disc	Cash	Bank
19x5		£	£	£	*19x5*		£	£	£
1 Mar	Balances b/d		250	1,200	8 Mar	B. Purvis	20		400
1 Mar	A. Harris			300	11 Mar	Wages		140	
9 Mar	C. Denver	10		150	19 Mar	D. Eversley	12		388
22 Mar	Sales		180		27 Mar	Cash banked		200	
25 Mar	E. Farrow	25		475	28 Mar	Balances c/d		90	1,197
27 Mar	Cash banked			200					
		35	430	2,325			32	430	1,985
1 Apr	Balances b/d		90	1,197					

Debit Discounts allowed £35, Credit Discounts received £32

10.3

Petty Cash Book

Debit	Date	Details	PCV	Total	VAT	Cleaning	Postage	Office	Ledger supplies
£				£	£	£	£	£	£
75.00	1 Mar	Balance b/d							
	3 Mar	Cleaner's wages	401	5.00		5.00			
	6 Mar	L. Lomas	402	14.00					14.00
	8 Mar	Postage stamps	403	3.00			3.00		
	10 Mar	Cleaning materials	404	11.75	1.75	10.00			
	14 Mar	Printer ribbons	405	4.70	0.70			4.00	
	18 Mar	Parcel post	406	8.00			8.00		
	23 Mar	Pens and pencils	407	7.05	1.05			6.00	
	26 Mar	Postage stamps	408	7.00			7.00		
	29 Mar	Stationery	409	2.35	0.35			2.00	
				62.85	3.85	15.00	18.00	12.00	14.00
	31 Mar	Balance c/d		12.15					
75.00				75.00					
12.15	1 Apr	Balance b/d							
62.85		Bank							
75.00									

10.4

Cash Book

28 Feb	Balance b/d	25	28 Feb	Halifax B/S SO	20
	L. Tudor C/T	100		Bank charges	40
				Balance c/d	65
		125			125

Bank Reconciliation at 28 February 19x6:

Balance per statement	10	Overdrawn
add Receipts not credited	300	
	310	
less unpresented cheques:		
440	150	
441	75	
		225
Balance per cash book		65

Chapter 11 11.1

Purchases journal

Date	Invoice No	Name	Net value	VAT	Invoice total
5 Jan	83	D. Evans	350.00	61.25	411.25
15 Jan	84	E. Ford	108.00	18.90	126.90
25 Jan	85	D. Evans	230.00	40.25	270.25
31 Jan		Totals	688.00	120.40	808.40

Purchase returns journal

Date	Credit Note no	Name	Net value	VAT	Credit note total
20 Jan	901	D. Evans	140.00	24.50	164.50
28 Jan	902	E. Ford	36.00	6.30	42.30
31 Jan		Totals	176.00	30.80	206.80

Ledger account entries:

D. Evans – debit with £411.25 (5 Jan); credit with £164.50 (20 Jan); debit with £270.25 (25 Jan)
E. Ford – debit with £126.90 (15 Jan); credit with £42.30 (28 Jan)
Purchases – debit with £688.00 (31 Jan)
Purchase returns – credit with £176.00 (31 Jan)
Input VAT – debit with £120.40 (31 Jan); credit with £30.80 (31 Jan)

11.2

Type of error; (a) commission, (b) compensating, (c) omission, (d) original entry, (e) reversal, (f) principle.

Journal entries:

		Debit		*Credit*
(a)	A. Hunt	£1,000	A. Hurst	£1,000
(b)	Motor Vehicles	£ 500	Sales	£ 500
(c)	A. Brunt	£ 600	Sales	£ 600
(d)	Rates	£ 100	Cash	£ 100

(e) Purchases   £ 800   L. Jones   £ 800
(f) A. Green   £ 100   Wages   £ 100

Revised trial balance:

Debits: Rates £150, Wages £100, Stock £1,000, Bank and cash £1,900, Purchases £4,800, Motor vehicles £1,500, Premises £5,000, Debtors £3,700
Credits: Sales £7,100, Capital £8,250, Creditors £2,800
Totals: £18,150

11.3

8 Jan   Debit Office equipment £340, Debit stationery £70, Credit H. Young £410
10 Jan Debit Office equip. dep'n £800, Debit B. Brownlow £250, Debit Disposals £1,000, Credit Disposals £800, Credit Disposals £250, Credit Office equipment cost £1,000
15 Jan Debit J. Ashworth (creditor) £250, Credit J. Ashworth (debtor) £250
21 Jan Debit Bad debts written off £300, Credit A. Briggs £300
27 Jan Debit Profit and loss account £180, Credit Provision for doubtful debts £180

11.4

Journal entries:

2 Jan   Debit Suspense £900, Credit Purchases £900
4 Jan   Debit Suspense £20, Credit Rent received £20
7 Jan   Debit Input VAT £350, Credit Suspense £350
9 Jan   Debit Stationery £500, Credit Suspense £500
10 Jan Debit Sales £1,000, Credit Motor vehicles £1,000

Suspense account:

Debit entries – opening balance £1,480, 2 Jan £900, 4 Jan £20
Credit entries – 7 Jan £350, 9 Jan £500
Closing balance – £1,550 debit

Revised net profit – £4,750 + £900 + £20 – £500 – £1,000 = £4,170
Revised net assets – £40,400 + £900 + £20 – £500 – £1,000 = £39,820

Chapter 12 **12.1**

Debit entries – Cheques paid £8,500, Discount received £500, Purchase returns £1,200
Closing creditors £3,800
Credit entries – Opening creditors £2,000, Credit purchases £12,000

12.3

Debit entries – Opening balance £125,000, Provision for doubtful debts £375
Credit entries – Discounts allowed £399, Error in credit note £1,175
Bad debts written off £500, Closing balance £123,400

Sales ledger balances – Original balances £124,600 less £1,600 =   £123,000
                                    add Dishonoured cheques   £1,200
                                    less balances listed as debits   (£800)
                                      Final balances   £123,400

Chapter 13 13.1   (a)   FIFO

Date	Receipts			Issues			Balance		
	Qty	Value each	Total value	Qty	Value each	Total value	Qty	Value each	Total value
		£	£		£	£		£	£
1 Jan							10	30	300
3 Jan	8	35	280				8	35	580
8 Jan				6	30	180	4	30	120
							8	35	400
15 Jan				4	30	129			
				3	35	105	5	35	175
23 Jan	10	40	400				10	40	575
30 Jan				5	35	105			
				7	40	280	3	40	120

LIFO

Date	Receipts			Issues			Balance		
	Qty	Value each	Total value	Qty	Value each	Total value	Qty	Value each	Total value
		£	£		£	£		£	£
1 Jan							10	30	300
3 Jan	8	35	280				8	35	580
8 Jan				6	35	210	10	30	300
							2	35	370
15 Jan				2	35	70			
				5	30	150	5	30	150
23 Jan	10	40	400				10	40	550
30 Jan				10	40	400			
				2	30	60	3	30	90

AVCO

Date	Receipts			Issues			Balance		
	Qty	Value each	Total value	Qty	Value each	Total value	Qty	Value each	Total value
		£	£		£	£		£	£
1 Jan						10	30	300	
3 Jan	8	35	280				18	32.22	580
8 Jan				6	32.22	193.33	12	32.22	386.67
15 Jan				7	32.22	225.54	5	32.22	161.13
23 Jan	10	40	400				15	37.41	561.13
30 Jan				12			3	37.41	112.17

(b)		FIFO		LIFO		AVCO
Sales		1.000		1,000		1,000
Opening stock	300		300		300	
Purchases	680		680		680	
	980		980		980	
less Closing stock	120		90		112	
Cost of sales		860		890		868
Profit		140		110		132

(c) In times of rising prices, the FIFO method gives a higher closing stock value than LIFO, and hence a lower cost of goods sold, and a higher profit. The AVCO method gives a result in between LIFO and FIFO.

13.3

(a) (i) Suppliers' statements should always be checked with the ledger accounts and any discrepancies discussed with the supplier. This should be done as soon as possible after the invoice arrives to avoid this situation.

(ii) The use of a sales ledger control account would highlight a discrepancy between the total of the individual debtors' accounts and the control account whose entries come from the books of original entry. The segregation of duties between accounts clerks would also help to ensure that such discrepancies were discovered.

(iii) A regular bank reconciliation would highlight the returned cheque as being omitted from the company's cash book. All bank transactions should be recorded before the documentation is filed.

(iv) Any petty cash payment should only be given on the production of a properly authorized petty cash voucher; this in turn should only be authorized if a receipt/invoice is available to evidence the payment. The person authorizing should check the customer's ledger to ensure that the amount is still outstanding.

(b)

Stock record card – FIFO

Date	Details	Receipts			Issues			Balance		
		Qty	Price	Value	Qty	Price	Value	Qty	Price	Value
			£	£		£	£		£	£
1 Apr	Balance							100	10	1,000
8 Apr	Sales				24	10	240	76	10	760
18 Apr	Purchases	38	12	456				38	12	1,216
20 Apr	Sales				50	10	500	26	10	260
								38	12	716
23 Apr	Sales				26	10	260			
					9	12	108	29	12	348
28 Apr	Purchases	20	13	260				20	13	608

Stock record card – AVCO

Date	Details	Receipts			Issues			Balance		
		Qty	Price	Value	Qty	Price	Value	Qty	Price	Value
			£	£		£	£		£	£
1 Apr	Balance							100	10	1,000
8 Apr	Sales				24	10	240	76	10	760
18 Apr	Purchases	38	12	456				114	10.67	1,216
20 Apr	Sales				50	10.67	533	64	10.67	683
23 Apr	Sales				35	10.67	373	29	10.67	310
28 Apr	Purchases	20	13	260				49	11.63	570

(c) Recording of an issue at too high a level would result in the stock record card showing a lower quantity than actual; Recording of a delivery at too low a level would result in the stock record card showing a higher quantity than actual.

13.4

		A	B	C	D
Gross pay		187.50	90.00	160.00	115.00
Deductions:					
Tax	30.50		8.75	23.75	12.50
Superann.	11.22		5.40	9.60	6.90
NI	18.75		9.00	16.00	11.50
Union fees	1.00		1.00	1.00	1.00
Savings	9.38		–	8.00	–
		70.85	24.15	58.35	31.90
Net pay		116.65	65.85	101.65	83.10

Ledger entries:

Wages expense – debit £552.50 (gross pay), debit £55.25 (employers' NI)
Tax and NI creditor – credit £75.50 (tax), credit £55.25 (employees' NI),
                 credit £55.25 (employers' NI)
Superannuation creditor – credit £33.12
Union fees creditor – credit £4.00
Savings scheme creditor – credit £17.38
Wages creditor – credit £367.25 (net wages)

Chapter 14 14.1

Debit entries – Payments to creditors £51,200, Closing creditors £18,000
Credit entries – Opening creditors £14,000
Credit purchases = Balance £55,200
Total purchases = Credit purchases £55,200 plus Cash purchases £2,500 =
         £57,700

14.2

Debit entries – Opening debtors £3,800, Credit sales £59,200
Credit entries – Closing debtors £4,800
Cash received = Balance £58,200

14.3

Debit entries – Opening prepayment £1,200, Paid £16,500
Credit entries – Refunds £800, Closing prepayment £1,400
Rent payable for the year = Balance £15,500

14.4

Cash balance at 1.1.x5			6,500
add receipts: Debtors		44,430	
Cash sales		1,000	
Loan account		10,000	
			55,300
less payments: Suppliers		32,000	
Fixed assets		14,000	
Stationery		1,500	
			(47,500)
			14,300
Balance at 31 December 19x5			12,000
Drawings			2,300

14.5

Plant cost	50,000
Depreciation to date	10,000
Net book value at 1 January 19x5	40,000
Purchase during year	12,500
	52,500
less Net book value at 31 Dec, 19x5	43,000
Depreciation for 19x5	9,500

14.6

Statement of affairs at 1 January 19x5:

Assets – Plant £30,000, Stocks £14,000, Debtors £8,000, Bank £24,000, Total £76,000

Less liabilities – Creditors £12,500, Heat and light accrued £500, Total £13,000

Opening capital = £76,000 – £13,000 = £63,000

Workings:

Bank – Opening balance £24,000, plus Receipts £82,000, less payments £109,400 = Closing balance £3,400 overdrawn

Purchases – Paid to suppliers £40,000, less opening creditors £12,500, plus Closing creditors £9,000 = Purchases £36,500

Sales – Receipts from debtors £80,000, less Opening debtors £8,000, plus Closing debtors £13,000 = Credit sales £85,000. Add Cash sales £2,000 = Total sales £87,000

Heat and light – Paid £3,800, less Opening accrual £500, add Closing accrual £700 = Heat and light consumed £4,000

Insurance – Paid £1,200, less Closing prepayment £250 = Insurance for the year £950

Depreciation – Plant = 10% of £30,000 = £3000; Premises = 5% of £50,000 = £2,500

Trading and profit and loss account:

Sales £87,000, less Cost of sales £42,000 = Gross profit £45,000
less Expenses £12,850 = Net profit £32,150

Balance sheet:

Fixed assets – Premises £42,500, Plant £27,000, Total £74,500
Current assets – Stocks £8,500, Debtors £13,000, Prepayments £250, Total £21,750
Current liabilities – Creditors £9,000, Accruals £700, Bank £3,400, Total £13,100
Working capital – £21,750 – £13,100 = £8,650
Total net assets – £74,500 + £8,650 = £83,150
Opening capital £63,000, plus Net profit £32,150, less Drawings £12,000 = Closing capital £83,150

Chapter 15 15.1

Subscriptions received				
1 Jan In arrears b/fwd	140	1 Jan In advance b/fwd		120
31 Dec In advance c/fwd	135	19x4 subscriptions received		140
19x5 subscriptions	1,135	19x5 subscriptions received		975
		19x6 subscriptions received		135
		31 Dec In arrears c/fwd		40
	1,410			1,410

15.2

Workings:

Subscriptions − 1,331 + 100 − 80 + 25 − 110 = 1,266
Purchases − 3,962 + 380 − 420 = 3,922
Bar expenses − 234 − 100 + 200 = 334
Raffle prizes − 60 + 10 = 70
Depreciation of pavilion − 10% × £6,000 = £600
Depreciation of equipment − 20% × £2,500 = £500

Bar trading account − sales £5,628 less Cost of sales £3,860 = £1,768
less Bar expenses £334 and Bar wages £624 = Profit £810

Income and expenditure account:

Income − Bar profit £810, Subscriptions £1,266, Donations £120,
Raffle profit £30 (£100 − £70) = £2,226
Expenditure − Wages £939, Repairs £348, Depreciation £1,100 = £2,387
Deficit − £2,226 − £2,387 = £161

Balance sheet:

Assets − Pavilion £5,400, Equipment £1,200, Stocks £558, Subscriptions in
          arrears £25,
Bank £1,036 = £8,219
Liabilities − Bar creditors £380, Expense creditors £200, Subscriptions in
          advance £110 = £690
Net assets − £8,219 − £690 = £7,529
Accumulated fund − £7,690 − deficit £161 = £7,529

15.4

(a)   *Receipts and payments account for the year ended 31 December 1990*

Receipts	£	Payments	£
Bank balance b/d	2,170	Equipment	250
Subscriptions	2,340	Miscellaneous expenses	473
Life memberships	2,000	Bank balance c/d	5,787
	6,510		6,510

(b)

Subscriptions				
1 Jan Balance b/d	800	1 Jan balance b/d		600
31 Dec Income and				
expenditure a/c	1,960	Bank		2,340
Balance c/d	500	31 Dec Balance c/d		320
	3,260			3,260

(c) *Balance sheet as at 31 December 1990*

Fixed Assets	Cost £	Depreciation £	NBV £
Equipment	4,250	1,225	3,025
Current assets			
Subscriptions in arrears		320	
Bank		5,787	
		6,107	
less Current liabilities			
Subscriptions in advance		500	
			5,607
			8,632

Financed by:	
Accumulated fund:	
Balance at 1 January 1990	1,070
add Surplus for the year	1,762
	2,832
Life membership fund	5,800
	8,632

Chapter 16 16.1   *Manufacturing account for the year ending 30 June 19x6*

	£000	£000
Opening stocks of raw materials		6,700
Purchases	8,000	
Carriage inwards	150	
		8,150
		14,850
less Closing stocks of raw materials		4,600
Direct materials		10,250
Direct labour		1,600
Power costs		1,300
Prime cost		13,150
Factory indirect expenses:		
Supervisors' wages	5,200	
Rent	400	
Depreciation of production machinery	300	
Heating and lighting	100	
Rates	800	
		6,800
Total factory cost		19,950
Work-in-progress		
Opening stock	3,600	
Closing stock	4,800	
		(1,200)
Factory cost of goods completed		18,750

Trading and profit and loss account for the year ending 30 June 19x6

	£000	£000
Sales		15,700
less Cost of sales:		
Opening stock finished goods	7,100	
Factory cost of goods completed	18,750	
	25,850	
less Closing stock finished goods	11,600	
		14,250
Gross profit		1,450
Less expenses:		
Office salaries	100	
Rent of offices	150	
Heating and lighting	150	
Depreciation of office machinery	200	
Rates	200	
Delivery costs	120	
General office expenses	180	
		1,100
Net profit		350

Chapter 17 17.1

Bert and Sid – appropriation account for the year ending 31 December 19x5

	£	£	£
Net profit			120,000
Loan interest – Bert			1,000
			119,000
Interest on drawings: Bert		150	
Sid		150	
			300
			119,300
Salaries: Bert	17,000		
Sid	8,000		
		25,000	
Interest on capital: Bert	2,800		
Sid	4,200		
		7,000	
			32,000
			87,300
Profit share: Bert 1/3		29,100	
Sid 2/3		58,200	
			87,300

Current accounts						
	Bert	Sid		Bert	Sid
---	---	---	---	---	---
Interest on drawings	150	150	Opening balances	25,000	5,000
Drawings	6,000	6,000	Loan interest	1,000	
			Salaries	17,000	8,000
			Interest on capital	2,800	4,200
Closing balances	68,750	69,250	Profit share	29,100	58,200
	74,900	75,400		74,900	75,400

Capital accounts

	Bert	Sid		Bert	Sid
			Opening balances	40,000	60,000

17.3

Dog, Cat and Mouse – Appropriation account for the year ending 31 December 19x5

	£	£
Net profit		1,000
Salary – Dog		4,000
Loss		3,000
Share of loss:		
Dog 1/3	1,000	
Cat 1/3	1,000	
Mouse 1/3	1,000	
		3,000

Current accounts

		Dog	Cat	Mouse			Dog	Cat	Mouse
19x5		£	£	£	*19x5*		£	£	£
31 Dec	Loss	1,000	1,000	1,000	1 Jan	Balances	5,000	6,000	500
	Drawings	2,000	2,000	2,000	31 Dec	Salary	4,000		
	Balances c/d	6,000	3,000			Balance c/d			2,500
		9,000	6,000	3,000			9,000	6,000	3,000

Capital accounts

	Dog	Cat	Mouse		Dog	Cat	Mouse
19x5	£	£	£	*19x5*	£	£	£
				1 Jan Balances	8,000	5,000	4,000

17.4

(a) Journal entries – Debit Land and buildings £48,000, Debit Goodwill £240,000
Credit X £108,000, Credit Y £108,000, Credit Z £72,000

(b) (i) Net assets – £280,000 + £288,000 = £568,000
Capital accounts – X £228,000, Y £204,000, Z £136,000

(ii) Net assets £328,000
Capital accounts – X £228,000 – £120,000 = £108,000
– Y £204,000 – £80,000 = £124,000
– Z £136,000 – £40,000 = £96,000

17.5

Journal entries – Debit Goodwill £30,000, Credit Peter £15,000, Credit Paul £15,000
– Debit Cash £35,000, Credit Pamela £35,000
– Credit Goodwill £30,000, Debit Peter £12,000, Debit Paul £9,000, Debit Pamela £9,000

Balance sheet – Net assets £60,000 + £35,000 = £95,000
– Peter £40,000 + £15,000 – £12,000 = £43,000
– Paul £20,000 + £15,000 – £9,000 = £26,000
– Pamela £35,000 – £9,000 = £26,000

17.6

Journal entries – Debit net assets £40,000, Debit Goodwill £50,000, Credit Brown £36,000, Credit Green £36,000, Credit Black £18,000
– Debit Black £48,000, Credit Cash £48,000
– Credit Goodwill £50,000, Debit Brown £25,000, Debit Green £25,000

Balance sheet – Brown £141,000, Green £91,000 = Net assets £232,000

17.7

In the old businesses' books:

David – Debit Goodwill £20,000, Debit Plant £20,000, Credit Capital £40,000
Dawn – Debit Goodwill £30,000, Credit Plant £5,000, Credit Capital £25,000

Balance sheet of new business

Plant £80,000 + £20,000 + £40,000 – £5,000 =	£135,000
Stocks	£ 25,000
Debtors	£ 32,000
Goodwill	£ 50,000
Creditors	(£ 24,000)
Net assets	£218,000
Capital – David £95,000 + £40,000	£135,000
– Dawn £58,000 + £25,000	£ 83,000
Total capital	£218,000

Chapter 18 **18.1**

RJA Limited – Trading and profit and loss account for the year ending 31 December 19x5

	£000	£000
Sales		10,000
less Cost of goods sold:		
Opening stock	600	
Purchases	7,700	
	8,300	
less Closing stock	400	
		7,900
Gross profit		2,100
less Expenses:		
Carriage outwards	50	
Auditors' fees	30	
General expenses	260	
Debenture interest payable	50	
Directors' salaries	150	
Depreciation	150	
		690
Net profit for the year		1,410
Taxation		130
Net profit after tax		1,280
Dividends:		
Preference	8	
Ordinary	80	
	88	
Transfer to general reserves	500	
		588
Retained profit for the year		692
Profit and loss account balance b/fwd		380
Profit and loss account balance c/fwd		1,072

RJA Limited – Balance sheet at 31 December 19x5

	£000	£000	£000
Fixed assets:			
Office machinery			2,390
Current assets:			
Stocks	400		
Debtors	1,000		
Bank and cash	600		
		2,000	
less Current liabilities			
Creditors	300		
Taxation accrued	130		
Dividends proposed	88		
Directors' salaries accrued	150		
Debenture interest accrued	50		
		718	
			1,282
			3,672
less Long-term liabilities			
Debenture			500
			3,172
Financed by:			
Ordinary shares		1,000	
Preference shares		100	
Share premium account		200	
General reserves		800	
Profit and loss account		1,072	
			3,172

18.3

Zed Ltd – trading and profit and loss account for the year ending 31 Decemebr 1993

	£000	£000
Sales		920
less Cost of sales:		
Opening stock	35	
Purchases	500	
	535	
less Closing stock	40	
		495
Gross profit		425
Operating expenses	368	
Depreciation – machinery	9	
– building	1	
Bad debts	5	
Debenture interest	8	
		391
Net profit		34
Dividends – preference	4	
– ordinary	26	
		30
Retained profit for the year		4
Profit and loss account b/fwd		34
Profit and loss account c/fwd		38

Balance sheet at 31 December 1993

	£000 Cost	£000 Dep'n	£000 NBV
Fixed assets			
Land (valuation)			130
Building	80	6	74
Machinery	90	52	38
			242
Current assets			
Stock		40	
Debtors		35	
Bank		56	
		131	
less Current liabilities			
Creditors		35	
			96
			338
less Long-term liabilities			
Debenture			50
			288
Financed by:			
Ordinary shares, £1 each			130
Preference shares, £1 each			40
Share premium			30
Revaluation reserve			50
Profit and loss account			38
			288

Chapter 19 19.1

(a) (i) Post-balance sheet events are events which occur between the balance sheet date and the date on which the accounts are approved by the board of directors.

(ii) Adjusting events are post balance sheet events which provide additional evidence of conditions which existed at the date of the balance sheet, but which were not originally included in the accounts at that time. The accounts must be 'adjusted' to reflect the true position.

(iii) Non-adjusting events are post balance sheet events regarding conditions which have arisen since the balance sheet date.

(iv) Contingency is a condition which existed at the balance sheet date, but where the result is conditional upon the occurrence or otherwise of an uncertain future event. A contingent gain or loss depends on the contingency.

(b) Examples of adjusting events include the insolvency of a debtor, the writing down of stock to net realizable value, the discovery of fraud, the reduction in valuation of a fixed asset. Examples of non-adjusting events include take-over bids, labour disputes, raising of capital, exchange rate changes.

(c) A material contingent loss should be accrued in the accounts if it is probable that the event will occur and the loss can be estimated with reasonable accuracy; it should be disclosed if its occurrence is only possible, and it can be ignored if the occurrence is remote.

A material contingent gain should be disclosed if it is probable that it will be realized.

Chapter 20 20.1   *TA Limited – Cash Flow Statement, year ending 30 April 19x6*

	£000
Net cash inflow from operating activities	74
Returns on investments and servicing of finance	5
Taxation	(13)
Investing activities	(78)
Net cash inflow before financing	(12)
Financing activities	1
Net cash inflow/(outflow)	(11)

Workings:

(i) Net cash inflow from operating activities:

	£000	£000
Net operating profit		78
Add back:		
Interest payable	2	
Depreciation	22	
Decrease in debtors	1	
		25
Less:		
Interest receivable	10	
Profit on disposal of plant	7	
Increase in stocks	8	
Decrease in creditors	4	
		(29)
Net cash inflow from operating activities		74

(ii) Returns on investments and servicing of finance:

Cash inflow from interest receivable	10
Cash outflow from interest payable	(2)
Cash outflow from dividends paid	(3)
	5

(iii) Investing activities:

Cash outflow on fixed assets:	
Cost at 30 April 19x5	180
less Disposal	(25)
less Balance at 30 April 19x6	(260)
Fixed assets purchased	105
Cash inflow from fixed assets sold	27
Cash outflow from investing activities	(78)

(iv) Financing activities:

Cash inflow from shares issued	13
Cash outflow from debentures repaid	(12)
Financing activities	1

20.3

Cash Flow Statement for the year ending 31 December 19x6

	£000	£000
Net cash outflow from operating activities		(76)
Returns on investments and servicing of finance		(21)
Investing activities		(120)
Net cash outflow before financing		(217)
Financing activities		100
Net cash outflow		(117)

Workings:

(i) Net operating profit:

Change in retained profit	89
Add increase in reserves	20
Add 19x6 dividend	18
Net operating profit	127

(ii) Cash flow from operating activities:

Net operating profit	127
Add depreciation	24
Less:	
Increase in stocks	(49)
Increase in debtors	(81)
Decrease in creditors	(97)
Net cash outflow from operating activities	(76)

(iii) Cash flow from investing activities:

Fixed assets purchased (15 + 29 + 24)	68
Investments purchased	52
Cash outflow from investing activities	120

(iv) Cash flow from financing activities:

Inflow from shares issued	150
Outflow from debentures repaid	(50)
Cash inflow from financing activities	100

Chapter 21 21.1

(a) £1,200
(b) Gross profit = £2,400; Sales = £8,400
(c) Gross profit = £1,000; Sales = £6,000
(d) Gross profit = £1,600; Purchases = £1,900
(e) Sales = £10,000; Gross profit = £4,000
(f) Cost of sales = £3,200; Gross profit = £800

21.2

	19x5	*19x6*
Gross profit %	10%	15%
Gross profit mark-up	11.1%	17.6%
Net profit %	4.9%	3.3%
Return on capital employed	9.1%	6.3%
Current ratio	2.15	1.7
Acid test ratio	1.04	0.89

	19x5	19x6
Stock turnover	7 times	7.8 times
No. of days' stock	52 days	47 days
Debtors' collection period	31 days	49 days
Creditors payment period	41 days	21 days
Fixed asset turnover	£2.33	£2.31

Comments:

Gross profit improved in 19x6, but net profit and ROCE worsened, indicating a larger expenditure on general running costs in proportion to sales and capital employed. Both current and acid test ratios worsened, although neither is critically low compared to the ideal ratios of 2 and 1. Stock turnover was faster, stock being tied up for less time, but the collection of debts was much slower, contributing to the overdraft situation. Creditors were paid more quickly, making the cash situation even worse.

21.4

(a) $\dfrac{\text{Debt}}{\text{Total capital}} = \dfrac{10}{48} \times 100 = 20.8\%$

(b) $\dfrac{\text{Profit before interest and tax}}{\text{Average capital employed}} = \dfrac{5.6}{46.25} \times 100 = 12.1\%$

(c) (i) The effect on profits will probably be in the future rather than next year, thus the ROCE will decrease as capital employed increases; the likely ratio based on current profit levels is 10.6% (5.6/53 × 100)

The gearing ratio would also decrease to 17.25% (10/58 × 100)

   (ii) If the capital was raised by a debenture issue, interest payable would increase and hence decrease profits. ROCE would fall, to perhaps 11.7% (6.6/56.25 x 100). Gearing would increase to 34.5% (20/58 × 100). If future profits are uncertain, then higher gearing is risky.

(d) Pure research is research 'for its own sake' where the outcome is unclear, not directed towards any specific profitable aim.; applied research is aimed at a particular area or product, but is not likely to lead to additional profits; development expenditure is aimed at producing future profits as a result of improved methods or products.

Prudence is the main concept which governs R&D expenditure; if profits are expected, the costs can be carried forward on the balance sheet to be amortized over the revenue-producing life of the project; otherwise expenditure should be written off, as there is no expectation of future profits. Matching is also concerned in that expenditure should be matched with the revenue it produces.

		1990	1991
(a) Liquidity ratios:	Current ratio	3.4:1	2.6:1
	Acid test ratio	3.1:1	2.1:1
Profitability ratios:	ROCE	5%	10.9%
	Gross profit ratio	40%	37.5%
	Net profit ratio	25.7%	25%
Efficiency ratios:	Fixed assets:sales ratio	0.17:1	0.42:1
	Stock turnover ratio	3 times	5.6 times
	Debtor collection period	188 days	165 days
	Creditor payment period	210 days	75 days

(b)	(i) Gearing ratio	42.1%	24.6%
	(ii) Dividend cover	1.5 times	1.5 times
	(iii) P/E ratio	10	4.8

Chapter 22 22.1

(a) The purpose of accounting records is to provide information for management and to safeguard the assets of the business. A double-entry book-keeping system, with controls, will enable the accountant to produce management information, e.g. profit and loss account, balance sheet, debtor analyses, etc. A full audit trail should be in place. The ledger accounts should enable all entries to be traced back to the source documents as evidence. The accounts provide historic information which can be used as a basis for forecasting the future.

(b) Characteristics of a good coding system include the following:

Uniqueness of each code (no duplication); certainty (reliability); capable of expansion for new items; brevity (few digits); capable of interpretation, e.g. mnemonic; incorporating checking facilities, e.g. check digits.

(c) Consistency – the method used should not be changed without good cause; this facilitates comparison; matching – expenses are matched with the revenue earned within the same period, thus stock is retained as an asset until it is consumed and its cost is set against the sales revenue earned; going-concern – assets are valued on the basis that the business will continue to trade, thus stocks are valued at the lower of cost or NRV.

22.3

(a) A computerized accounting package would consist of a series of modules to record and analyse all the transactions of the business, e.g. sales ledger, purchase ledger, nominal ledger as well as modules for payroll, stock control and other areas. Some packages are 'integrated', which means that a single input is required to update several different ledgers. The procedures to be used can be described by using a sales ledger package for illustration. The package will contain details of all customers, their names, addresses, etc., credit limits, balances or outstanding invoices. As transactions occur, they can be entered (input) either one-by-one (on line) or in batches to the computer, which may update (process) the files at once (real time) or periodically. Modern systems use 'menus' to guide the user through the various parts of the system. The first menu might include the major areas of the package, e.g. Ledger processing, Payments, Enquiries, Customer updating, Statements, Period end, Report, Exit. If you choose Customer updating, a second menu appears which might include Create new customer, Delete customer, Amend customer, Print customer details, Return to main menu. Choose Create new customer and you will be given a screen which shows the layout of a customer record.

(b) The advantages of using a computerized package include speed, accuracy, neatness, flexibility of reporting, inclusion of automatic controls, less space, instant access.

Index

Account, 8
  capital, partnership, 141–3
  capital, sole trader, 7
  current, partnership, 141–3
  income and expenditure, 124
  manufacturing, 133–7
  profit and loss, 6, 24
  receipts and payments, 126–7
  trading, 6, 23
  trading (clubs), 125
Accounting, 2
  adjustments, 33–8
  codes, 190–1
  computerized, 187–93
  concepts and conventions, 61, 63
  equation, 7–8, 27
  financial, 2
  management, 2
  policies, 61
  profession, 2
  ratios, 174–83
  standards, 3, 61
Accounting ratios, *see* Ratios
Accounting information, users, 1
Acconting packages, 188–9
Accounts, interpretation, 174–83
  limited company, 151–7
  partnership, 139–48
  published, 155–6
Accruals, 33–38
Accrued revenue, 33–38
Accumulated fund, 124
Acid test ratio, 178
Amortization, 47
Analysed cash books, 86–7
Analysed journals, 97–8
Appropriation accounts, companies, 153,4
  partnerships, 140–2
Assets, 7
  current, 26
  depreciation of, 41
  fixed, 26,41
  intangible, 47
  net current, 26
Asset turnover ratio, 180
Auditing, 153, 156–7

  external, 157
  internal, 157
Average cost (AVCO), 111–112

Bad debts, 14
  provision for, 46–7
  recovery of, 15
Balance sheet, 7, 25–7
Bank reconciliations, 89–92
Batch, processing, 189
  totals, 189
Book-keeping, 2, 5–16
  other methods, 80
Business documents, 72–76

Capital, 7
  authorized, 152
  employed, 177
  expenditure, 28
  introduced, 15
  issued, 152
  maintenance, 63–4
  share, 152
Capital accounts, sole traders, 7
  partnerships, 141–3
Capital structure ratios, 175, 180–1
Carriage, 11
Cash books, 79, 83–92
  analysed, 86–7
  petty, 87–9
  three column, 85–6
  two column, 83–5
Cash discounts, 68–70
Cash flow statements, 165–9
Characteristics of good information, 192–3
Cheques, 83
Codes, accounting, 190–1
Clubs and societies, 124–30
Computers in accounting, 187–93
  accounting codes, 190–1
  accounting costs, 189
  accounting packages, 188
  advantages and disadvantages, 192
  databses, 192
  processing methods, batch, real time, 189
  security precautions, 189–90

segregation of duties, 189
spreadsheets, 191–2
Contingencies, 163
Contra entries, 107
Control accounts, 105–8
    purchase ledger, 105–8
    sales ledger, 105–8
Cost of goods sold, 32–3
Cost, classification, 133–4
Corporation tax, 154
Credits, 8–9
Credit notes, 73
Creditors' payment period, 179–80
Current account, partnerships, 141–3
Current assets, 26
Current cost accounting, 64
Current liabilities, 26
Current purchasing power accounting, 64
Current ratio, 177–8

Databases, 192
Day books, *see* Journals
Debentures, 153
Debits, 8–9
Debtors' collection period, 179
Deficits, 124
Depreciation, amortization, 47
    fixed assets, 41–7
    ledger entries, 43–4
    methods, 41–3
    reducing balance, 42–3
    revaluation, 43
    straight line, 42
Direct costs, 133
Directors, 153
Discounts, 68–70
    cash, 68–70
    trade, 68
Disposal of fixed assets, 44–6
Dividends, 152, 154
Divisions of the ledger, 79–81
Double entry book-keeping, 10
Doubtful debts provision, 46–7
Drawings, partnership, 140
    interest on, 141–2
    sole trader, 7, 15, 25

Efficiency ratios, 175, 178–80
Errors, affecting the trial balance, 100–2
    correction, 99–101
    effect on profit and loss account, 102
    not affecting the trial balance, 98–100
    suspense account, 101–2
Expenses, 6
Extended trial balance, 55–7

Factory, cost of goods completed, 134, 136–7
    direct costs,
    indirect costs, 133
    prime cost
Final accounts, 51–5
Financial accounting, 2
First In First Out (FIFO), 110–1
Fixed Asset Register, 46
Fixed assets, 26
    depreciation, 41–47
    disposals, 44–6
    revluation, 43
Folio columns, 80
FRSs, 3

GAAP, 3
Gearing ratios, 175, 180–1
General purpose packages, 188
Goodwill, 47
Gross profit, 6, 23

Hardware, 187
Historical cost, 63

IASs, 3
Imprest system, 87–9
Income and Expenditure account, 124, 129
Incomplete records, 117–21
Information, characteristics, 192–3
Intangible assets, 47
Interest on drawings, 141
Interpretation of accounts, 174–83
Investors' ratios, 175, 181–3
Invoices, 72–3

Journals, 95–102
    analysed, 97–8
    general, 95, 98–102
    purchases, 95
    returns, 95, 96–7
    sales, 95, 96–7

Last In First Out (LIFO), 111
Leases, 48
Ledger accounts, 8
    balancing, 30
Liabilities, 7
    current, 26
    long-term, 26
Life memberships, 126
Limited company accounts, 151–7
    appropriation of profits, 153–4
    auditing, 153, 156–7
    published, 155–6
    share capital, 152–3

shareholders' funds, 154–5
Liquidity ratios, 174, 177–8
Long-term liabilities, 26

Management accounting, 2
Manufacturing accounts, 133–7
Margin, 176
Mark-up, 176
Matching concept, 33

National insurance, 133
Net book value, 42
Net current assets, 26
Net pay, 114
Net profit, 6, 25
Net realisable value, 112
Nominal accounts, 27
Nominal ledger, 79
Not-for-profit organizations, 124–130

Ordinary shares, 153
Overheads, 133–4

Partnership accounts, 139–48
   act 1890, 130
   agreement, 139
   admission of new partner, 146–7
   appropriation account, 140–2
   capital accounts, 141–3
   changes in profit-sharing ratios, 143–8
   current account, 141–3
   drawings, 140
   formed from 2 sole-traders, 147–8
   goodwill, 144–8
   goodwill elimination, 148
   partners' liabilities, 140
   partners' loan accounts, 141
   retirement of partner, 145–6
   revaluation of assets, 143–8
PAYE (pay as you earn), 113
Paying in slips, 83
Payroll accounts, 114
Pension contributions, 113–4
Performance ratios, 174, 175–7
Personal accounts, 27
Petty cash, 87–9
Post-balance sheet events, 162
Preference shares, 152
Prepayments, 33–8
Prime cost, 134
Profit, 6
   gross proft, 6
   net profit, 6
Profitability ratios, 174, 175–7
Provisions, 141–7

Purchase ledger, 79
   control account, 105–8

Quick asset ratio, 178

Ratios, 175–83
   capital structure, 180–1
   efficiency, 178–80
   gearing, 180–1
   investors', 181–3
   liquidity, 177–8
   performance, 175–7
   profitability, 175–7
   security, 181–3
   solvency, 177–8
   use of assets, 178–80
Raw materials, 135
Real accounts, 27
Real-time processing, 189
Receipts and payments accounts, 126–7
Reconciliations, bank, 89–92
   suppliers' statements,   74–5
Regulatory framework, 3
Research and development, 48
Reserves, 153–4, 163
   capital, 152, 153, 163
   revenue, 153–4, 163
Return on capital employed, 177
Returns, 13–14
   inwards, 13–14
   outwards, 13–14
Revaluation, of fixed assets 43
   reserve account, 163
Revenue, 6, 27
   expenditure, 27–8
   receipts, 28
   reserves, 28

Sales ledger, 79
   control account, 105–8
Sales revenue, 6
Security precautions in computerized systems, 189
Security ratios, 175
Segregation of duties, 189
Separate entity concept, 8
Share capital, 152–3
Share premium account, 152, 163
Share values, 152
Shareholders' funds, 154–5
Shares, preference, 152
   ordinary, 153
Software, 188
Solvency ratios, 174, 177–8
SORPS, 3
Spreadsheets, 191–2

SSAPs, 3
  SSAP2, 61
  SSAP12, 41
  SSAP17, 162
  SSAP18, 163
Statement of affairs, 117–8
Statement, bank, 89–92
  suppliers, 74–5
Stock turnover ratio, 178–9
Stock valuation methods. 100–112
  AVCO, 111–112
  FIFO, 110–111
  LIFO, 111
  Net Realizable value, 112
Subscriptions, 125
Subsidiary books, 79
Surpluses, 124
Suspense account, 101–2
Taxation, corporation, 154

Trade discounts, 68
Trading account, 23
  for clubs, 125
Trial balance, 21–3
  extended, 55–6
  errors affecting, 100–2
  errors not affecting, 98–100
True and fair, 3

Use of assets ratios, 175, 178080
Users of accounts, 1
  external, 2
  internal, 1

Value added tax, 70–1

Wages and salaries, 112–4
Work in progress, 134, 6, 7